SECOND EDITION

■ THE LAWYER'S GUIDE TO
Marketing Your Practice

James A. Durham

Deborah McMurray

Editors

(First Edition entitled *The Complete Guide to Marketing Your Law Practice*, edited by Hollis Hatfield Weishar and James A. Durham)

MARKETING • MANAGEMENT • TECHNOLOGY • FINANCE

Commitment to Quality: The Law Practice Management Section is committed to quality in our publications. Our authors are experienced practitioners in their fields. Prior to publication, the contents of all our books are rigorously reviewed by experts to ensure the highest quality product and presentation. Because we are committed to serving our readers' needs, we welcome your feedback on how we can improve future editions of this book. We invite you to fill out and return the comment card at the back of this book.

Cover design by Jim Colao.

Nothing contained in this book is to be considered as the rendering of legal advice for specific cases, and readers are responsible for obtaining such advice from their own legal counsel. This book and any forms and agreements herein are intended for educational and informational purposes only.

The products and services mentioned in this publication are under or may be under trademark or service mark protection. Product and service names and terms are used throughout only in an editorial fashion, to the benefit of the product manufacturer or service provider, with no intention of infringement. Use of a product or service name or term in this publication should not be regarded as affecting the validity of any trademark or service mark.

The Law Practice Management Section, American Bar Association, offers an educational program for lawyers in practice. Books and other materials are published in furtherance of that program. Authors and editors of publications may express their own legal interpretations and opinions, which are not necessarily those of either the American Bar Association or the Law Practice Management Section unless adopted pursuant to the bylaws of the Association. The opinions expressed do not reflect in any way a position of the Section or the American Bar Association.

© 1999, 2004 American Bar Association. All rights reserved.
Printed in the United States of America.

Library of Congress Control Number: 2004101701
ISBN 1-59031-355-0

08 07 06 05 04   5 4 3 2 1

Discounts are available for books ordered in bulk. Special consideration is given to state bars, CLE programs, and other bar-related organizations. Inquire at Book Publishing, American Bar Association, 750 N. Lake Shore Drive, Chicago, Illinois 60611.

Contents

Acknowledgments	xi
Introduction	xiii

SECTION I:
DEVELOPING YOUR APPROACH 1

CHAPTER 1
Overcoming Objections and Obstacles:
Persuading Your Pessimistic Partners 3

Terri Pepper Gavulic and Susan Raridon Lambreth

Identification of Barriers to Marketing	3
Internal Institutional Obstacles	4
Internal Individual Obstacles	6
External Obstacles	7
Understanding Why Obstacles Exist	9
Insecurity	9
Rapid Change	9
Lack of Solid Business Management	9
Overcoming the Obstacles	10
Correct the Incentives	10
Provide Marketing Education	10
Promote Internal Communication	11
Strengthen Practice Management	12
Provide Early Success Experiences	12
Obtain Client Feedback	13
Improve Marketing Leadership	13
Summary	13

CHAPTER 2
Strategic Marketing Planning — 15

Hollis Hatfield Weishar (with James A. Durham)

Background	15
Simplified Process	16
The Strategic Marketing Planning Process	16
Purpose of a Strategic Marketing Plan	16
Now That We Know What to Do, Where Do We Begin?	18
How Do We Apply the Knowledge We Have Gained?	20
The Strategic Marketing Plan	22
Overview of the Plan	22
Specific Elements of the Strategic Marketing Plan	23
SUPPLEMENT A: THE FIRM STRATEGIC PLANNING PROCESS	30
Some Thoughts on Why Law Firms Lose Their Way	30
Leadership Is Important	30
In Planning Your Strategy, Set Clear Rules of the Game	30
Designing a Strategy: How Not to Do It	31
Designing a Strategy: How to Do It	31
The Six Levels of Strategic Planning Success	31
SUPPLEMENT B: A SAMPLE STRATEGIC MARKETING PLAN	33
Marketing Plan and Background	33
SUPPLEMENT C: A STRATEGIC PLANNING SUCCESS—	
BUILT UPON THE "VOICE OF THE CLIENT"	46
The Situation	46
The Solution	46
Four Components for Developing the Plan	47

CHAPTER 3
The Client Feedback Program: A Proven Strategy for Winning New Business, Improving the Bottom Line, and Creating a "Delighted and Loyal" Client Base — 49

Linda LaBrie

Client Value—The Link Between Satisfaction and Loyalty	50
How Client Loyalty Improves Your Bottom Line	52
Critical Elements of a Results-Driven Client Feedback Program	54
Client Selection	54
Client Feedback Methodology	54
Who Should Conduct the Interview?	55
The Client Interview	57

Follow-Up Strategy—The Critical Success Factor!	60
Role of the Marketing Director	61
The Bottom Line	62
Other Ways to Bring the *Voice of Your Clients* into Your Firm	63
Summary	63

SECTION II:
ENHANCING YOUR IMAGE   65

CHAPTER 4
Public Relations for Lawyers   67

Richard Levick and Elizabeth Lampert

A Spotlight on Public Relations	67
How Has PR for a Law Firm Changed in the Last Decade?	
Beyond the Press Release . . .	68
Activities	68
To Make It All Happen	72
Structuring an Internal Public-Relations Function	72
Using External Agencies	73
Models	74
The Next Step	75
A Bold Communications Program Would Stun the Legal Market	75
How Can PR Support Firm Strategy?	77
Business Development Media Demand a Two-Tiered Approach: Use Advertising to Position the Firm, and Public Relations to Reach Targeted Buyers	77
What Can You Do?	78

CHAPTER 5
Developing Your Visual Image   83

Burkey Belser

The Real Goal of Marketing Communications	83
How People Find and Choose Their Lawyers	84
Finding Lawyers	84
Choosing Lawyers	85
Buyer's Remorse	86
What Works, and Why and How It Works	86
The Firm Brochure	87

Enhancing Memory	90
Yes, Your Clients Read Newsletters	95
The Designer's Art May Offer Your Only Chance to Be Read	96
Web Sites and Other New Media	96

SECTION III:
IMPLEMENTING MARKETING STRATEGIES   101

CHAPTER 6
Marketing with the Written Word   103

Roberta Montafia

Why Write?	103
How to Begin	104
Steps in Creating a Plan	105
What to Write	105
How to Write—Your Style	106
Where to Publish	107
Leverage	109
Other Forms of Writing for Lawyers	110
Letters and Notes	110
Firm Brochures and Collateral Materials	111
Résumés and Biographies	112
Newsletters and Advisories	113
Announcements	114
Press Releases	114
Putting It All Together—One Lawyer's Story	116
Conclusion	117

CHAPTER 7
Marketing Through the Spoken Word:
Conversations and Public Speaking   119

Robert N. Kohn and Lawrence M. Kohn

Sales Dialogue for Lawyers	119
Sales Dialogue with Clients	120
Sales Dialogue with Friends	121
Sales Dialogue with Strangers	123
Sales Dialogue with Qualified Prospects	126
Conclusion	132
Public Speaking as a Marketing Technique	133

Meet the Audience	133
Prepare Your Introduction for the Host	133
Prepare Your Speech	134
Content	135
Overcoming the Fear of Public Speaking	138
Arranging Speaking Engagements	139
Conclusion	140

CHAPTER 8
Proposals and Responding to Requests for Proposals — 141

Suzanne Donnels

Are Proposals Worth the Investment?	142
How to Get on That RFP List?	142
To Propose or Not to Propose	143
Relationships Change	146
You Have Decided to Propose	147
Refine Your Strategy	147
Conduct Preproposal Research and Gather Competitive Intelligence	148
Develop Themes, Strategies, and Key Points of Differentiation	149
The Process	150
Draft the Outline	150
Select the Team	150
Complete All Sections of the Proposal	151
Eye Candy—What Should the Proposal Look Like?	153
Good Content	153
Continuous Improvement	155
Conclusion	155

CHAPTER 9
Using Win-Win Pricing As a Marketing Advantage — 157

Felice C. Wagner and Peter D. Zeughauser

About Fee Arrangements	157
Impediments to Change	159
Risk/Reward Allocation	160
The Alternatives	161
Relationship-Building Fee Arrangements	164
The Impact of Fee Structures Upon Quality	165
The Proper Role of Discounting	166
Best Practices in Pricing	168

CHAPTER 10
Let Strategy Drive Your Internet Marketing — 171

Deborah McMurray

The First Step: Strategy	171
Interview or Survey Your Clients	173
Your Site	174
Domain Names	174
Traditional Marketing Tools That Drive Traffic to Your Site	175
Online Marketing Tools	175
More Online Marketing—Making Your Firm "The Expert"	176
Search Engines—An Important Part of Your Strategy	176
Grow Your Site	176
What Do Clients and Prospects Want from Your Site?	177
Practice Descriptions and Industry Strength	177
Lawyer Résumés—Still a Critical Part of Your Strategy	178

CHAPTER 11
Weblogs — 179

Richard P. Klau

Overview: What Are Weblogs?	179
Third-Party Endorsements	180
Weblogs as Marketing Vehicles	180
Google	181
What to Say on Your Blog	184
Where Should the Blog Reside?	185
Publicizing Your Weblog	186
Enhancing Your Weblog	186
Tips and Tricks	188

SECTION IV:
MAINTAINING YOUR PROGRAM — 189

CHAPTER 12
Business Development, Sales, and Marketing Training — 191

James A. Durham

Introduction: Setting the Stage	191
The Advent of Training	192
Making the Case: Why Do Training?	193

The Nature and Extent of Training	194
The Training Process	194
Selecting a Trainer	195
Management's Role	196
Flexibility and Costs	196
Managing Expectations	197
Business Development Training: A Case Study	197
Conclusion	198
Types of Marketing-Related Training Programs You Might Offer	199

CHAPTER 13
Ethical Aspects of Client Development   201

William E. Hornsby, Jr.

An Overview of the Ethics of Lawyer Advertising, Solicitation, and Marketing	201
Limitations on the Content of Marketing Material	202
Housekeeping Rules	205
Solicitation Rules	207
Special Issues	209
Specialization	209
Firm Names and Trade Names	209
Domain Names	210
Multijurisdictional Compliance	210
Disciplinary Actions	211
Resources	211

APPENDIX
Research: The Foundation of Intelligent Marketing   213

Mark Greene, Ph.D., and Ann Lee Gibson, Ph.D.

Afterword	**277**
Resources	**279**
About the Editors	**281**
About the Authors	**283**
Index	**289**

Acknowledgments

This book has many authors. We've chosen to include them in this second edition because they are legal marketing and management thought leaders. While we served as editors, facilitators, motivators—and also authors—this book wouldn't have been possible without their extraordinary and meaningful contributions.

Thanks to Burkey Belser, Suzanne Donnels, Terri Pepper Gavulic, Ann Lee Gibson, Mark Greene, Will Hornsby, Rick Klau, Lawrence M. Kohn and Robert N. Kohn, Linda S. LaBrie, Elizabeth Lampert, Susan Raridon Lambreth, Richard S. Levick, Roberta Montafia, Felice Wagner, Hollis Hatfield Weishar, and Peter Zeughauser.

We also thank the legal marketing professionals who continue to pioneer change in their firms and in the industry. And thanks to the best lawyers in the legal profession—who understand that all the credentials, talent and drive mean little without a client to represent.

Finally, a heartfelt thanks to Beverly Loder, Tim Johnson, and the other ABA Law Practice Management Section Publishing Board personnel who kept us energized and on schedule. Thanks to Heather Jefferson for her insightful review comments. And to our families and friends, who unfailingly keep us grounded and inspired to be the best we can be.

Deborah McMurray
James A. Durham

INTRODUCTION

James A. Durham

Soon after I was asked to be an editor of the first edition of *The Complete Guide to Marketing Your Law Practice,* I left the business of law firm marketing to work for Major League Baseball. When I returned to my business as a legal consultant two years later, I was convinced that lawyers everywhere would already have learned what they needed to know about marketing legal services. My thought was that I would not be very busy as a trainer or marketing strategist. So imagine my surprise when I learned that there was a greater demand than ever for the work I and other law firm consultants do! What this illustrates is an increasing awareness by lawyers that they are working in a mature marketplace; it also reflects the acceptance of what was written in this space four years ago: "The practice of law has not really changed all that much in the past decade, but the *economics of the business of law* have changed dramatically."

Lawyers are slowly, but surely, coming to accept that it is no longer sufficient to rely exclusively on excellent technical skills to succeed as a lawyer. Law firms that have a large number of lawyers making large amounts of money by contributing nothing more than billable hours are bringing a much more strategic approach to how they compete for work, and they are asking everyone to contribute to the firm's success by developing new business, offering value-added services, and ensuring client retention.

More and more firms are accepting that they are not immune from the business pressures that are driving lawyers to focus much more on marketing and client development. Some high-profile law firms have folded, in part because of economic pressures, and in part because they have lost sight of "the client" in all of their practice and promotional efforts. This book will help you avoid both pitfalls. Moreover, globalization is putting incredible new pressure on lawyers to have a wide network of resources, to be able to practice much more efficiently, and to respond to worldwide business and political developments at lightning speed. Much of what you will learn here can help you in all of those areas.

With such dramatic market and geo-political changes, an increasing awareness of the importance of marketing and business development, as well as the dramatic advances in the tools for marketing legal services, it was imperative that we update *The Complete Guide to Marketing Your Law Practice* by bringing together the best and most current thinking on the subject. *The Lawyer's Guide to Marketing Your Practice,* Second Edition, represents that effort.

Even the best strategic or creative thinking, however, does not displace the most important, long-standing, and timeless marketing concept of "learning what clients want and delivering it." There is value, for example, in knowing that you need to use technology more effectively in your practice and your marketing, but you will have even greater success if you know the specific ways in which technology might be better used to deliver more value to clients. Similarly, it does no good to know that you need to get client feedback, if you have never learned the best way to conduct a client interview and respond to expressed client concerns. Similarly, the impact, quality, and value of ideas can be greatly enhanced if you know from other's experience what to expect and what is possible. This book is intended to provide these valuable insights, and more.

The list of things you will learn from reading this book is nearly as long as the book itself; it is packed with practical ideas, outlines, strategies, and even some so-called "big-picture concepts." All this wit and wisdom is presented in the relevant context of practicing lawyers and busy law firm managers; it is not just "textbook" information.

Although we have made every effort to offer a comprehensive guidebook to marketing legal services, I am compelled to remind you of Dr. Wayne Dyer's observation in *You Will See It When You Believe It:* "You cannot *taste* water simply by reading the word water.... You cannot see a sunrise simply by saying the word sunrise. In order to *taste* water and *see* the sunrise, you must touch the former to your lips and gaze upon the sun at the crack of dawn." Obviously, no amount of talking or reading about marketing will draw clients to your practice—you must **do** something if you want to attract, keep, and grow client relationships.

Law firm marketing has been described, appropriately I think, as "a contact sport." It involves getting face-to-face with clients and prospects, asking questions, and listening to the answers. You can, however, listen and respond better if you have read about what is going on in the industry and studied what the very best legal marketers have done. This book will help you do that.

Marketing Versus Business Development

I always start a business development training program by making a clear distinction between those things that I perceive to be "marketing tools"—brochures, advertising, public relations, articles, Web sites and speeches, and those things that "create clients"—having face-to-face business conversations, networking effectively, serving super-satisfied clients, cultivating referral sources, giving referrals, and creating client-specific products and service strategies. This book addresses both sides of the spectrum, however, and the terms "marketing" and "business development" will be used interchangeably.

Whether we call it marketing or business development, it is helpful to define the specific goals of these activities. I believe the overriding *goal* of marketing and business development activities is to generate satisfying, profitable work and to increase revenue for the firm. There are a variety of measures that will tell you if you are meeting this goal. Are you:

- Keeping all of the existing work that clients are currently giving to you?
- Turning "first-time" client matters into future work? (Get a case, make it a relationship.)
- Ensuring that clients who use the services of a specific practice area are giving you as much of their work as possible in that area?
- Expanding beyond practice areas? Turning litigation-only, business-only, employment-only, or other single-practice-area clients into "firm clients" who work with lawyers in other parts of the firm?
- Ensuring that your clients are referring their business colleagues to you without qualification or reservation?
- Increasing and maximizing the profit margin and realization from all of the work you are doing for clients?
- Attracting new clients to all areas of the firm?

The best way to accomplish all the above is *to provide extraordinary value in all of your professional relationships.* You can do this by taking the following actions:

1. Communicate clearly and consistently with your clients:
    - Discuss in advance the scope, cost, and strategy of all work, and keep the client informed of all developments, including actual fees versus budget.
    - Manage the client's work cost effectively: that means recognizing the difference between "bet-the-farm," important, and routine ("commodity") work, and approaching each type of work accordingly.
    - Seek feedback regularly, so you know the client's level of satisfaction with your work and service; respond to client's expressed concerns.

2. Get to know your client and prospects so well that you can identify creative ways to help them achieve their business goals; offer them referrals and new ideas (for example, preventative law, product development, training, case disposition strategies, business introductions, etc.).
3. Develop risk-sharing arrangements and cooperative relationships with clients by learning what "partnering" really means, and offering some "win-win" arrangements to clients.
4. Make sure everyone in your organization understands how important it is to give extraordinary client service at every point of contact, and train them to deliver that level of service.
5. Use your network of contacts and relationships as an asset; put people together, give referrals, do favors for people, and be available as a resource.

You Will See Myriad Examples of Management's Role in Marketing

There is an obvious connection between a firm's marketing success and the support and direction marketing initiatives get from management. But it is often of greater import than we realize. If your firm rewards only billable hours or the one lawyer whose initials appear next to a new client's name, then much of what you read here will fall on deaf ears. Similarly, if your firm does not measure non-billable time, or if the lawyers in your firm are not willing to contribute 2,500 to 2,600 hours a year to their professional lives, it will be hard to get them to invest time "off-the-clock" enhancing client relationships. Simply stated: if there are firm policies that are anathema to a marketing culture, then you will not benefit institutionally from the many great ideas and concepts set forth here. Individual lawyers will, nevertheless, learn a lot of marketing skills and strategies that they can apply whether they are in a marketing culture or not.

It is possible, of course, that by reading the work of the superb authors who have contributed to this book you might be inspired to change your management policies and procedures to create a more marketing-friendly culture. It is hard to argue with the value of a well-developed strategy, good training, market and client research, professional communications, and business innovation. These concepts will jump out of these pages. I challenge you to read this book and **not** change the way in which you understand and approach business development. Please use this book not only as a resource guide, but also as inspiration; use it to help you see the future better, and to determine the steps you need to take to move from where you are today to where you want to be tomorrow.

Although many of the best legal marketing people in the world have contributed their best thinking to this book, what you learn here is only part of *the story*. We can all learn the rest of the story by listening to clients. Clients are actually quite good at developing business strategies, and they certainly know what they want from their lawyers. If you read this book and then listen to the voice of the marketplace, you will know exactly what to do—whether you do it is then up to you. Our law schools do not teach us business development or client service skills, and most firms have not done a very good job of teaching it either. To keep up with the dynamic changes in the legal industry, we must become students of the business of law. This book offers a terrific, advanced course of study.

Section 1

Developing Your Approach

Overcoming Objections and Obstacles: Persuading Your Pessimistic Partners

Terri Pepper Gavulic
Susan Raridon Lambreth
—*Hildebrandt International*

In the past, law firms needed to be convinced of the importance of marketing themselves. Today, most lawyers realize they must market their services, but many are still unsure about how to do so most effectively. In many firms, lawyers remain frustrated with or skeptical about the whole process.

Part of the skepticism—or even cynicism—results from the many obstacles lawyers and law firms can face in developing and implementing marketing programs. Many of these obstacles can be removed, or at least minimized, however, by following these steps:

(1) Identify the apparent barriers or obstacles to marketing—both real obstacles and excuses.
(2) Understand why and how the real obstacles inhibit marketing and why the excuses exist.
(3) Take steps to overcome the obstacles.

Identification of Barriers to Marketing

There are both external and internal obstacles to marketing. The external barriers include competitors (many with increasingly sophisticated sales programs), ethical constraints, client reactions, and community attitudes. Though generally these are out of our control and cannot be addressed directly, they are usually less problematic than internal obstacles.

Internal obstacles—which are actually more troublesome—generally fall into one of two categories: those that affect the marketing of the firm as a whole (institutional barriers) and those that hinder the implementation of marketing tactics by individual lawyers (individual barriers). Institutional barriers include firm cultures or mind-sets that do not support marketing, complacency, compensation systems that are not linked to marketing efforts, insufficient communication and practice management, lack of accountability, and lack of marketing leadership. Individual barriers include lack of time, discomfort, fear, and lack of understanding. All internal obstacles can be overcome, however, by employing specific strategies.

Internal Institutional Obstacles

Institutional obstacles can include the following types of problems.

Firm Culture or Historical Mind-Set That Does Not Support Marketing

The majority of lawyers grew up in law firms that disavowed marketing as unprofessional, placed the responsibility in the hands of a few designated rainmakers, or discouraged it as unnecessary: "Don't worry about bringing in business—we've got plenty." "Just get the work done and keep the clients happy." Even though these same firms now encourage or even require marketing, years of nay-saying are not remedied by a simple mandate. Change requires firmwide education, the right (and not mixed) messages from firm management, and incentives for team marketing and cross-selling.

Complacency

Some lawyers still think they can avoid marketing. However, the next few years will continue to "shake out" firms that are mismanaged and lawyers who underperform. Look for more dissolutions of firms that fail to develop clearly identified market positions and follow through on them. Complacency can be addressed by the messages sent by firm leadership, changes in incentives, and education. Understanding the "marketplace imperative" helps overcome complacency, too. Firms that recognize we have moved from a client-focused business model to a *client-driven model*—in which clients call the shots—will more quickly recognize the need to develop effective marketing.

Ineffective Compensation System

Compensation systems that are primarily production oriented ("eat-what-you-kill" or "billable-hour-as-king" types) discourage lawyers from co- or cross-selling, delegating or working as teams in developing business, or even ensuring client service. Systems that reward origination, but not teamwork and cross-selling, are also divisive and hinder effective team marketing. Similarly, even if a compensation system rewards production, marketing efforts, and results, there must still be a way to ensure accountability, to prevent "worker bees" from being as highly compensated as those who produce revenues and new business. Too many firms provide incentives for the wrong things, such as

(1) bringing in new clients rather than expanding existing ones,
(2) landing clients individually rather than working with others as teams,
(3) allowing individuals to keep contacts with clients and prospects to themselves rather than sharing them freely with others or making them part of the firm's contact database, or
(4) attracting new pieces of marginally profitable work for which individuals get credit, rather than working with teams to land more profitable matters for which teams share credit.

Compensation systems must reward at least some business development and practice management activities and efforts, not just results.

Lack of Internal Communication
When lawyers do not communicate well with each other, firms—particularly midsize and larger firms—miss some terrific opportunities. Knowledge management and client relationship management (CRM) tools are essential for marketing success, yet in many firms the lawyers know little about each other's practice strengths, selling points, clients, or success stories. These firms fail to cross-sell well, do effective team marketing, and integrate laterals or other offices because internal communication is lacking. Typically, the failure to communicate is due to three factors: (1) the firm's compensation system does not encourage internal communication, much less require it, (2) the firm's value system does not monitor, measure, or reward cross-selling or the expansion of existing clients, and (3) the firm does not use technology efficiently to capture and then communicate this critical information.

Lack of Practice Management
Today's frequent purchasers of legal services have become sophisticated consumers, demanding efficient, cost-effective service, *as they define it*. However, study after study shows that without good practice group management, service does not meet client expectations of excellence. Good practice management means more than paying lip service to associate training and annual evaluations. It includes devoting substantial attention and resources to workload allocation, case management, delegation, supervision, training, mentoring, peer review, and more. As a result, practice group management—includ-

ing workload monitoring, lawyer development programs, business planning, and quality control—has become a higher priority in many firms. Marketing without effective practice management dilutes the marketing message and disappoints clients.

Lack of Accountability
Poor follow-through is probably the most prevalent problem hindering law firm marketing. Lawyers make the mistake of going through "fits and starts" or bursts of marketing activity after firm meetings or annual retreats. The pervasive mantra, "It doesn't matter what you do, just do something," encourages people to select the least personally painful options rather than the strategies and tactics that would accomplish their goals and objectives. Carefully planned, ongoing, and regular follow-through is necessary for business development success.

This follow-through does not happen without individual and firm *accountability*. Accountability means measuring, monitoring, and rewarding marketing, which in turn requires (1) establishing tracking systems, (2) developing plans and budgets, (3) instituting policies, procedures, and guidelines to help monitor effectiveness, (4) communicating regularly about efforts and results, and (5) providing strong compensation incentives.

Lack of Marketing Leadership
In many firms, the role of "marketing director" includes a heavy emphasis on performing tactical implementation, as opposed to helping shape effective strategies. Marketing directors—even chief marketing officers—often have neither a "seat at the table" nor a voice in firm management. Furthermore, they are frequently overwhelmed with providing "concierge" services—planning holiday parties, organizing boxes at sporting events, and the like. Finally, they do not have enough substantive knowledge to be pragmatic in the advice and counsel they provide to lawyers in their firms. This demotes marketing to the lowest common denominator, encouraging a continuing emphasis on ineffective activities that do not lend themselves to measurement or realization of a return on the investment of lawyer time and dollars.

Internal Individual Obstacles
Individual obstacles to marketing—including the following—are also significant.

Lack of Time
This is the most frequent excuse lawyers give for not marketing. It often masks more deep-seated reasons, such as compensation disincentives, lack of

accountability, fear of operating outside perceived levels of competence, or problems with time management.

Discomfort
Even though marketing is now "accepted" (and even expected) in most firms, there are lawyers in every firm who are not comfortable with the idea. Some mistakenly equate marketing with advertising, which they find offensive. Others accept public relations and image campaigns, but do not want to meet personally with clients and prospects "one-on-one." They may want the firm to spend countless dollars on image building, but they are unwilling to take maximum advantage of that image by embarking on systematic business development and client-care initiatives.

Many lawyers believe that only good "schmoozers" or natural salespeople are effective marketers, and if they do not have these skills, they should be relieved of any obligation to bring in business. To help combat this problem, some firms have hired sales leaders to develop sophisticated programs for targeting and teaching lawyers how to sell to clients and prospects effectively—these firms will rapidly gain a competitive advantage over lawyers who fear going face-to-face with these constituents.

Fear
Closely related to discomfort is outright fear—fear of failure or rejection. Lawyers mention fear as an obstacle in almost every sales training program.

Lack of Understanding
Many unnecessary battles are fought in law firms because lawyers simply do not understand basic marketing concepts and tools. Some who view marketing as little more than advertising or slick salesmanship fight every proposed marketing initiative. Lawyers who recognize that the keys to marketing are outstanding client service, excellent personal relationships, and strategic business development efforts (such as face-to-face pitches, cross-selling and co-selling initiatives, and client teams) cannot understand why all lawyers do not embrace it.

External Obstacles
Potential external obstacles include strong competition, ethical constraints, fear of clients' reactions, and community culture or attitudes.

Strong Competition
Aggressive efforts by competitors can sometimes dilute the effectiveness of marketing efforts. Competition often raises client awareness of all marketing,

however, and competitors' efforts can shake the complacency of some lawyers and motivate them to market more. If you feel your competitors are "beating" you by being more aggressive, you can use several strategies to respond. Because it is unlikely your competitors are doing all these things, you can achieve a marketing advantage by

(1) improving internal cross-selling efforts by implementing "key client" plans that lead you to understand everything about a client and suggest creative ways to meet the client's needs;
(2) ensuring a large number of your partners are trained in the latest relational selling techniques (many firms who believe they are "marketing aggressively" are actually doing the wrong things); and
(3) targeting niche markets or specialties, rather than trying to be all things to all people.

Ethical Constraints

The ethics rules were not designed to protect sophisticated business executives from the persuasive wiles of lawyers. They were designed to protect injured persons or unsophisticated laypersons. To our knowledge, there is not one example of a law firm being disciplined for "business-to-business" marketing. Most lawyers who raise ethical limitations as obstacles to marketing are actually using them as excuses to avoid marketing. Nevertheless, ethical rules do govern a variety of lawyer marketing activities, and they must be understood and respected.

Fear of Clients' Reactions

Despite some lawyers' fears to the contrary, many clients—particularly businesses—react positively to appropriate law firm marketing. In client interviews, we've heard CEOs make statements such as, "Lawyers are so arrogant they think they don't have to sell like the rest of us. Every successful businessperson sells something, whether it's products, services, or ideas." Clients expect law firms to tell them about their areas of expertise, and they rarely react negatively to substantive business-to-business marketing. Individual (nonbusiness) clients respond favorably as long as the marketing is understandable and not intrusive or condescending.

Community Culture or Attitudes

Most communities not only accept law firm marketing (other than tacky billboards or some television ads), they expect it. Law firm contributions to charitable organizations have grown rapidly, despite data showing this is often not good use of a firm's *marketing* budget. Research data suggest that as long as law firm marketing is tasteful and professionally executed, negative community reaction is not an issue.

Understanding Why Obstacles Exist

Before exploring ways to overcome obstacles, we must understand why they exist. The major causes of law firm marketing obstacles are insecurity, rapid change, and lack of solid business management and knowledge.

Insecurity

There is tremendous insecurity in the legal profession due to increased competition, consolidation (the big firms have gotten bigger and more formidable), and the rapid change that has characterized the industry in recent years. This causes many lawyers to adopt a "bunker mentality" or to stick their heads in the sand because they are overwhelmed by the prospect of even more change ahead. Psychologists tell us that you *can* "teach an old dog new tricks." It is next to impossible, however, to teach "scared dogs" new tricks. The legal profession is full of "scared dogs." Insecurity leads to the following reactions (that is, obstacles):

- lack of follow-through
- discomfort and fear of marketing
- lack of understanding
- perceived lack of time
- complacency

Rapid Change

Although rapid change can be a reason for insecurity, the rate and pace of change has resulted in firms with management and leadership structures that do not yet support marketing efforts. This is reflected in obstacles such as the following:

- historical mind-set
- out-of-date compensation systems
- lack of accountability
- lack of internal communication
- insufficient practice management

Lack of Solid Business Management

Despite all the talk about management committees, increased use of professional legal administrators, and the growing use of management consultants, many law firms are only beginning to implement what the business world considers basic management principles and structures. This results in many obstacles, such as the following:

- lack of strong practice group management and leadership
- insufficient management support for marketing

- lack of management, marketing, and technology training
- insufficient compensation incentives and accountability
- ineffective marketing leadership
- no "seat at the table" for marketing professionals

Overcoming the Obstacles

Although there are no magic bullets to eliminate marketing obstacles, there are some sound ways to attack the problems. It should be noted, however, that the solutions are hard to apply in many law firms, because they require willingness to change, time commitments, strong leadership, and proactive approaches (in what are typically reactive environments). Several suggested solutions follow.

Correct the Incentives

One of the most important ways to overcome obstacles is to ensure that the firm's incentive system supports the right behavior. If you tell lawyers to cross-sell, but the compensation system discourages them from doing so, your efforts will lead to frustration, not success. In fact, in firms with compensation systems that do not provide accountability for marketing, less than 25 percent of the partners typically make sufficient efforts to market.

Incentives can be monetary or nonmonetary, but the best systems use both. Monetary incentives reward not only new-client origination, but also marketing efforts (within clearly defined guidelines), such as cross-selling initiatives and team marketing. Many firms now use partner "models" or personal annual business plans to provide accountability and measure performance.

In addition, firms should set realistic expectations for individual and group marketing efforts, and for the results to be achieved. Frustration arises when unrealistic goals and expectations give lawyers a sense that they are not experiencing success. Research shows a typical partner should spend three to four hundred hours per year on marketing and should understand that it takes three to five years of efforts before significant results are seen. Some lawyers get so discouraged before they reach this point that they quit doing much marketing. Many lawyers spend enough time, but because their efforts are unfocused or they are unskilled, the time does not pay off and frustration levels rise.

Provide Marketing Education

To build acceptance and enthusiasm, it is important to create a common understanding of marketing within the firm. This can be accomplished through programs and presentations—either by outside experts or knowledgeable people within the firm—at firm retreats, firm meetings, seminars, and practice group meetings, and by frequent circulation of articles or other marketing information.

All education efforts should emphasize that legal marketing depends upon personal contacts and relationship building. The education should also provide guidance on the most effective tools for advancing personal relationships and managing networks. Many firms use antiquated marketing approaches that have lost their effectiveness.

Lawyers must learn that they each can play a valuable role in business development. Many times, lawyers' discomfort with marketing stems from their misconception that only certain models of behavior work, and that effective rainmakers have a unique style. In fact, there are many routes to take. Each lawyer can take a different approach to building relationships and developing contacts—one that suits his or her talents and interests. Often, when lawyers see comfortable roles for themselves in the process, they are more willing to participate in the efforts.

Finally, marketing education should include specific skills training. Because the most effective law firm marketing is personal contact, lawyers must feel comfortable with—and be effective at—making contacts and building relationships with existing and prospective clients. They must be good at personal "selling." Many of them also need presentation skills training to help them respond to Requests for Proposals (RFPs) and "beauty contests." For more information about RFPs, see Chapter 8, "Proposals and Responding to Requests for Proposals."

Promote Internal Communication

Because most firms miss their best marketing opportunities through a failure of internal systems, internal communication should get some serious attention.

Simply stated, lawyers do not know enough about each other's strengths, success stories, networking contacts, prospecting efforts, and the like. We have yet to see a law firm that spends *too much* time or money on internal communication. Some of the most effective marketing programs consist principally of internally focused efforts (such as cross-selling plans and seminars, internal newsletters, and lawyer skills databases).

Though many law firms now have internal marketing newsletters, others resist, claiming "lawyers won't read it" or "it's only a brag sheet." An internal marketing newsletter (or intranet) is one of the easiest, least expensive, and most effective ways to improve marketing. It works in firms that have fifteen to more than a thousand lawyers, and can be produced without the aid of outside consultants—in smaller firms, even without an in-house marketing professional.

With or without an internal newsletter, lawyers must communicate marketing success stories to each other on a regular basis. These success stories should include information about new clients attracted through team marketing, positive feedback after competitive bidding contests, business acquired or contacts made through speeches, and significant outcomes and wins for clients, such as deals completed, cases won, or partnering structures achieved, just to name a few.

Another important element of internal communication is making sure that marketing activities have a high profile and a perceived *high priority* within the firm. Marketing should be an agenda item for most management committees, and partner, firm, practice area, and staff meetings. Individual lawyers should report their successes at regular meetings. The entire firm should receive the message that marketing is important. The managing partner should be visible in his or her support of marketing, as should the practice group managers.

Strengthen Practice Management

Strong practice group managers who have been trained in their roles and who have accountability can help overcome obstacles by implementing training and development programs for the associates and partners in their groups, by encouraging individual and practice group plans, by using quality control systems, by applying new technologies, and by creating model documents and other initiatives that bring lawyers and clients together through improved communication and service.

Provide Early Success Experiences

Many lawyers are skeptical about marketing because past marketing "failures" or fits and starts have fueled cynicism (or fear) about the subject. Although education and internal communication are extremely important, firms must find ways to measure and then point to marketing successes—both large and small. You should begin your marketing program by identifying projects that, if implemented, are almost guaranteed success (such as face-to-face meetings with clients, small industry-focused seminars with built-in follow-up plans, or targeted-industry speeches with direct audience follow-up).

Identify two or more lawyers and staff persons with the best track record of follow-through and get them involved in one of these projects. Begin pilot projects with smaller groups, rather than launching firmwide programs from the start. After each project is completed successfully, communicate the success widely and regularly throughout the firm. Success breeds success. When lawyers see their colleagues succeeding, some will be encouraged to get on the bandwagon.

Obtain Client Feedback

Another excellent way to overcome some of the obstacles to business development is by obtaining client input. It can be gathered through formal client interviews, informal client visits by the relationship partners, clients speaking at retreats, or personal visits by managing partners. When clients tell lawyers what they want and expect, it is a powerful motivator—and most of what clients request, from legal updates to creative fee structures, is simply marketing.

Improve Marketing Leadership

Firms appear to be in the beginning stages of overcoming lack of leadership by hiring marketing professionals who have expertise in business development and client care, instead of relying upon promotions and communications specialists. Some firms are creating positions with titles such as Chief Marketing Officer, Director of Strategy, or Director of Sales. These people have a seat at the management table and focus on strategically positioning the firm and then arming the lawyers with the skills and processes necessary for business development success.

But, just having the leadership in place is not enough. Marketing professionals can strengthen their positions significantly by doing several key things:

- Understand law firm economics and the individual firm's compensation system.
- Focus on the big picture and not the minutiae.
- "Walk the walk" and "talk the talk"—that is, understand the practices, products, and services the firm offers to the marketplace.
- Talk with the firm's clients to develop a deep understanding of the mind-set of the purchasers of the firm's services.

Summary

The chart on the following page summarizes specific marketing obstacles and some suggested ways to overcome them. There is much overlap—you cannot view a particular obstacle in a vacuum, and there are various strategies to address each one. Adapt these and other ideas you will find throughout this book to your firm's culture. Do not let the apparent barriers to marketing become *real* obstacles—the marketplace demands change.

Ways to Overcome Marketing Obstacles	
Obstacle	**Ways to Overcome**
Historical mind-set	Incentives/accountability, education, internal communication
Complacency	Incentives/accountability, education, early successes
Inadequate compensation system and accountability	Incentives/accountability
Lack of internal communication	Education, firm meetings to focus on marketing, internal newsletters
Poor practice management	Incentives/accountability, strong firm and practice area leadership and management
Lack of follow-through	Accountability, internal communication, early successes, monitoring by administrator or in-house marketing professional, training
Lack of time	Incentives/accountability, education, realistic expectations, finding right role for each lawyer
Discomfort	Education, training, realistic expectations, finding right role for each lawyer
Fear	Education, training, realistic expectations, finding right role for each lawyer
Lack of understanding	Education, training, realistic expectations, finding right role for each lawyer, internal communication
Lack of marketing leadership	Hiring professionals with business development and client care expertise, understanding firm's products and services, being pragmatic, talking to clients

Strategic Marketing Planning

2

Hollis Hatfield Weishar
(with James A. Durham)

Background

If you are a managing partner, marketing partner, or marketing director of a law firm, then you may be faced with the task of developing a strategic plan or a strategic *marketing* plan for your firm or for a key specialty area of practice. Hundreds of articles have been written on the subject of strategic planning. It seems that everywhere we look, seminars are offering advice on how to grow, manage, position, and market law firms; and dozens of formulas, frameworks, and processes have been suggested for making strategic planning work in law firms. You can learn a lot from all this scholarship, but it is not easy to apply any of the plans or outlines to the cultures typically found in law firms.

What we call strategic "planning" is really the beginning of strategic "change," and change does not come easily in any environment—particularly in a law firm. Experience tells us that firms can spend countless hours and tens of thousands of dollars to develop strategic plans that include many goals and action items, but only a few are ever achieved or implemented.

Lawyers have a tendency to avoid change by spending a lot of time meeting, talking, and planning, but in the end, strategy implementation is "spotty" at best (assuming the lawyers actually articulate a strategy, and not just create a "to do" list).

There is great value in the discussion and critical thinking that usually occur in the planning process, but many lawyers think there is real value in the resulting document. They will almost inevitably be disappointed. Strategic planning might be viewed by firm management as the process of creating the structure and organization necessary to adapt to changing marketplace conditions and changing client needs and demands. It should be viewed as the foundation for flexibility, not an "end game."

Included as "Supplement A: The Firm Strategic Planning Process," at the end of this chapter is a detailed overview of a firmwide strategic planning process. It is the rare law firm, however, that can actually follow through on an elaborate plan. This chapter focuses upon strategic *marketing* planning, to assist you in creating a road map for new business, revenue, and market position.

Simplified Process

If you believe in practical simplification, then you could approach the process somewhat informally by having discussions related to the following few questions, and writing the general conclusions:

> A. How is the firm known in the marketplace?
> B. How do we want the firm to be known?
>> (Though the lawyers' opinions are relevant, the only way to *really* know the answer to question A is to ask clients and others in the relevant marketplace. Will the firm undertake the necessary research, by talking to clients and other businesspeople? Should it hire someone to do a quality market study?)
>
> A. What clients are we serving now?
> B. What clients do we want to serve?
>
> A. What types of services are we offering now?
> B. What types of services do we want to offer?
>
> A. How are we selling services and growing revenue now?
> B. How do we want to do it?

If $A = B$, keep doing what you are doing. If $A \neq B$, then do whatever is necessary to make $A = B$.

Realizing this approach will not satisfy the more sophisticated strategic thinkers—those who appreciate a more formal and detailed process—we have set forth below a more advanced (and more traditional) explanation of the strategic *marketing* planning process.

The Strategic Marketing Planning Process

Purpose of a Strategic Marketing Plan

A variety of factors in today's business environment make practice development and marketing efforts vital for any law firm—not only as a means of expansion, but also to prevent loss of the firm's existing client base.

Survival (The Big-Picture View)

Any professional practice is caught in a never-ending process of losing clients for perfectly valid and acceptable reasons—companies expand, merge, relocate, and close. To stay at the same level of fee income, at the very least, a firm must replace these "natural" losses, whatever their causes, and continue to provide high-quality, world-class service. By taking a "big-picture" view of marketing and by placing the client at the center of that picture, you come to realize that marketing is a means of survival. Never forget that a strategic marketing plan should have clients—both existing and potential—as the center of all efforts.

Ability to Compete

The marketplace is becoming more competitive. Clients are more sophisticated and have higher expectations. Law firms are reporting 15 percent more marketing hours than ever before. All this makes for a highly competitive marketplace. Further, many types of legal work have become commodities in the marketplace. To compete effectively, law firms must develop and market unique selling features, and substantiate billing rates by emphasizing the value-added services the firm can provide.

Personal Fulfillment

The purpose of strategic planning and an ongoing marketing program is to improve the flow of high-quality clients into the firm and increase client satisfaction with the firm's services. However, marketing should also fulfill the needs of professionals and staff persons to work at a firm they feel is a successful and productive member of the community and the profession. Marketing is not advertising or cold calling, but rather, a continuing and sophisticated combination of ascertaining the ongoing legal and business needs of target groups, and organizing people and services to meet those needs in a first-class manner at an appropriate profit.

Meeting Future Needs

An equally important aspect of marketing is determining the services clients will want in the future, which the firm may not currently provide. A strategic marketing plan must identify hot markets for work in the next five to ten years, and move in the direction of capitalizing on these opportunities. At the same time, the firm should be aware of any practice areas that may be on the wane.

Clear Direction and Control

A good strategic marketing plan can provide control and direction as growth of the firm is maintained and increased. A plan should detail growth objectives and the strategies and actions required in achieving those objectives.

The implementation of the actions will result in a stronger, healthier, and more fulfilling practice.

Now That We Know What to Do, Where Do We Begin?
Step 1: Situation Analysis; Meeting with Key Individuals
Call a meeting with key individuals, including the managing partner, management committee members, director of marketing, and others who are interested in the process and important to the law firm's marketing program. Also, review the firm's current marketing literature and determine how members of the firm use it.

Step 2: Vision Session or Retreat; S.W.O.T. Analysis
It can be helpful to have either a half-day retreat or a ninety-minute "vision session" over lunch in the office. In larger law firms, it is necessary to do a series of vision sessions. The purpose of the retreat or vision session is to get information from the group and build consensus.

Typically, a S.W.O.T. (Strengths, Weaknesses, Opportunities, and Threats) analysis is performed during either the retreat or vision session. This analysis must be facilitated by an individual who can use a variety of exercises to help the group focus on (1) the perceived position of the law firm in the marketplace and in the minds of the clients, (2) desired growth patterns and potential for the law firm, and (3) opportunities to cultivate new clients.

Planning a Marketing Retreat or "Vision Session"
(1) First, identify your goals.
- ❑ Encourage open discussion.
- ❑ Solicit ideas from the *entire* group.
- ❑ Build consensus.
- ❑ Encourage out-of-the-box thinking.
- ❑ Ask the hard questions.
- ❑ Formulate conclusions for each session.
- ❑ Keep the discussion focused.
- ❑ Cut off the discussion when necessary.
- ❑ Make sure you have fun.
- ❑ Provide a written plan for follow-up.

(2) Then, look back for a brief historical overview.
- ❑ Why are we here? How has the legal environment changed over the last _____ years?
- ❑ What types of changes have we experienced in the last ten years, in terms of practice areas, clients, and personnel?

- ❏ What have been the primary forces generating this change? What have been our marketing "actions" and firm "reactions"?
- ❏ What has given us the ability to adapt successfully? Have we experienced some cultural success with marketing?
- ❏ What are the key strengths and weaknesses of our firm?
- ❏ How does our firm differ from our competitors' firms?
- ❏ Why do clients use our firm?
    - ◆ performance/quality of work
    - ◆ personal relationships
    - ◆ competence/experience
    - ◆ special skill
    - ◆ knowledge of client industry/business
    - ◆ written and verbal communication skills
    - ◆ professional image/reputation
    - ◆ location
    - ◆ cost/fees/price
    - ◆ financial terms and conditions
    - ◆ dependability/reliability
    - ◆ persistence
    - ◆ availability
    - ◆ bottom-line results
- ❏ How has our financial *growth* been affected?

(3) Now . . . look forward.
- ❏ What are the primary forces that will change our firm or areas of practice in the next ten years?
    - ◆ physical issues
    - ◆ clients
    - ◆ competitors
    - ◆ economic issues
    - ◆ technological changes
    - ◆ social issues
    - ◆ political issues
    - ◆ legal issues
- ❏ Where do we want to be in three to five years?
- ❏ What are our major opportunities and threats?

(4) Develop a unified approach.
- ❏ Summarize three to five key points relating to your discussion.
- ❏ List your desired client types.
- ❏ Discuss how you can develop new programs, including key-client focus, creative partnering, risk-sharing arrangements, legal budgeting for clients, and advanced case management.

❑ Identify *ten* priorities to accomplish over the *next six* months.
❑ Plan how to communicate the goals and key priorities.

(5) Finally . . .
❑ Create a written, strategic marketing plan.
❑ Identify your goals (for example, "Grow intellectual property (IP) practice by 10 percent").
❑ List the tactics planned to achieve goals (for example, "Develop new brochure for IP practice, establish client teams for key IP clients, sell service to firm clients who do not presently use IP").
❑ Set priorities.
❑ Budget appropriately.
❑ Develop a detailed marketing calendar.
❑ Implement, monitor, and revise.
❑ Measure your success *every* three months.

Step 3: Client Feedback and Analysis

Client interviews—which are generally necessary to evaluate clients' views of the firm—can be performed during the strategic planning process. Personal visits are best. In addition, an analysis of the firm's existing client base is essential. Through a client analysis, the law firm should identify which clients provide 80 percent of revenues in any single area of practice. From this list of clients, the firm can identify industry strengths, geographic strengths, and practice area strengths, and can also explore which clients are profitable. Client profiles can be developed for each partner's top clients, illustrating billing trends over the past three years, areas of law provided to the clients, pertinent information about the clients' businesses, and other law firms that the clients use regularly. These client profiles can then be reviewed, and opportunities to expand the client relationships can be included in the marketing plan.

Step 4: Market Research and Analysis

Information about the marketplace is essential to any law firm, and this information is easily obtainable. Several companies execute market research studies and can provide valuable data about the marketplace. Every law firm should also have an active "prospect" list of up to a dozen companies that the firm would like to secure as clients. Research on these companies can be performed (often by the firm's librarian) and a one-page marketing plan can be developed for each prospective client. This makes it easier to track marketing success or failure.

How Do We Apply the Knowledge We Have Gained?

At this point in the process, your firm or practice group will have a clear view of where it is. Moving forward, you should ask, "What are the opportunities for the law firm or group?"

Step 5: Crafting the Mission Statement; Positioning

The mission statement communicates the goals of the law firm in a simple statement. It is communicated internally within the firm, as well as externally to the world. The mission statement should go beyond "wordsmithing" to form an image of the law firm. It should be the "headline" about your business, and is important because it defines you and sharpens your focus. A clear mission statement enables you to clarify your purpose to anyone you engage—from your banker to prospective clients. It differentiates you from the pack, which is an important aspect of your ability to compete. The mission statement should clearly describe (1) the nature of your practice or service, and (2) the markets you want to serve.

Sample Mission Statements

Our firm's mission is to assist our clients in achieving their legal, business, and financial goals. We provide creative solutions that are cost-effective and consistently exceed client expectations. The firm's commitment to excellence is reflected in our long-term relationships with our clients, in the professional development of our people, and in our reputation in the community.

We strive to be a preeminent, New York business law firm that delivers consistently high-quality, responsive, and cost-effective legal service. We will work to build lasting client relationships based upon honest dialogue and the timely exchange of information. We will always treat others with dignity and respect. We will share with our community a portion of the leadership, skill, and other resources we enjoy, and will fulfill our ethical and professional responsibilities to the legal system, our clients, and the public.

Your mission statement is one method by which you can position your firm, or differentiate it from other firms in the marketplace. Positioning the law firm to the external world is very important. Law firms can own any number of market positions—positions based upon geographic location, industry expertise, price, and so on. Many law firms base positions upon their business sense, service, value to the client, spirit of innovation, or an individual lawyer's reputation. To position your firm effectively, and differentiate it from all other law firms, you should explore service offerings, professional and employee attitudes, and marketing communications (every piece of paper published by the firm—letters, forms, advertisements, and brochures—reflects the firm's market position), as well as the community involvement efforts of the firm's lawyers. Most importantly, the position should be as specific as possible (for example, "a Florida firm serving middle-market businesses in every region of the state and in Latin America").

Step 6: Planning on Many Levels—Firm, Practice Group, Niche Area, and Individual

Strategic Marketing Plan for the Firm
The final step in the strategic marketing planning process is the development of a written marketing or strategic plan (or plans) for the law firm. The written plan should be concise (no one will read 300 pages) and address client relations, firm-specific activities, plans to develop marketing support materials, any planned advertising, and a public-relations program, as well as a comprehensive "action items" list, an implementation schedule, and a budget. The plan should contain defined goals and targets, as well as key-result areas, which should be achievable and measurable. (See "Supplement B: A Sample Strategic Marketing Plan," at the end of this chapter.)

Strategic Marketing Plans for Practice Groups or Niche Areas
You may also find it helpful and meaningful to develop strategic marketing plans for specific practice groups, niche areas, or even individual clients. Use your firm strategic marketing plan as a model (so you have consistency in format), and remember that these plans should be goal oriented and concise.

Strategic Marketing Plans for Individuals
Each lawyer in the firm should complete an individual marketing plan. This is valuable for three reasons: (1) it helps the individual articulate goals, organize efforts, and set priorities, (2) it helps identify clients or prospects that more than one individual is marketing, so the firm can establish client or prospect "teams" to facilitate the marketing and development of clients, and (3) it provides a way to assign marketing budgets to individuals. Individual plans can also be evaluated for opportunities to cross-sell new services to existing clients. Ideally, the individual plans will complement, support, and be an extension of the firm strategic marketing plan. (See the section entitled "Individual Marketing Plans" near the end of this chapter for ideas regarding what to include in such plans.)

The Strategic Marketing Plan

Overview of the Plan
A comprehensive marketing plan is inclusive, beginning with the marketing goals of the firm, continuing with an implementation schedule, and ending with a marketing background section and budget. Most marketing plans contain three major components:

> (1) *Marketing Goals, Priorities, and Action Plan*: Specific marketing goals should be developed from information gathered and analyzed during meetings with lawyers, the management committee, or marketing

committee. The overall goals should cover no more than a three-year period. Specific priorities should be clearly identified for each year, and immediate priorities can be listed in boldface type (or placed in a separate marketing summary for the given year). An action plan should follow each goal and provide a step-by-step strategy to achieve it.

(2) *Marketing Background*: The marketing background section includes the vision and mission statements for the organization, as well as a list of present areas of expertise, and the market segments and potential niche strategies for the firm.

(3) *Budget*: This simply details the costs associated with implementing the tactics contained in the plan.

Remember that the objective of any strategic marketing plan is to establish order, control marketing activities and expenditures, and provide direction for the management and growth of the firm.

Specific Elements of the Strategic Marketing Plan
Market Position

You should identify the market position the firm occupies at present. This could include information about the size of the firm, its location, the strength of its position in its current market, the types of clients it serves, and the services provided those clients. You may also want to include information about any law firm networks or alliances with which you are affiliated.

The Six Market Segments

Every law firm should direct its marketing activities in six market segments, which should be reflected in the strategic marketing plan. These market segments are the sources of new clients for the firm, and include firm members, existing clients, local prospective clients, general prospective clients, in-house counsel, and other referral sources.

Firm Members

This group includes all professional and support staff, as well as lawyers. The lawyers must make everyone in the firm aware of all capabilities and expertise, and get everyone in the firm involved in client relations and business development, to the greatest extent possible.

Existing Clients

Existing clients should be a firm's best referral source. If you provide prompt and high-quality service, as well as value, you will obtain referrals. Cross-selling is part of this. You must make a concerted effort to educate clients about the firm's services. Research shows that clients typically are not aware of the range of services available from their law firms. Lawyers must thoroughly analyze the needs, expectations, and desires of clients, and model their service offerings accordingly.

Local Prospective Clients

This group includes potential clients that the firm does not presently represent, but with whom the firm would like to do business. A list of prospects for both the short term and long term should be included in the individual marketing plan of each lawyer, and the firm should have a meaningful number of firmwide prospects as well.

General Prospective Clients (International, National, Regional)

Your firm wants to represent those included in this group because they currently do business in your state or region or may do so in the future. The firm could offer practice areas in which it has built—or could build—sophisticated expertise that is not easily replicated, or practice areas in which the firm's lawyers have the ability to do high-quality work nationally, but at far less expense than other firms.

In-House Counsel

Members of in-house counsel staff frequently make decisions about which firms to retain for legal services. Your firm should (1) develop a database of those businesses in your market area that have in-house legal departments and the need to use outside firms, and then (2) develop a program to make those businesses aware of your firm's capabilities in specific areas that may interest them.

Other Referral Sources

Last, but not least, general referrals may turn out to be the most important part of the firm's marketing efforts. A major push should take place to maximize specific referral sources and build relationships with key individuals who can send your firm business. Individual members of the firm should make a concentrated effort in this area, which includes building strong relationships with accountants and other lawyers through trade associations and similar organizations. Individuals in your firm must do significant courting of these individuals, particularly on the local level, to make sure they know your firm wants new work, has a desire to develop new clients, and has a dedication to client service. Your firm should make these referral sources aware of your full range of capabilities.

Niche Strategy

To build a successful niche strategy, it helps to isolate a specific number of practice areas that are likely to grow and develop needs during the next five years. This could include service niches (such as estate planning, litigation, healthcare, or intellectual property), geographic niches (defined by city, state, region, or country), and specialty-market niches (such as closely held businesses, physicians, construction companies, or corporations). Individual lawyers can consider these broad niches in their marketing plans. By focusing marketing efforts upon a select number of niche areas, each lawyer can create a successful and *manageable* marketing program. If lawyers try to be all things to all people, they will fail. Your firm should build a reputation for having specialized expertise in select areas, and strongly market the services in those areas.

Overall Strategies for Success

Strategies are courses of action necessary to achieve firm goals, capitalize on firm strengths, and overcome firm weaknesses. Every strategic marketing plan needs them. Strategies cover the following areas:

- people
- product (service)
- place
- promotion
- price

People

In a service business, people are the most important asset. Clients judge services by the professionalism and technical competence of the firm's people. Because a law firm does not necessarily have a "product," and the services that a firm provides are intangible, clients, prospective clients, and contacts will search for clues by which to judge the firm. Among those clues is the image projected by people. The professional dress and conduct of staff persons, and the manner in which the phone is answered and clients are greeted, are extremely important. Therefore, your firm should continue to stress professionalism, attentiveness, and concern at all levels of the organization, at all times. Your firm should also stress the importance of working as a team. *This is a priority.* Implementing your strategic marketing plan should be the responsibility of *all* members of the firm, from the managing partner to the receptionists and mailroom workers.

As part of your marketing plan, you should establish a philosophy that encourages the continued professional growth and development of all personnel—maximizing their potential and thereby maximizing client service.

Product (Service)

Expanding the range of services the firm can provide clients, and focusing upon *specific* services that clients desire, are necessary steps to addressing clients' needs. Through a survey of selected clients and regular client contact, your firm can better understand the additional services clients may desire. All lawyers should strive to serve these evolving needs by developing current personnel, hiring necessary expertise, or establishing relationships with qualified individuals to whom they will refer clients to ensure needs are met.

Place

Your firm should clearly articulate the location of your marketplace. Some lawyers may have practices that are national in scope, while others may focus their energies upon the local marketplace.

Promotion

Your marketing objectives are probably focused upon client satisfaction, retention, and development, and your marketing efforts should not lose sight of that. Marketing should be divided between maintaining existing clients and adding new ones. Generally, as a rule of thumb, you should spend about 75 percent of your "marketing time" on taking care of and expanding existing client relationships. The other 25 percent should be devoted to establishing new relationships and business development.

Your firm should support individual participation in community and professional groups, as deemed appropriate. Lawyers should be encouraged to develop individual marketing plans, which serve as outlines for individual participation in the firm's marketing program. Activities such as writing articles, speaking, participating in seminars, and contributing to community projects should be detailed in these plans.

Price

In comparing your firm's fees with those of other firms, on both a local and national basis, your firm should strive to maintain a "value-added" philosophy, to offer clients more for their money, and to create positive feelings in clients (especially when they are paying your bills). Pricing is an important component to consider when developing any marketing plan. You may want to get some feedback from your clients regarding their comfort level with your fees.

Individual Marketing Plans

Key questions for any individual marketing plan include the following:

- How many hours per week, on average, are you willing to devote to business development and client retention activities?
- Are there areas of practice in which you specialize? If so, what areas?
- Are there other areas in which you would like to become more specialized?

- List three clients or prospects who might benefit from your existing—or new—area(s) of expertise. How will you present this specialization to these clients or prospects?
- List the five most valuable clients with whom you work.
- Identify which of the following activities you will do to improve your relationship with these clients: (1) increase communication (take the client to lunch or dinner, visit the client's place of business, send the client advisories), (2) learn more about the client's business or industry, and present business ideas to the client, (3) conduct a client satisfaction interview, and look for ways to cross-sell new services, and (4) list other ways in which you could improve your level of service to the client.
- If you were to target three potential clients this year (to whom you could sell firm services other than your own), who would they be?
- List one step you will take to move each of these prospects closer to "client status."
- List your three most valuable sources of referrals.
- To whom do you make the most referrals?
- List one or two new people to whom you can refer business.
- List one way you will thank or acknowledge each in the next thirty days.
- In which organizations are you active (including professional/business/civic)?
- Write one goal for increased leadership or contribution this year.
- In which other organizations would you like to become active this year?
- If you were required to write an article on two topics this year, what would they be?
- On which topic will you try to speak or write this year?
- If you were to follow up on three clients that you or the firm lost, who would they be?
- Describe other business development/marketing activities not mentioned that are important or of interest to you.
- Based upon the above questions and answers, what will be your primary marketing goal for the year?

Weekly Marketing Plan Checklist

It can be helpful to your program to provide individuals with *gentle reminders* that they should be marketing. Offer them laminated cards or something to post in their offices to remind them to market—every week! An example follows.

✓ *Check those items accomplished every week:*

80% OF YOUR TIME SHOULD BE SPENT ON "RELATIONSHIP BUILDING"

___ Contact your **existing clients** at least weekly.

___ Make a list of and call or visit your **referral sources** on a regular basis.

___ Make a list of at least **three targets** and contact your target clients at least every two weeks—remember it can take seven contacts before they remember you.

___ Have your library or a member of your support staff do some **research** about your target clients and think of ways you could help them solve their problems or capture opportunities.

___ Make your **friends/family/social contacts** aware of the capabilities of the firm.

___ Work to build relationships and communicate with **other partners/ professionals** in the firm.

___ Create a list of **other professionals outside the firm** who might be referral sources.

___ Have someone else do a **client interview** with one of your clients.

___ Send your clients, contacts, and referral sources an **article** of interest to them.

___ Take someone to **breakfast, lunch, or dinner.**

___ Invite someone to a **sporting or cultural event, or to play golf or tennis.**

___ Send out your card, **a firm profile**, or information on a specific practice area or area of expertise.

___ Invite selected contacts to a **seminar.**

___ Send **personal notes** of congratulations for accomplishments.

___ **Join organizations** that are meaningful to your clients and contacts.

___ Update your **mailing list.**

___ Send **holiday cards.**

___ Send **thank-you notes** for referrals.

___ Become actively involved in the **community.**

___ Involve your **secretary/support staff** in your marketing efforts.

___ **Track your results** and remove unproductive prospects, referral sources, and clients.

___ Think about ways you can expand services to clients; **cross-sell** other firm professionals.

___ Develop a **client service team** and prepare a marketing plan for an individual client.

___ Offer to help clients with **project/case management and budgeting.**

20% OF YOUR TIME SHOULD BE SPENT ON "REPUTATION BUILDING"

___ Identify three newsworthy matters about which you can **write** an article or client alert.
___ **Read** a variety of industry publications to learn what issues are important to your clients and contacts.
___ **Join** an association that supports your practice specialty.
___ Obtain the **mailing list** for group(s) in which you participate.
___ **Send** at least one article, letter, or client update per month to those individuals on your mailing list.
___ Update your **résumé and bio** to include recent achievements.
___ **Speak** when you can on your area of expertise.
___ Send a **letter to editors** who might be interested in publishing articles prepared by you; include a list of topics for them to consider, and then stay in touch and get to know them.
___ Get more involved in **industry groups** related to your area of expertise.
___ Make sure a **press release** is issued for your accomplishments.
___ Make sure your accomplishments are **communicated internally** in the firm.
___ Contribute to your **Web site**; announce areas of interest, important accomplishments, or developments.
___ Make sure you are aware of **conferences/seminars/trade shows** to attend within your area of expertise; offer to speak or moderate a program.
___ Respond to **RFPs** if this is appropriate for your area of practice.
___ Watch for **upcoming events in the community** that will provide you with an opportunity to meet people.
___ Work on preparing a **"twenty-second infomercial"** about the firm and your practice.
___ Attend a **networking event** and really network.
___ Make a list of ways that your **practice is different** from your competitors' practices.

Supplement A: The Firm Strategic Planning Process

To engage in strategic planning, you need a clear understanding of who you really are, what you are capable of, what business you are in, what value you create for your clients, and how you differentiate yourself in winning and keeping your clients. The key is to create the means to make the most of whatever the business environment presents. The task is to use *strategic thinking* and create a strategic plan to create success.

Some Thoughts on Why Law Firms Lose Their Way

Many law firms appear to be no more than a collection of individuals practicing under one roof. Sometimes it seems that midsize or large firms have fifty different businesses operating at once. Often these businesses fail to enhance one another, and can even compete for a firm's marketing budget and resources. Remember, if a law firm is at war with itself, it can never be very effective on the battlefield of business! This is an important concept to accept and explore when you enter the strategic planning process.

Leadership Is Important

In the process of developing a plan, answers come through a careful process of creative thinking and logical reasoning that must be unique to each firm. The process of strategic planning or goal setting has fundamental features that make it relevant to almost any challenge facing any law firm, but leadership is necessary to achieve success. Someone must work hard to craft the vision and define the direction. Someone must put the right people in the right places and build a "marketing team." Someone must build consensus about the plan and communicate it widely and frequently, and at least one individual must face difficult issues and make tough decisions.

In Planning Your Strategy, Set Clear Rules of the Game

Sure, you could probably assemble a dozen of your best and brightest lawyers around a conference-room table in your office and work for a day to develop a strategic plan. Every law firm is full of highly intelligent people who love to offer their opinions and expertise regarding marketing. But maybe it is smarter to do some external research (in addition to your internal conference-table sessions with your best and brightest) to identify some driving patterns, including economic considerations, demographics, client feelings and preferences, and the ways in which information technology and globalization are changing the way we do business.

Designing a Strategy: How Not to Do It

Many law firms have planning systems that are bottom heavy. They spend a great deal of time and effort getting all the practice group, departmental, and individual tactical plans written, but little or no time thinking about the basic strategy or direction of the business. To correct this strategy, law firms must try to set some firmwide goals. These can include tactics that involve the entire firm, such as starting a client interview program, or beginning a marketing training program for lawyers or support staff, or sending out regular press releases. These are examples of marketing tactics that benefit the whole firm. Firms must then go beyond simply planning, and begin doing. Many firms create grandiose strategic plans, supported by elaborately detailed budgets, resource estimates, tactical plans, and timetables, most of which ultimately have little connection to the success of the business.

Designing a Strategy: How to Do It

Think about the future. Where does your firm want to be in three years? In five years? Focus on "futuring," instead of just *planning*. A forward-thinking approach can help law firms form pictures of where they are going. Ask the tough questions: Is our labor practice becoming obsolete? Should we still be focusing on serving labor unions, or should we train our people to focus on the growing areas of employment law, such as sexual harassment in the workplace and age discrimination? Although developing a plan is necessary, it should be focused on the future "picture" and how to achieve that picture. Law firms should not get caught up in the process of planning, but should be able to move beyond process.

The Six Levels of Strategic Planning Success

(1) *A Vision*: Who is ABC Law Firm and who do we want to become?
(2) *A Mission Statement*: It is helpful to create a written statement of how the firm must do business, how it defines clients, what value it creates for clients, how it will keep clients' business, and how it can work with clients to get critical feedback regarding their desires and the firm's performance. Many firms come up with documents to serve as their strategy statements, philosophy statements, value statements, or company policies, but too often even the most basic

document of this kind never gets far beyond the management committee. Your mission statement should go beyond "wordsmithing" to *form an image of the firm*. Someone who is reading the statement should be able to ascertain the qualities that make your firm unique relative to other firms. Your statement should be short, memorable, and catchy so that people can remember it!

(3) *External Information about the Market*: You need some indication about what is going on in the *external* world—with your competitors and throughout the economy—concerning technological, political, and social changes within your defined geographic market.

(4) *Internal Information about Your Strengths, Weaknesses, Opportunities, and Threats*: Work with your lawyers to obtain their perspectives about your firm and your practice. Ask questions including these: Who are we? What are we good at? Are we a team? What are we committed to? What are our best opportunities?

(5) *Goals for Growth*: These can include both qualitative goals (such as, "We want to become the number-one healthcare firm in Kansas City") and quantitative goals (such as those having revenue/growth targets, market-share targets, or cost-reduction targets). These goals should be as specific as possible, and be supported with detailed tactical plans.

(6) *Implementation and Measurement*: Do not keep your plan a secret! Set realistic targets, provide training to individuals who are responsible for implementation, keep the strategic marketing plan as simple as possible, and try to make it measurable. And remember, success is never final, and neither is the strategy.

Supplement B: A Sample Strategic Marketing Plan

Marketing Plan and Background

Following is a sample strategic marketing plan that you can adapt for your own firm. In your plan, you may want to include a section on marketing background, such as a summary of your client interview program, market research data, economic reports, or any other materials you used in developing the plan.

Marketing Goals, Priorities, and Action Plan

The goals and objectives will be revised on an ongoing basis, as needed, and are an important part of the long-range planning effort of the firm. These marketing goals reflect specific activities that presently are viewed as offering the best opportunity and highest payoff for the firm. The goals presented here are for a two- to three-year period. In an effort to identify a manageable level of activity, and to establish priorities for the next year, all headers, capped and listed in **boldface** type throughout the plan will be executed in [year].

This marketing plan was created for ABC Law Firm as a formal outline of planned marketing activity for the next two to three years. The marketing plan, as a whole, details a very comprehensive approach to marketing. Considering personnel, time, and monetary constraints, it is necessary to prioritize activities to ensure successful completion of this plan.

Overall Objectives for ABC Law Firm

GOALS FOR GROWTH
1. 5%–7% net increase in chargeable hours per year
   ($_____ x 6% = $_____ additional revenue)
2. Increase in chargeable hours for all personnel per year as follows: one-half from new business and one-half from existing clients
   ($_____ new and $_____ existing)

MARKETING GOALS

1. Maintain client satisfaction, develop central client database, and develop new business from existing client base.
2. Cultivate active referral sources and develop a program to maximize referral opportunities.
3. Target market-specific niches and develop a specific prospect list of clients from whom the firm will generate new business.
4. Position the firm to expand and strengthen awareness of ABC Law Firm in our market.
5. Internal marketing—build a marketing culture and improve marketing firmwide.

Goal # 1: Maintain Client Satisfaction, Develop Central Client Database, and Develop New Business from Existing Client Base

ABC Law Firm will strive to retain the firm's existing client base and to continue building on the satisfaction of those clients by providing superior client service. This also includes generating new business from those clients through cross-selling of new services. The firm will strive in [year] to improve communication with existing clients and referral sources.

The firm will focus on expanding relationships with existing clients in an effort to (1) further develop the "value-added" concept, (2) strengthen key client relationships and cultivate our primary source of new business, (3) expand our services to existing clients, (4) better understand how clients view us, and (5) specifically promote selected niche areas.

EXISTING CLIENTS

Existing clients continue to be our most valuable new-business source. We must constantly recognize the importance of providing *high-quality* service to them. This includes proper use of the telephone and voice mail. Clients should be given options when calling the office, and voice mail should be used appropriately. High-quality service—a much broader concept than high quality in the technical sense—entails providing our services to clients on a timely basis at a reasonable cost. High-quality service means assisting clients in improving their profitability and operations through value-added legal services. We must be proactive with our clients and help them plan their legal strategies. The specific programs relating to existing clients follow.

CLIENT CONTACT PROGRAM

- We will emphasize ongoing involvement at both partner and associate levels in this program. Reporting of these efforts should be a requirement.

- An initial minimum goal of the client contact program will be one client meeting of a practice development nature per week, with a further goal of meeting with each client every six months.
- "Welcome to Our Firm" letters from the engagement partner will be sent to new clients.
- Targeted seminars will be held for selected clients, prospects, and referral sources.
- A client satisfaction/needs survey will be developed and conducted.
- A checklist will be developed and used as a reminder about additional services to provide existing clients.
- Exit interviews will be conducted, as an analysis of lost clients. A memorandum should be prepared and forwarded to the marketing committee whenever a client is lost.

STRATEGIES TO ACHIEVE GOAL #1 IN [YEAR]
Maintain Client Satisfaction, Develop Central Client Database, and Develop New Business from Existing Client Base

ACTION STEP	RESPONSIBILITY	PRIORITY	DATE
EXISTING CLIENTS			
◆ Mail "Welcome to Our Firm" letter for all new clients, which will be sent to them from the managing partner.	_____	_____	_____
◆ Conduct yearly client satisfaction survey:			
Develop survey and obtain principal approval.	_____	_____	_____
Send survey to clients, and perform personal interview.	_____	_____	_____
Tabulate results and report.	_____	_____	_____
◆ Implement key principal visibility program, which involves having each principal meet with existing clients to ask, "How are we doing? What can we do better? How can we improve our service to you?" It is important to report results (a memo to the marketing committee), which can be summarized and reported on an ongoing basis.	_____	_____	_____
◆ Send birthday greetings to clients.	_____	_____	_____

- Conduct exit interviews for outgoing clients. _____ _____ _____

- Develop a strategy to deal with transition issues resulting from retirement of partners. _____ _____ _____

- Update client listing to include bank name and key bank contact, law firm and principal lawyer, and SIC codes. _____ _____ _____

- Institute program where professional staff write letters (samples available on system) to selected in-house counsel and other referral sources, thanking them for their assistance during the engagement. These letters go to agreed-upon individuals at least once a year. The engagement partner approves these letters. _____ _____ _____

- Consider conducting a seminar for our clients and potential clients before [date]. _____ _____ _____

- Conduct in-house seminars once or twice a year in the office to address specific topics of interest to clients. _____ _____ _____

- Design a more complete "client service opportunities" or "client needs analysis" checklist in an effort to further develop and cross-sell the practice. Tie this to a client-education program. _____ _____ _____

Goal #2: Cultivate Active Referral Sources and Develop a Program to Maximize Referral Opportunities

By using a well-established network of referral sources, the firm can generate new business. Individuals must ask for the business! For all referral sources, specific programs include the following:

- Interfacing with our counterparts (partners and associates, middle management)
- Encouraging referral sources to view us as a resource
- Inviting referral sources to conduct training sessions for our staff on what they do
- Joining their trade associations (if possible)

- Making targeted technical presentations to their trade associations or to their companies
- Referring business to key referral sources on a selected basis and making sure they know who referred it

ACCOUNTANTS/CPAS/OTHER LAW FIRMS

We must expand our network of professional service firms to focus on relationship building with the following referral sources:

- Targeted law firms, including those that specialize in specific practice areas in which we do not practice
- Specific CPAs who want to conduct seminars for or with our firm

BANKS

Commercial bankers continue to be one of our major referral sources, and we will keep targeting and networking with them. It is critical that our professionals interact with their counterparts at these banks. Our lawyers must make it a point to know the loan officers assigned to their clients and should begin developing relationships with them (one bank at a time).

- Targeted banks include ____, ____, and ____
- We will hold at least one bank reception in the fall of each year

STRATEGIES TO ACHIEVE GOAL #2 IN [YEAR]
Cultivate Active Referral Sources and Develop a Program to Maximize Referral Opportunities

ACTION STEP	RESPONSIBILITY	PRIORITY	DATE
REFERRAL SOURCES			
◆ Update database of referral sources.	_____	_____	_____
◆ Develop a specific plan regarding how to market referral sources, including accountants, other lawyers, brokers, and insurance consultants.	_____	_____	_____
◆ Identify and create a list of specific referral sources.	_____	_____	_____
◆ Organize receptions to be held in our office for the following banks: _____	_____	_____	_____

- Host cocktail receptions for the following CPA firms: _____

- Host a dinner or reception with one or more of the following stockbroker firms: _____

- Host a dinner or reception with one insurance agent: _____

- Identify banks or groups of commercial lenders for a seminar, and conduct one seminar before the end of the year.

- Ensure that significant emphasis is placed upon the cultivation of referral sources, particularly bankers and other lawyers, but also existing clients, in all individual marketing plans.

  Develop a referral card system to track referrals.

Goal #3: Target Market-Specific Niches and Develop a Specific Prospect List of Clients from Whom the Firm Will Generate New Business

The firm must take a more proactive approach to business development. If the right process is followed within key niche areas, the firm will secure new clients. The firm must bring in a constant flow of new clients to survive. Specific prospect lists will be gathered and contacts will be made. Brochures or flyers describing niche services will be developed. Specific mailings will be done to target niches and prospect lists. The firm has a particular interest in increasing market share of small to medium-size emerging companies, which typically have $5–$50 million in revenue and in-house legal staffs.

SPECIFIC PROSPECTIVE CLIENTS
[Include a meaningful list. A large or even midsize firm should have at least ten or twelve.]

NICHE MARKETING PROGRAM
Specific marketing plans will be developed for specialized services (niches), and partners and associates will be encouraged to increase their credibility and name recognition to develop a "famous person" concept within niche

areas. The "famous person" is the one whom potential clients consider the expert in any given area of practice. As part of this effort, the firm will expand and continue to develop skills, materials, and other resources needed to broaden service offerings in consultative areas. The following areas will be explored and evaluated:

[List areas.]

STRATEGIES TO ACHIEVE GOAL #3 IN [YEAR]
Target Market-Specific Niches and Develop a Specific Prospect List of Clients from Whom the Firm Will Generate New Business

ACTION STEP	RESPON-SIBILITY	PRIORITY	DATE
TARGET AND NICHE MARKETING			
◆ Obtain a written action plan from niche leaders for marketing business niche services through [date].	_____	_____	_____
◆ Meet with all lawyers and legal assistants to develop written individual marketing plans and finalize them.	_____	_____	_____
◆ Expand the mailing list for newsletters and consider developing specific newsletters or "legal briefs" for various industries.	_____	_____	_____
◆ Develop a top-ten desired-client list within each niche area, and perform research to develop a marketing plan for each. Target ten prospective clients, and have individuals gather information on them (their bankers and lawyers, for example). Make an attempt to secure a meeting or, at least, to get them on our mailing list for newsletter mailings.	_____	_____	_____
◆ Use the newsletters to "sell a theme," such as estate planning or health care.	_____	_____	_____
◆ Implement a system to track proposals (proposal control sheet), to monitor the status of proposals, and to determine the win/loss ratio and the principal reasons for success or failure.	_____	_____	_____

- Review the existing proposal letter format and narrative, evaluate it, and revise it if necessary. _____ _____ _____

- Create "model" proposals for specific services and client types. _____ _____ _____

- Target dental schools and other health care providers as a prospective client group. _____ _____ _____

- Identify all reports and procedures required in tracking marketing. _____ _____ _____

- Develop specialty-area marketing brochures or collateral materials, develop a direct-mail list, and execute the direct-mail program. _____ _____ _____

- Implement an eighteen-month follow-up program for new business development. _____ _____ _____

Goal #4: Position the Firm to Expand and Strengthen Awareness of ABC Law Firm in Our Market

ABC Law Firm must clearly identify a position in the marketplace that differentiates the firm from all other legal service providers and highlights the firm's unique capabilities and diversity. Using a consistent "look" or corporate identity is an important part of this process. The firm will continue to strengthen the market's overall awareness of who it is and what it does.

ABC Law Firm will be positioned as experienced, knowledgeable, and professional, and as providing close personal attention and high-quality service, particularly as business advisor to closely held business owners and privately held companies. The firm's mailing list of clients, contacts, and community leaders is a key part of this effort. The firm will explore improved processes to ensure the mailing list is updated and expanded on a regular basis.

COMMUNITY INVOLVEMENT

- Active participation in business, charitable, and civic associations, with emphasis on enthusiastic and regular participation, will be strongly encouraged.
- Every member of the professional staff will be encouraged to participate in at least one organization, which could be a business, charitable, recreational, or religious organization.

PUBLIC RELATIONS

- We will issue press releases for significant accomplishments.
- We will work with the press for potential feature-story coverage and to develop opportunities for writing articles.

NAME RECOGNITION/IMAGE

- The firm will design and develop "institutional" firm advertisements for publications and program book usage on an as-needed basis.
- The firm will identify various trade shows in which it will participate during the coming year.
- The firm will keep its Web site up-to-date.

COLLATERAL MATERIALS

- The firm will develop product brochures for the selected niche areas.
- More individuals in the firm will use the firm brochure in appropriate ways.
- The firm will continue quarterly publication of its newsletter.
- The firm will consider promotional items for client/staff use, such as coffee mugs or T-shirts.

SEMINARS AND SPEAKING ENGAGEMENTS

- The firm will hold at least three seminars per year and will follow each one with a specific contact program.

STRATEGIES TO ACHIEVE GOAL #4 IN [YEAR]

Position the Firm to Expand and Strengthen Awareness of ABC Law Firm in Our Market

ACTION STEP	RESPON-SIBILITY	PRIORITY	DATE
AWARENESS OF FIRM IN MARKET			
• Issue regular press releases, for items such as promotions, major appointments, speeches or presentations, and firm anniversaries. Information for press releases is to be generated by the marketing staff and/or committee.	_____	_____	_____
• Design and develop industry niche brochures for selected niches.	_____	_____	_____

- Determine and formalize a process that will ensure the quarterly update of the firm's mailing list. Expand the mailing list for the newsletter to include closely held companies not presently serviced by the firm.   _____ _____ _____

- Develop more-formalized materials to be used in proposal presentations (such as PowerPoint, or preprinted flip charts with graphics).   _____ _____ _____

- Through contacts at appropriate business and industry media, arrange for articles to be written by the firm or quote certain principals as appropriate. A "media guide" could be prepared and sent to key editors, listing resources in the firm.   _____ _____ _____

- Identify publications in which the firm will advertise in the coming year, and develop ads that can be used in a variety of situations.   _____ _____ _____

- Identify various industry trade groups that the firm, as well as specific individuals, should join. Encourage attendance at meetings, and hold seminars sponsored by these groups.   _____ _____ _____

- Identify three firm individuals who, as part of their individual marketing plans, will write articles for local business or trade publications on selected niche areas of practice:

    Each individual identified above will write at least one article before [date].   _____ _____ _____

Goal #5: Internal Marketing—Build a Marketing Culture and Improve Marketing Firmwide

There is a desire to improve marketing on all levels at the firm. A marketing culture must be initiated, and each firm member must be involved as an active participant in client relations and business development. Training and ongoing exposure to marketing concepts is key.

Active, focused, and enthusiastic participation in practice development is considered a positive characteristic of those individuals who will advance within our firm. Practice development always will represent much more than selling—or even marketing—the firm. It also will encompass the concept of providing high-quality service to our clients.

The firm will encourage staff persons to participate in the firm's marketing, in whatever manner is most comfortable for them. We will emphasize that marketing is everyone's responsibility. We will determine specific roles for each individual in fulfillment of the firm's marketing program.

INDIVIDUAL MARKETING PLANS

- The firm will assign [name] to act as a facilitator in the development of individual marketing plans.
- An "Individual Marketing Plan" will be completed by every lawyer and will become part of the ongoing counseling process.

MARKETING TRAINING PROGRAM

- Training will be provided regarding the variety of services the firm provides.
- Presentations on the basics of client relations will be held for partners and associates.
- Client-relations training will be conducted for all members of the support staff.

ANNUAL FIRM MEETINGS

- Annual meetings will be held to discuss marketing success and set marketing goals for the upcoming year.
- Marketing incentives will be offered and communicated.
- Short presentations on significant new clients will take place quarterly.
- Short presentations on new products or services will take place regularly.
- A monthly new-client list will be distributed via the weekly bulletin.
- Members of the staff will serve on the marketing committee.

STRATEGIES TO ACHIEVE GOAL #5 IN [YEAR]
Internal Marketing—Build a Marketing Culture and Improve Marketing Firmwide

ACTION STEP	RESPONSIBILITY	PRIORITY	DATE
INTERNAL MARKETING			
♦ Organize and locate all marketing materials in one area of the firm and notifying personnel.	_____	_____	_____

STRATEGIC MARKETING PLANNING

- Train firm professionals on marketing related matters. Such training would begin in the first year of an individual's career and continue each year. Training programs would include, but not be limited to, developing a marketing plan and personal marketing style, enhancing listening skills, improving oral and written communication, strengthening referral networks, and developing practice expansion skills. _____ _____ _____

- Include a section in weekly online bulletins, currently being developed, that is devoted to marketing-related activities. The marketing section would include cross-selling activities, "wins," seminars, articles, community service, networking opportunities, and similar items. _____ _____ _____

- Use e-mail to notify all personnel of prospective-client activity. _____ _____ _____

- Hold biweekly meetings of the marketing committee. The meetings will begin at 8:30 a.m. and last approximately one hour. _____ _____ _____

  Expand the marketing committee to include professional and support staff representatives. _____ _____ _____

  Upon approval of the marketing plan by partners or the management committee, present it the the rest of the firm. _____ _____ _____

- Encourage personnel to write newsletter articles. _____ _____ _____

- Encourage personnel to write for the Web site. A monthly tax column or legal tip will be included on the Web site. _____ _____ _____

- Institute quarterly brown-bag luncheon meetings to discuss marketing topics. All lawyers and support staff will be invited to the meeting, attendance will be optional, and the discussion will be informal, relating to any area of marketing or practice development, such as new clients, proposals outstanding, or marketing ideas. _____ _____ _____

◆ Issue a monthly marketing calendar to all personnel, which will indicate all action items targeted for that month, as well as any other marketing activities occurring during the month. _____ _____ _____

Supplement C: A Strategic Planning Success—Built upon the "Voice of the Client"

The Situation

A law firm with two offices and 125 lawyers came to a marketing consultant, seeking assistance with strategic planning on a firmwide basis. Although the firm had been successful, the lawyers felt that as a group they needed to identify a "shared" vision for the future of the firm. Key questions included these:

- Where are we going in the next five years?
- What is our mission?
- Do we want to grow or remain the same size?
- Should we maintain two offices or consolidate?
- What makes us unique compared with other firms?
- How do we effectively position ourselves?
- What are our strengths?
- Where does our future lie?
- Are we a group of individuals practicing together or a firm?

These are questions that law firms routinely face. So, how does a firm facing these questions respond? Can a large law firm develop a meaningful direction and strategic plan for the *entire* firm?

The Solution

The consultant worked with the firm to form a strategic marketing committee. The goal of the committee was to work in concert with the consultant to develop a more cohesive direction and more clearly defined objectives for growth.

Achieving consensus by committee is no easy task. In the initial meeting, it was made clear that although there was no doubt this committee could sit around a conference-room table and come up with a strategic plan for the firm, this was not the desired outcome of the process. The consultant suggested that this firm base its marketing plan upon something meaningful and concrete—the "*voice of the client.*"

Four Components for Developing the Plan

The following four components were analyzed in developing the plan:

(1) Personal interviews with twenty-five of the firm's clients
(2) A market research study of the top two hundred purchasers of legal services in the firm's market
(3) A "macro" economic analysis of the regional trends
(4) An internal analysis of key lawyers in the firm

Through this research, the firm identified and considered what its clients want and expect, what the market demands for legal services, and the general economic trends that could affect its business. A strategic plan was developed that summarized the major goals of the firm for the next three years, based upon these variables. The firm is reporting a great deal of success in implementing the plan.

Remember, success is never final, and neither is the strategy for achieving it.

The Client Feedback Program: A Proven Strategy for Winning New Business, Improving the Bottom Line, and Creating a "Delighted and Loyal" Client Base

3

Linda LaBrie

It is safe to say that all aspects of your firm—including market image, growth in profits, and ability to attract top-quality legal talent—are tied closely to your ability to retain and expand your existing client relationships. Ensuring highly satisfied, loyal, and profitable clients continues to be the best strategy for improving your firm's bottom line.

Experienced legal marketing professionals have long understood that a successful marketing program of any kind hinges first on properly identifying client needs, and then helping clients appreciate the firm's ability to provide the best solutions for meeting those needs. Businesses outside the legal profession demonstrate an understanding of this fundamental underpinning for keeping and getting more business with their heavy reliance on *quantitative* and *qualitative market research*. They use this data to uncover, predict, and confirm the variables that influence the "buy" decisions of their customers and prospects.

Still, most law firms remain reluctant to invest in any type of market research on a consistent basis. A growing number of law firms have, however, added client-focused, *qualitative* research programs to their strategic marketing plans and budgets. Market-savvy legal professionals—from managing partners and marketing partners at megafirms to in-house marketers and firm administrators at smaller firms—have successfully "sold" their firms on the bottom-line benefits of a *Client Feedback Program* (also referred to as Client Interview, Client Survey, or Client Satisfaction Programs).

This chapter focuses upon the tangible and intangible benefits derived from well-crafted client feedback initiatives. With an emphasis on the development and successful execution of a formal Client Feedback Program involving face-to-face interviews with your key clients, you should recognize and appreciate the value in both the tangible impact to your firm's bottom line and the intangible benefits derived from earning clients' accolades and long-term loyalty.

Client Value—The Link Between Satisfaction and Loyalty

Since the early 1980s, most businesses have focused upon customer satisfaction as a way to improve customer loyalty and profitability. However, in 1995, Jones and Sasser explained that "[m]any managers assume that there is a simple linear relationship between satisfaction and loyalty. But in markets where customers/clients have choices, the difference between the loyalty of completely or highly satisfied and *merely* satisfied clients was tremendous. . . . [P]roviding clients with outstanding value may be the only reliable way to achieve sustained customer/client satisfaction and loyalty."

If the level of client satisfaction appears to be the most obvious route to achieving client loyalty, we need to know how to get there. Consider that clients are satisfied only when value—*as defined by the 'client*—meets or exceeds expectations. So, how does the client define "value"? On the most basic level, value for a client involves (1) perceived product quality, (2) perceived value-based pricing, and (3) perceived service quality.

The results from hundreds of face-to-face interviews with clients (conducted by the writer) confirm that "perceived quality service" represents the most critical element of the value proposition for clients—*over the long term*:

- ◆ Clients value "high-level responsiveness" more than any other behavior attributed to their lawyer or law firm. "Lack of responsiveness" also continues to be the primary reason lawyers and firms are fired by clients, according to most surveys.

- The importance of service is further supported by a belief espoused by the majority of clients that work-product quality (except in "bet-the-company" matters) is not measurably different between competing firms—a presumption that renders "perceived work-product quality" a neutral factor, at best, in defining value for most clients.
- Finally, "perceived value-based pricing" may get your firm's foot in the door, but the client's perception of the service experience with your firm—beyond the initial matter or transaction—remains the true driver of that client's long-term loyalty.

So, how do we create and deliver value to the client? There is only one way, according to Tom Peters, a leading authority in service excellence: "Perception is everything. Value is whatever the client tells us it is. And we find out by asking them—over and over again. And having asked, we move heaven and earth to meet their expectations."

Yet, most law firms continue to identify and meet their clients' needs through a research methodology I have come to refer to as "incestuous guesswork." This approach typically involves a group of lawyers sitting around and asking each other what they think their clients think, and what they think the market wants! Even if you get some of it right, this is a risky and inefficient strategy.

My colleague, Jim Durham (who also is the co-editor of this book), is fond of saying, "If you listen to the marketplace, you will know what to do." When was the last time you talked with your clients about a new business or marketing strategy that you were considering? Did you get client input *before* launching that niche practice initiative; or *before* acquiring that smaller firm or merging with that firm on the opposite coast (likely a firm unknown to many of your clients); or *before* establishing your firm's new brand/market position; or more importantly, *before* hiring new lawyers to service a long-standing client, only to have the client defect to a competitor soon thereafter? Jim has also been heard to say, "To guess is cheap, to guess wrong is expensive." That really says it all!

Many important—and costly—firm decisions receive "lukewarm" responses from clients, prospects, and referral sources, simply because they miss the mark on what is important. David Maister, international management consultant and author, advises his audiences of professional service providers to follow *the basic rules of romance* in their marketing: "Shut up and really listen." To be successful marketers, we must spend time asking clients about *them,* seeking first to understand *them,* and then to be understood.

If you are convinced that it is a poor business practice to "guess" what your clients are thinking, feeling, expecting, or experiencing, then you will likely need to embark on the journey of "selling" your firm on the concept of conducting face-to-face interviews with selected clients. It is worth the effort, though, as Client Satisfaction Interviews can be the core of a powerful strategic marketing plan for law firms that want to experience long-term success.

How Client Loyalty Improves Your Bottom Line

The experience of those firms that have implemented Client Interview Programs proves that most feedback from clients is positive. It is not uncommon for a client to comment that the lead partner on the client team "walks on water" or "jumps through hoops." And, clients are always impressed with the time, effort, and resources invested by the firm to conduct client interviews—at no cost to the client, of course! The process creates a "halo effect," with the firm getting—in addition to critical information—kudos from the client just for asking to meet with them.

Though this "feel good" aspect of the interview process is valuable in enhancing the firm's relationships with clients, the more convincing argument for a Client Interview Program is the positive impact it can have on the proverbial *bottom line*. Fortunately, the experience of those of us who conduct (or teach lawyers to conduct) client interviews proves unequivocally that the investment of time, money, and political capital needed to launch a Client Satisfaction Program is miniscule when compared with the new revenue the program can yield. So, what are these revenue-enhancement opportunities? The resources cited at the end of this book support the following:

(1) *Improved Profitability*: Loyal clients or highly satisfied clients typically pay their bills on time, are less apt to haggle over fees, and are less inclined to ask for discounts. Firms that enjoy high levels of client satisfaction and loyalty can charge as much as 10 to 15 percent more for their services.

(2) *Reduced Marketing Costs*: It costs five to eight times more to generate revenue from a new client than to generate the same amount of new revenue from an existing client. Knowing what your clients think makes it possible to grow the business intelligently and appropriately.

(3) *Increased Market Share*: Loyal clients tell an average of five to seven other individuals about their positive experiences with a firm, resulting in the best and cheapest form of advertising—referrals. (Most unhappy clients, however, do not tell you they are unhappy, they just tell a lot of other people . . .)

(4) *Application of the 80/20 Rule*: Eighty percent or more of your firm's business and revenue comes from a limited number of existing *key* clients. Talking with them about how you are doing and what is important presents a unique reward/risk reality.

(5) *Creation of "Deep Water" Relationships*: Research confirms that most clients do business with a firm because of a relationship with one key partner. This does not bode well for firms, because they are rendered vulnerable if that individual leaves the firm or the principal client contact leaves the company. "Shallow water" relationships are one-dimensional and easy to exit. When the client relationship involves several professionals or practice areas, it is not that easy or convenient to walk away.

(6) *Measurement of Marketing's Return on Investment (ROI)*: Most traditional law firm marketing efforts do not provide immediate or even measurable cause/effect results. In a service-oriented, relationship-based industry, it is difficult to identify one event or contact that led to or solidified the "sale." Getting clients is usually a cumulative process that can take several years of effort to bring to fruition. Feedback from clients about what they value, need, or desire from the firm becomes valuable market research for allocating limited marketing resources and ensuring desired results. Moreover, in the process of conducting hundreds of interviews, my colleagues and I have learned that interviews can uncover the *potential* for lost business or new revenue opportunities.

(7) *Gaining a Competitive Edge*: A critical by-product of interviewing your clients is the "straight from the source" competitive intelligence you often get. Most clients do not mind talking about the various law firms they use, or sharing their perceptions of other firms' strengths and weakness. Most firms would pay a lot for such invaluable proprietary research—you can have it just by asking.

(8) *Becoming a "Client Satisfaction" Leader*: Demonstrating the firm's desire to "super please" clients can become a distinctive, competitive advantage as word of the effort percolates through the marketplace. Also, the firm's Client Satisfaction Program clearly communicates to all lawyers and staff that the firm is serious about achieving service excellence.

(9) *Leveraging of Client/Industry Information*: When a client tells you about potential changes in the company, industry, or economic/political/social environment, it is highly likely that such changes will also affect other clients and prospects in that industry. This insight not only can (and should) drive efforts to address existing client needs, it can fuel new business development opportunities with prospects in the industry.

(10) *Prevention of Client Defections*: Many clients have quietly left firms for reasons as basic as "poor chemistry" (though "poor service" still ranks as the leading cause of defections). Whatever the reason

might be for a client to consider changing firms, you get a chance to address it if you actually talk to the client. Also, as client companies merge, acquire, get acquired, reengineer, or downsize, new decision makers emerge. Without the benefits of client interviews, it can be difficult to know whether you might survive as counsel, and how you might need to "tweak" or even change the client team to maintain your position.

Critical Elements of a Results-Driven Client Feedback Program

Now let's discuss the critical components of a successful Client Interview Program.

Client Selection

It is extremely important to start the interviewing process with clients who are "perceived" as highly satisfied. Usually, these are long-term clients of the firm who reside in the top-ten to top-twenty client list, based upon revenues. Getting positive results early in the program will only strengthen the firm's long-term commitment, reduce partner resistance, and reinforce the point that clients are willing to participate in the program.

Ideally your Client Interview Program will achieve some momentum as a result of the recognition and credibility that flows from these early, positive results. Be aware, however, that even some of the firm's perceived *best* clients will have constructive suggestions for improved performance, and, in some cases, can have some surprisingly negative comments for the interviewer—which proves the value of the program in another way!

In addition to selecting the firm's highest-revenue clients, determining which clients you should interview can be governed by factors such as these:

- clients who have left the firm
- clients within a particular industry or sector
- start-up companies with high growth potential
- highly profitable clients
- key clients of a particular practice/industry/niche
- newly acquired clients (two years or less)
- clients with a strong market or industry presence

Client Feedback Methodology

In my opinion, and in the opinion of most clients, the only survey method that produces meaningful and measurable results is a face-to-face meeting. Only through personal interaction can you get a comprehensive (you might say, "holistic") interpretation of a client's experience with your firm. The trained interviewer uses a combination of active listening and keen observation skills, knowing that important information is communicated nonverbally. Critical insight is lost (not to mention the lost opportunity to enhance relationships) if an impersonal survey method is used.

Years of personal and industrywide experience prove that most clients welcome—are even "delighted" to have—the opportunity to meet interviewers face-to-face, preferably in their own offices. Clients recognize and appreciate fully the firm's investment of time, effort, and resources, and look forward to meetings that focus on them, their needs, and improvement in the level of service they get from the law firm.

If you are unable to meet in person—due to time constraints, location, or just personal preference—clients usually express willingness to participate in telephone interviews. The telephone interview is the second most effective survey method. Although the interviewer cannot observe the client's nonverbal behavior, the client's tone, pauses, and other cues are readily understood by the experienced interviewer.

In the last couple of years, "online" surveys, particularly strong in non-legal commercial sectors, have emerged in the professional services arena as well. This may be a useful method of obtaining feedback, especially among a growing cadre of technically savvy, time-starved executives. But frankly, this (and *written* survey instruments) should be used only for more modest, "end of matter" surveys, and as supplements to periodic in-person meetings. It can be insulting to important clients to ask them to complete standard form surveys about their level of satisfaction with the firm's services. If they are important enough to the firm to be clients you want to keep, they are important enough to talk to.

Moreover, written, mailed surveys are least likely to produce (1) in-depth, client-specific insight, (2) meaningful improvement in client relationships, and (3) response rates sufficient to provide reliable, valid data from which to draw meaningful conclusions. While clearly the least costly method—utilizing only paper and postage—written surveys aimed at determining client satisfaction are "Exhibit A" for the proposition that you get what you pay for! (Written surveys may be useful for gathering exploratory, general marketplace data—to help launch a niche practice or new service, for example—but this goal differs significantly from that of developing super-satisfied clients.)

Who Should Conduct the Interview?

It is well documented that a client's candor about her or his experience with a firm increases dramatically when the interviewer brings "third-party" objectivity to the experience. An independent third party can probe more deeply and has the capacity to maintain a neutral response when the client expresses concerns about the firm or its lawyers. This objectivity may be provided by a consultant who specializes in this area, a professional in the firm (such as the chief marketing officer or executive director), or the managing partner of the firm or another senior partner in the firm who does not directly service the client being interviewed.

A firm may also choose to use a third-party interviewer in combination with the lawyer responsible for overseeing the client's work. It should be noted, however, that the presence of any member of the firm might intimidate some clients. Invariably, a skilled, independent third-party interviewer will get better data from a client than one of the firm's partners.

The decision about who conducts the interview should be a function not only of the experience and skills of the interviewer, but also the firm's desired results. For example, assume your firm selects the managing partner as the ideal third-party interviewer. It is quite likely that the clients selected to meet with your managing partner will conclude they are valued clients, and will accept the invitations without hesitation. In this scenario, your firm achieved an outcome from the interactions *even before the interviews were conducted*—key clients of the firm "feel" extremely valued by the firm. If your goal was to have clients know they are valued and appreciated, as well as to get some feedback, then you achieved your primary goal just by sending the right person. (The same message can be sent, of course, by having someone else conduct the interview, but probably to a lesser degree.)

When a less-significant client is selected because it represents real potential for expanded work, the managing partner may not be the best person to conduct the interview. Given the daily demands on her or his schedule, consider whether your managing partner can do the following:

- spend the considerable time necessary to digest fully the total client/firm relationship from historical/financial viewpoints
- schedule and lead the essential meetings with the client's key partner and other lawyers on the client's team to "learn" the critical nuances of the relationship and agree upon the interview goals
- adhere to the essential 90/10 rules (regarding listening versus talking—see below) when meeting with the client, keeping the focus upon client satisfaction, not selling
- record accurately the client's comments and possible requests during the interview
- dictate or write a complete synopsis of the interview with the client
- conduct a debriefing session with the client's key partner/team and formulate a follow-up action plan and timetable
- monitor and track the follow-up action plan and timetable

- revisit the client sometime in the future—either in person or by telephone—to determine if the client is satisfied with the firm's response to his or her needs, desires, and expectations

It is often hard to get this level of commitment from managing partners even when dealing with major clients, so think seriously about your goals and level of commitment to the process before deciding upon the right interviewer.

You can help your firm select the best interviewer(s) by doing the following:

(1) requiring that the interviewer(s) be trained in effective listening and probing skills
(2) ensuring that the interviewer(s) be thoroughly knowledgeable about the firm/client relationship
(3) selecting "internal" candidates only when they possess
- the requisite third-party objectivity
- the ability/time to achieve the firm's objectives with each client
- the necessary firm status, credibility, and authority to orchestrate any changes/modifications in the client/firm relationship, if needed

The Client Interview
Preparation

It is imperative that the individual selected to conduct client interviews be thoroughly versed and knowledgeable about the total relationship the firm has had with the client to be interviewed. This assessment involves a complete review of the historical and current relationship with the firm, including the following:

- types and numbers of transactions/matters
- average annual billings
- types of legal services provided
- past performance issues or "chemistry" issues with any team members
- all firm lawyers who have serviced the client and for how long
- current team of lawyers servicing the client, including key partner(s)
- person affiliated with the client who makes the "buy" decision for professional services
- the senior management team and board of directors
- overview of the client's business and the industry
- the client's strategic plan (expansion, consolidation, relocation)
- other law firms the client uses and the services they provide
- the client's total legal budget, if known

Ideally, interview preparation should involve the interviewer, the key client contact or team leader, and as many of the client team members as possible and appropriate. This preparation results in an evaluation of the past and present quality of the firm/client relationship—*from the firm's perspective*—as well as a realistic assessment of the future potential of this client to the firm. Often this is a group discussion facilitated by the interviewer, but it can be a series of meetings, or even e-mail messages, if necessary to get the information.

The 90/10 Rules

The firm's intent must be *client-centered*. Client satisfaction meetings are intended to assess the client's experiences and perceptions about working with the firm's lawyers and staff and, of course, the results and value of the services. It cannot be emphasized enough that the *primary objectives* of a Client Feedback Program must be to pinpoint (1) what each client "values" and (2) what the firm can do to increase value and satisfaction. Clients are savvy and can easily sense if the meeting is focused upon them and their needs or some other firm goal—such as marketing. Therefore, it is imperative that the interview proceed along the following 90/10 rules:

- The interviewer listens 90 percent of the time and asks questions or speaks only 10 percent of the time.
- The interviewer poses open-ended questions 90 percent of the time and closed-end questions only 10 percent of the time.
- The interviewer places the client in the active communicator role at least 90 percent of the time and the passive observer role only 10 percent of the time.

Achieving the highest level of client candor, insight, and information is directly related to the client's comfort level during the interview—comfort in understanding the firm's objectives, comfort in the level of attentiveness provided by the interviewer, and comfort in believing the firm will respond immediately and appropriately to any concerns the client may share.

A host of ancillary objectives can also be achieved subtly by interviewing your clients. These include the following:

- identifying cross-selling opportunities
- gaining reactions to new/planned initiatives
- uncovering problem areas in client service or specific products
- improving the brand/market positioning of the firm
- anticipating changes or trends in the client's industry
- determining sensitivity to fees or desired alternative pricing strategies

- building alliances with other organizations that also service the client
- evaluating the results of selected marketing efforts
- documenting the strengths and weaknesses of the competition

Whether you can achieve these *secondary* objectives is a function of the current client/firm relationship, the depth of understanding of the client's definition of value, and the ability of the firm to satisfy or exceed these value expectations. In the right circumstances, a set of questions can be asked to elicit this information.

Interview Questions

The key to a successful interview with a client is to ask *open-ended questions* that place the client in the communicator role and the interviewer in the listener role.

The questions posed to each client clearly depend upon the objectives of the interview. The interview can be structured around just three primary questions: "What are we doing well?" "What could we be doing better?" "What are the most important issues in your business in the near future?" Each answer should be followed by an active-listening remark, such as, "Tell me what you mean by that," "Could you give me an example," or "In other words, ..." Some interviewers take the view that more specific and detailed questions should be asked to help establish some baseline information in particular areas of interest or concern to the firm. These questions might uncover a client's perceptions about matters such as the following:

- the firm's image in the marketplace (as compared with competitors)
- criteria used to select the firm initially
- assessment of client service—on current matters, overall performance issues, level of social contact, overall communication, use of technology, support staff service, and similar items
- referrals to the firm
- fees and billing issues
- improvement needs
- assessment of the firm's marketing communications and efforts

Some tailored questions, which go beyond satisfaction, might be focused upon secondary objectives such as these:

- type of business referrals desired from the firm and level of importance
- expanding the existing relationship—what, who, how?
- ways to improve the firm's communication efforts
- assessment of the client's industry influence

- assessment of the client's participation in industry/trade groups/conferences
- "must" reading—what? and why?
- desired value-added services
- "partnering" opportunities
- unique alternative fee or billing arrangements

Follow-Up Strategy—The Critical Success Factor!

Ultimately, some firms do not achieve the maximum benefits that can be derived from this powerful, qualitative research because the focus remains too much on the firm—and its internal dynamics—and not enough on the client's service and relationship needs and expectations.

Most feedback from clients is positive. Some clients may be highly satisfied with the relationship, but still request that some personnel or operational change be made, such as implementing a billing format that would be easier to track internally. Feedback from a small percentage of clients may, in fact, be quite negative and require significant modifications in relationships. In all cases, the firm must be prepared to respond after a client expresses dissatisfaction of any kind.

During the initial design phase of your program—*and long before the first client meeting takes place*—your firm's follow-up strategy must be developed. This strategy should articulate that your Client Feedback Program is an important part of the strategic plan. It establishes and reinforces your firm's commitment to improved client satisfaction and, when executed on a consistent basis, ensures maximum bottom-line results. More specifically, your firm's follow-up strategy should:

(1) define the accountability process—the who, what, when, and how of an efficient and effective client response system,
(2) institute an appropriate internal communication process for sharing client feedback (positive, negative, and neutral) inside the firm—often tailored from client to client, and
(3) ensure a timely and "on-point" response to your clients' current service issues, ensuring satisfaction in meeting future product, service, and relationship expectations. ("Timely" means responding immediately after the interview, not merely when it is convenient.)

The following questions should be considered in the early stages of the interview planning process, because the answers provide the road map to your follow-up strategy:

- Will lawyers be given choices about whether "their" clients become interview candidates?

- Who will interview the clients? People from the firm or an outside consultant?
- Who will be responsible for analyzing client survey information to determine common themes, strategic opportunities, or firm infrastructure improvement needs?
- Who in the firm will have total access to all client survey information—uncensored notes, thank-you letters to clients, summary reports, recommended action plans, and ongoing follow-up information?
- Which parties will meet with the client interviewer to learn the outcome of a specific client interview? How soon after the client interview should/will this meeting take place?
- What time frame will the firm establish as the deadline for responding to each client? Who will be the "timekeeper"?
- Who will meet with the client to discuss the firm's response; that is, what, how, and when changes will be made?
- Who will be responsible for managing "follow-up accountability" (ensuring the action plan for each client is executed) and tracking the client's overall relationship going forward?
- How will the firm guarantee consistency of service improvement for these clients over the long term; that is, establishing a program of "end of matter" audits or discussions with clients?
- Will a summary of client survey results be shared with the firm's clients? If so, what is the purpose of this, and what will the summary look like?

Remember, your firm's answers to these "process" questions (as well as other issues that may be unique to your firm) will shape the outcome of your Client Feedback Program. At a very basic level, the interviewer or responsible lawyer should get back to the client within days with a summary of the concerns they heard, and a promise to get back to the client promptly with suggested solutions.

Role of the Marketing Director

What role should/can the firm's senior marketing professional play in your firm's Client Feedback Program? The marketing professional's role in this endeavor depends upon a number of factors, including the individual's

(1) current role/definition and position/level in the firm,
(2) interest, experience, and skills related to the process,
(3) level of influence that he or she currently enjoys or aspires toward,
(4) management/supervisory responsibilities (number of staff reports), and
(5) other demands/expectations deemed critical to the firm.

Whether this individual is new to the firm or enjoys years of tenure will also affect his or her role and level of credibility. More important, perhaps, is the risk of sending a mixed message to the client by having someone with a "marketing" or "business development" title conduct the meeting, which should be focused only upon client satisfaction. It is a factor for consideration, though there is no dispositive answer.

Depending upon the firm's responses to these and other considerations, there are at least four different roles the marketing professional can assume:

(1) *Catalyst*: The marketing professional becomes the agent of change—a conduit of information to and from firm management about the benefits of gaining client feedback. He or she may help shape the critical elements of the program.

(2) *Manager*: The marketing professional is the overseer and proprietor of the program and ensures that the program, particularly the firm's follow-up strategy, is implemented effectively and in a timely manner. He or she reports results on a consistent basis.

(3) *Facilitator*: The marketing professional becomes both the catalyst and launchpad for the firm's program. His or her interpersonal skills and influence help "drive" the critical elements of the program, including guiding management in adopting the most effective follow-up strategy.

(4) *Leader*: The marketing professional "owns" the program and assumes some combination of all four roles. He or she ensures the program's design, execution, and results; proposes the critical elements of the program; meets with client teams to strategize follow-up actions; monitors changes and modifications desired by clients; tracks new business from clients; and perhaps conducts the client interviews.

The Bottom Line

A well-designed Client Feedback Program can and will significantly affect your firm's bottom line. In addition to the obvious and critical impact of client retention, loyalty, and referrals that come from client interviews, you can further maximize the ROI by using client insights (appropriately, of course) in the development of the firm's strategic marketing plan and budget. Law firm marketers should consider using the insights from client feedback on marketing initiatives such as the following:

- developing promotional materials for a new product or service
- testing internal assumptions about marketplace needs and wants

- using client testimonials (with approval) as "message makers"
- leveraging proven ideas and concepts with other clients
- uncovering fee and pricing floors and ceilings
- maximizing competitive analyses
- launching brand/market position

The ultimate, bottom-line value of talking with your clients is the way in which it will reinforce throughout the firm that the greatest competitive advantage is in delivering extraordinary service—*as the client defines it!*

Other Ways to Bring the *Voice of Your Clients* into Your Firm

As a supplement to in-person interviews with your key clients, participation in client or industry-specific events will also allow you to garner valuable insights. Such efforts result in learning about your clients' businesses, challenges, service needs, expectations, potential networks, partnering opportunities, and more. The following are just some of the ways firms of all sizes have brought their clients' voices into their firms:

- client presentations at practice meetings, particularly those meetings in which associates participate
- key-client panel discussions at partner retreats
- reverse seminars or executive briefings—sessions conducted by client representatives to educate their outside lawyers
- client advisory boards
- strategic planning sessions with clients
- brown-bag lunches and on-site client visits (off the clock, of course)
- key industry or trade meetings/conferences, attended jointly
- roundtables that bring several clients together to discuss topics of interest
- cosponsored seminars or events
- brief, informal interviews with one firm client in each internal newsletter

Summary

In today's highly competitive legal environment, obtaining feedback from your clients through a formal Client Interview Program is no longer an option—it is a requirement. What you don't know *can* hurt you. And be assured, if your firm is not listening to its clients, some other firm is!

Section II

Enhancing Your Image

Public Relations for Lawyers

4

Richard Levick
Elizabeth Lampert

A Spotlight on Public Relations

It used to be that only large New York law firms received serious media attention, but this has changed dramatically in recent years. Today, from sole practitioners to boutiques to global behemoths, firms are setting trends and being referenced in the press on a daily basis.

Take into account the amount of space newspapers dedicate to business, trade, and current affairs stories. Is your law firm getting the attention from the print media you feel it deserves? If you answered yes, congratulations—you are on your way. If you answered no, then maybe your approach is not working. Ask yourself the following questions:

(1) Is media relations included in my firm's marketing and business development strategy?
(2) How many of the firm's lawyers have been crisis or media trained?
(3) Has the firm put a disproportionate share of the marketing budget into advertising?
(4) Has the firm engaged in media-generating activities other than writing press releases?

Here are some practical tips—points of view and information about public relations that should increase your understanding and explain how it can all come together.

How Has PR for a Law Firm Changed in the Last Decade? Beyond the Press Release . . .

Once a media and marketing industry standard, press releases were the first step in most PR campaigns. In fact, the release once comprised the beginning and end of the campaign itself. Today, press releases are diminishing in popularity, primarily because of their diminishing returns.

The press release is an overused form of communication. Lawyers often regard it as an opportunity to communicate with the media, when, in fact, most releases get tossed before they are read. We recognize, however, that for a variety of firms, press releases are *the* way that news gets into the marketplace. That said, a number of other tools have entered the PR realm, and many of these are underutilized. The activities below are designed to raise the profile of a practice group or firm. They can be rolled out nationally to provide a broader firmwide message, or tailored to specific geographic markets, individual buyers, and/or industry sectors.

Activities

Publicity for Deals and Cases

Firms should publicize as many deals and cases as possible. Many publications now publish comprehensive summaries of recent deal and case activity.

When any practice or industry group is involved in a significant case or deal, the firm's marketing and communications department should be alerted—*long before* the deal closes or the jury is deliberating. Once the case or deal reaches conclusion, the department can contact reporters at targeted publications. Depending upon state bar rules and only with your client's permission, you may contact reporters to work toward in-depth articles on the merits and ramifications of the case or deal.

It is imperative to understand that when dealing with the media, timeliness is critical. It makes or breaks your relationship with reporters. Providing advance notice of upcoming cases and decisions and allowing time to coordinate an effective strategy could be the difference between getting into a publication or missing out.

An effective way to stay informed about current matters is to encourage lawyers to submit brief synopses of important matters. A suggested submission form for a lawsuit is displayed at the top of page 69.

Reporter Meetings

In-person meetings with reporters allow discussions between lawyers and key legal and business correspondents about the firm's successes, structure, and strategy moving forward. Come armed with details of recent successes and news that can be shared with the reporters.

Litigation Submission Form

Please provide a brief synopsis of the case, including, but not limited to, case merits, ramifications, and similar matters.

Firm partners involved; phone #s	
Opposing counsel	
Case number	
Industry	
Settlement amount	
Court/District	
Filing date	
Settlement date	
What is interesting or unique about this case?	
Is it precedent setting?	
Lawyer quote	

Keep in mind that the national press looks for "hard" news stories and information that will interest their readers. The firm will compete for valuable space, so it is crucial that it establish itself as a valued and consistent source for press comment. To do so, identify issues on which the firm's lawyers can provide different or unique viewpoints. This might include comments on industry sector issues related to the firm's areas of expertise (such as utilities, engineering, or food/beverage) or issues affecting the wider business community, such as dispute resolution, insolvency, privacy, employment, or intellectual property.

It is worth remembering that at first these reporter meetings will probably not result in immediate press coverage—the main objective is to create awareness of the firm and begin building relationships with the reporters and publications. As with any relationship, building trust takes time. By establishing relationships, it becomes more likely that firm spokespersons will be interviewed and quoted, or have their byline articles published in target publications. Reporters who have had personal interaction with firm members are invariably more receptive to news of the firm's successes.

When the firm has bad news, the investment you have made in reporter relationships can help you. If the reporters like and trust you, they are more likely to seek a balanced story—and ensure that your side of the story gets reported.

First- and Third-Party Commentary

Look to create opportunities for firm spokespersons to be interviewed or published. As mentioned earlier, develop first-party commentary opportunities for spokespersons on firm developments or, when possible, on deals and cases in which the firm has played a key role.

At the same time, do not overlook the value of third-party commentary. This occurs when a lawyer is asked to comment about a case or legal issue in which the firm is not directly involved. For example, if you are aiming to secure coverage for your antitrust practice, research and follow closely any related legal issues that are topical or have arisen in the press. Once identified, promote the spokesperson as a legal expert on antitrust. There were hundreds of news stories about the Microsoft antitrust case that quoted lawyers who had nothing to do with the litigation. The only requirements are that the lawyer be up-to-the-minute on the developments and peripheral issues (sometimes the most interesting parts of the story), and return phone calls and e-mails immediately.

Opportunities for third-party commentary may also arise when a new law or regulation is passed, when a legal decision is made, or when a large-scale deal with important implications arises (and the firm does not act for the parties involved).

Publishing Opportunities

Identify industry trade publications, which often commission articles from industry experts. Also, lawyers may have written articles for internal publications that they can easily refresh and publish externally. Articles can address a specific business purpose, such as the following:

- providing a new solution to an old problem
- offering words of caution and explaining how companies can protect themselves
- providing a different point of view for a subject already in the news
- introducing a local or national angle
- showing a new or established trend (giving statistics, if possible)

Use the following guidelines when writing an article for publication:

(1) Avoid legalese. Use a journalistic style; include who, what, where, how, and why.
(2) Remember your audience—they may not be lawyers. Focus upon business and industry angles.
(3) Do not use footnotes. If a case is cited, provide the full citation.
(4) Talk to your readers, not about them.

(5) Generally, keep your articles to between 1,200 and 1,500 words. However, each publication has different length requirements, so check first.
(6) Know the deadline and be maniacal in meeting it.

Once an article is accepted, it will be reviewed by the editor, who will discuss recommended changes with the author.

The firm's marketing and communications department should maintain a bank of published articles—the Web site is a perfect repository for these. Articles that relate to the needs of a client or potential client should be included in information packets mailed to clients. Attach a "with compliments" card. Doing this not only demonstrates the firm's predominance in specific practice areas, but also provides clients with a feeling that they are constantly on your mind.

Round Table Discussions

Picture this: A firm lawyer and several of her prominent industry or business colleagues discuss a timely topic for a couple hours. A few of your clients and client prospects also participate. Many sound bites later, the discussion is featured in a publication, the transcript is posted to the publication's Web site (as well as your own), and a hyperlink to your Web site is provided. If nothing else, the time spent discussing a current, relevant topic with these people justifies your investment.

The topic you choose for such discussions should be focused. For example, though you should not propose a round table discussion on employment issues because the topic is too broad, you could be more specific and suggest a discussion of privacy issues in the workplace. The press coverage can be packaged and sent to interested clients and provide, in part, the justification for future client round tables. Relevant subject matter is the key to success and should be decided jointly between the firm and other panel members.

Research Studies

Commissioning research studies also offers excellent PR opportunities. As with round table discussions, careful thought is needed regarding the subject matter. It is almost always advisable to employ the services of a professional market research firm. Though often costly, this decision is critical to ensuring the integrity of the data collection process and analysis.

Research findings can be pitched as a story to specific reporters, disseminated to the press, mailed to clients and contacts, and form the basis for follow-up seminars or round table discussions.

Speaking Opportunities

Speakers are naturally viewed as experts on the topics they address. Whether speaking engagements occur at leading industry events or at monthly luncheons of professional organizations, they enhance the firm's profile and increase its potential client base.

Join two or three organizations in the industries you want to target. Attend their meetings and assist the program committee chair. Let the committee know you are interested in speaking, and assist in the creation of a program that fits your practice *and* serves the goals of the program committee and organization.

Beware: A lot of lawyers assume that speaking is a worthwhile business development activity and they speak *everywhere*. Most of these speaking commitments result in nothing. Choose wisely, and do not expect business to walk in the door the day after you appear on the dais. Speaking can result in new and good client relationships—but you must hit a specific nerve with the listeners, and then engage in crucial follow-up activities.

To Make It All Happen

Structuring an Internal Public-Relations Function

Endless scrutiny of return on investment (ROI) for marketing initiatives is nothing new to law firm marketers. While marketing budgets are shrinking, the demand for public-relations support is growing—a need compounded by the challenges facing law firms in the post-Enron, post-Andersen milieu.

Marketing departments of professional service firms work best when structured with the firm's clients—not the firm itself—in mind. There is no "one size fits all" solution to the question of how to best structure public relations internally. Clearly, a one-stop international law firm with a thousand lawyers will require a different marketing structure than a small litigation boutique. But there are fundamental elements that must be in place for both to function effectively.

Firms that have seen results from their public-relations initiatives have systems in place for gathering information (editorial calendars, reporter queries, and case updates) and for making partners aware of where to turn with PR queries. These systems are critical for effective PR functioning.

To ensure the marketing department's ability to stay on top of it, PR managers remain in close contact with the firm's managing partner and/or executive committee. They continuously reassess the firm's business goals and objectives. The PR manager must also be active within the individual practice areas and work with lawyers to identify opportunities to highlight achievements and expertise.

Using External Agencies

Many law firms also find that once the PR function of an internal marketing team is organized, and goals and responsibilities are defined, additional success is realized through an outside agency. Agencies are able to focus upon specific projects or goals, resulting in heightened visibility through solutions that are faster and less expensive than handling projects internally in piecemeal fashion. This is a widely valued solution: according to a study conducted by the Legal Marketing Association in 2002, public relations is one of the top two marketing functions that is outsourced, and 44 percent of firms surveyed hired outside PR agencies. Firms that go this route range from a six-lawyer firm to one of the largest global firms in the world, with more than twelve hundred lawyers.

When embarking on a relationship with an outside agency, the first step is to delineate the roles. The ideal situation is for the external and internal communications teams to work together in a cohesive and seamless fashion. Cohesion guarantees that the firm's messages remain consistent in all communications and that efforts are not duplicated. It is important that everyone understand who is accountable for doing what.

The law firm's internal marketing department should be a facilitator rather than a gatekeeper, thereby maximizing opportunities. Facilitating includes keeping external publicists updated with the firm's news, regardless of whether it directly affects the specific task on which they are working at that time. A simple weekly call between external and internal PR team members is an effective way to keep everyone updated and on the same page. Brief daily communications supplant this.

The external agency should focus upon developing opportunities to highlight specific practices areas and important cases or deals. Typically, law firms handle press releases, partner announcements, surveys, lists, and deal releases internally, as these are not cost-efficient ways of utilizing an external PR agency. However, it is also important not to give the agency all the firm's more "strategic" work—this can be demoralizing for in-house professionals who may feel relegated to "second string." By involving the internal staff in the process from the start, they will accept the process and be helpful in its execution.

In addition to offering the advantages of cost efficiency and speed, agencies develop and maintain close relationships and access to the media, and use these relationships to the firm's benefit. As outside publicists are somewhat removed from the firm, they are often able to see the larger picture and trend stories, which can sometimes be overlooked internally.

Similarly, there are advantages to internal PR. These include close access to the firm's lawyers and the ability to access information quickly. Both internal and external PR groups rely upon each other, and the best situations arise when both groups work together to meet the firm's business development goals.

Models

There are, then, a number of elements consistently employed for an effective law firm PR function, regardless of firm size or structure. But beyond this, there are different structures and systems that can work effectively. To illustrate the various ways in which a law firm can successfully structure its PR function, several models are listed below. Many firms engage in combinations of these structures, and some engage in all:

(1) *Partner-in-Charge*: Those that use this method—typically small and boutique firms—often do not have formal internal marketing departments. The partner-in-charge works with a managing partner or executive director and may have an assistant who serves as a coordinator. Firms that use this method without the assistance of an outside PR agency have difficulty developing press contacts and obtaining media placements. Lawyers rightly focus their energy on their clients, and have little time to develop publicity opportunities proactively.

(2) *Marketing Committee*: Again, used most often by small and boutique firms, this method is similar to the partner-in-charge. The difference lies in the fact that several partners—most likely from different practice groups—share the responsibility.

(3) *Everyone Does Everything*: One tactic is for all employed firm marketers to engage in all functions, including PR. One Chicago firm decided to pool senior-level talent and place the priority on the talent rather than on job functions. At this firm, members of the marketing department engage in all marketing functions, from Web site design to PR.

(4) *Practice-Area Focused*: The trend has moved toward marketing departments being structured around practice/industry areas, rather than mere geographic locales. In this structure, PR specialists are assigned to one or more practice groups and work closely with practice group heads to identify and target opportunities for expertise that resides in these groups.

(5) *Client Focused*: Some firms have begun to develop client-driven marketing teams. With this approach, a team performs marketing and PR functions around the work of various clients, rather than focusing on specific lawyers, practice areas, or offices. The firm identifies top clients, teams are organized around them, and marketing and PR initiatives are tailored appropriately.

(6) *Job-Function Focused*: Many firms divide their departments by job functions; for example, individuals are responsible for PR, marketing,

business development, Web sites, or advertising. The benefit of this design is that the firm can designate people who have expertise in specific areas. To supplement this approach, some firms hire outside PR agencies for their expertise in legal media or specific practice areas, and to utilize their reporter contacts. This also helps reduce the workload of the internal team.

(7) *Geographically Focused*: Some firms choose to separate PR duties by office locations. In this structure, one person is responsible for one or more offices. If the firm has several offices and widespread practice areas, this can overlap with practice group marketing.

The Next Step

A Bold Communications Program Would Stun the Legal Market

Marketing-smart law firms and their CMOs have been identifying new, fresh ways to maximize their marketing dollars. The recent appearance of sales directors as firm employees is just one of the innovations that signal a sea change. Many diverse business development initiatives are being introduced and embraced. Can communications be far behind?

Ponder Firm XYZ: It has an internal staff and an outside agency that has garnered the firm more and better media attention than most law firms its size. But as firms increasingly compete on a global scale and, therefore, compete against global players, the requirements at all operational levels—information technology, marketing, recruiting, and media—are heightened. What if Firm XYZ were to reconfigure its communications strategy decisively, to adapt to a new global strategy? That would be a true legal-marketplace "story." By taking such an aggressive step, Firm XYZ would send a strong message that it is on the move—and a contender with which to reckon—and a message that reinforces its ongoing brand development.

The idea proposed here exceeds the efforts of most law firms' internal communications teams. It involves the reconfiguration of Firm XYZ toward a new world communications paradigm. Plan A and Plan B, outlined below, are alternative paths toward that paradigm.

Such a paradigm is not unlike how corporations structure their various professional services purchases, including legal services. There is an in-house department, with delineated roles and tasks, interfacing on a daily basis with "outside counsel," which also has its delineated roles and tasks.

Plan A: The Incubation Approach

In this model, the outside agency hires two PR professionals in one of its offices. These hires are dedicated to Firm XYZ's account. Their charge is to work full-time on Firm XYZ's placements and develop diverse media opportunities. They would research possible story ideas, contact Firm XYZ spokespersons to confirm interest or develop other ideas, and then pitch them aggressively. Their dedicated work will decisively increase the number of media appearances.

More "boilerplate" work (like press releases) that the firm normally does internally can now be farmed out to Firm XYZ's team at the agency. Why is such an arrangement attractive? Because if you choose the right outside agency, these two PR professionals would be mentored at the highest level, and bring experience not available to newer media associates.

The dedicated PR pros would work on crisis situations at the highest level. They would handle transatlantic mergers and rollouts. They would help develop regional and global media strategies. In fact, these associates would gain experiences in one year that, at most law firms, could only happen in two or three years—if at all! The agency would incubate seasoned pros on Firm XYZ's behalf, and, at the end of the day, the firm would have the option of hiring these associates or, if the arrangement is working too well to justify changing, continue to keep them on staff at the agency.

The firm would gain predictability of resources, plus have maximum flexibility.

Note that we are not aware of any firm that has embraced this arrangement. However, the potential is extraordinary, in terms of the quality and quantity of opportunities that could be generated. Firm XYZ would gain a decisive advantage over other firms without having to train its own personnel. The arrangement also has the benefits of simplicity and economy: the firm pays the agency a lump sum, and the agency worries about health benefits, office space, hiring, training, and similar matters.

As part of any arrangement, the incubated staff should personally visit the firm on a weekly basis (or more or less often as appropriate), while the team leader would be available to consult with any Firm XYZ lawyer to discuss work-in-progress or ideas for new initiatives.

Because the staff is dedicated to only one firm, the scope of the campaign can broaden. There could be more of everything—interviews, reporter meetings, speeches, and roundtables. Naturally, the campaign would involve a greater number of lawyers and offices. The concentration of seasoned PR professionals for one law firm would inevitably lead to greater internal interest and buy-in.

Plan B: The In-House Model for Larger Firms

In this model, Firm XYZ increases its internal resources by hiring two or three new staff members dedicated to media and communications. But, because of the need for training and management, at least one would need to be a high-level staff person.

The firm would have a permanent in-house media team (with the accompanying management responsibilities and costs). The same level of media attention as in Plan A would probably be achieved. Control and flexibility are the salient advantages under Plan B. Firm XYZ could use these new employees for whatever purpose it wants—exclusively on internal communications, for example, or on a variety of other projects, depending upon need.

The disadvantage of this model is that it requires recruitment, hiring, and training. It would cost more, and result in less intensive relevant training.

Alternative Plan: Don't Fix It

While we believe that Plan A is conspicuously innovative, and that Plan B provides an unthreatening alternative, Firm XYZ's current arrangement may have yielded tangible benefits. As such, the firm may not have a pressing need to change.

Regardless of the plan it chooses, the firm can pursue specific PR goals and subjects immediately:

(1) *Neglected Offices*: Firm XYZ has not been on the map in several of its core regions. Third-party commentary, roundtables, reporter meetings, and a substantial increase in the number of media mentions would be effective ways to highlight what the firm is doing in these crucial markets.

(2) *Firm Chair or Managing Partner*: We suggest consultations and, ideally, formal media training to revive media interest in what the firm chair or managing partner has to say.

(3) *Business Crisis*: Let's say Firm XYZ is well positioned to become a go-to law firm for commentary on the current corporate meltdown. We suggest substantially increasing the number of opportunities for the firm's bankruptcy, litigation, and corporate governance lawyers to comment publicly when possible.

How Can PR Support Firm Strategy?

Business Development Media Demand a Two-Tiered Approach: Use Advertising to Position the Firm, and Public Relations to Reach Targeted Buyers

When we talk about the two-tiered approach, we are talking about how clients choose legal services at a most fundamental level.

Positioning and branding—as opposed to advertising tag lines (which law firms too frequently confuse with brands)—have always demanded a two-tiered approach, at the firm and practice area (or lawyer) levels. Unfortunately, law firms often ignore the dual approach and focus exclusively on one or the other.

Observe how your corporate clients employ a dual approach to positioning and branding. How much do you know about Proctor & Gamble, SmithKline Beecham, or Johnson & Johnson? These are the parent companies for thousands of products, each one with its own separate brand. What is the image in your mind for each of these organizations? As an investor in the stock market, you may have received impressions through research and earnings reports. Without this, though, you may have little or no view of them.

Contrast that with the mental images you associate with products such as Mr. Clean®, Ivory, or Cheer. You certainly know the precise consumer problems these products solve. All you know about the holding companies is that their products are safe, tested, and returnable—extremely important information, considering how unlikely you are to switch to Joe's Generic Cleanser, but not enough by itself to make you write on your shopping lists, "Buy Johnson & Johnson products." Similarly, general counsel do not write on their shopping lists, "Hire that Canadian brand-name firm." They list problems and seek solutions.

Every lawyer who has shopped in a grocery store knows where we are going with this. Many law firms spend considerable resources attempting to "brand" the *law firm*, without focusing any attention on the *practices* or *lawyers*. But it is the lawyers and their problem-solving capabilities that motivate general counsel to buy. The branding and positioning of the firm is supposed to raise awareness and set the stage for these other marketing activities, not be a substitute for them. Corporate clients have been branding products for nearly a century and a half; law firms have been attempting it for just over a decade. To whom are you going to look for lessons in the art?

What Can You Do?

If you want to obtain the business you are now leaving behind, build a dual-focused marketing campaign that positions the firm *and* lawyers/practice areas by industry. In other words, take the umbrella approach of building the law firm brand or position, but do not stop there. Focus your communications strategy on identified buyers—this is where PR comes in. Determine their most pressing problems and identify how you can partner with these companies to fix those problems. Communicate this expertise in the media they read. Start with the leading industry trades. Advertise, write, and speak in ways that appeal to the readers of these publications, not to other lawyers (unless increasing lawyer referrals is a key part of your business model).

Drill down further to the individual company publications. Identify with specificity the few associations or speaking engagements that your clients and prospects care about. Participate and speak at those events. After you have started communicating at this level, then you can focus on the *Wall Street Journal*. Nearly all law firms do this backwards—hoping for the front-page story in the *Wall Street Journal* or *New York Times*, without first (or ever) getting to the direct-communications phase.

Integrate your sales and marketing efforts so the specific plans developed by sales-trained lawyers are supported by specific, focused, marketing and PR efforts.

It is not enough to try to be *the* international trade, corporate, intellectual property, or capital markets law firm. Most markets are now too crowded. You must drill down to your specific clients' and prospects' needs. This is not a marketing crisis, as all markets mature. But it does mean you must aim more narrowly, specifically to those companies most likely to be in need of your services. As a general rule, broad marketing is accomplished by advertising, and narrow marketing by public relations.

Firms that want to succeed in an increasingly competitive legal market can no longer risk the high opportunity cost of "fractured marketing"—one year a little PR or advertising; the next year, maybe some market research; then two years later, maybe a little sales training. Though such fragmentation looks satisfactory from a budgetary point of view, it has little value beyond allowing a law firm to *feel like* it is marketing. You want more than this.

What you want is to be more profitable.

PROTECTING YOUR CLIENTS IN A CRISIS

Welcome to the age of corporate enlightenment, where new levels of stockholder and journalistic inquiry demand heightened responsiveness from in-house counsel. "What did you know and when did you know it" is now the standard by which executives, including in-house counsel, are judged. Be vigilant in spotting issues that may soon become headlines. Here are ten rules to live by:

(1) *Time Is Not on Your Side*: Defending the Bastille is always easier with advanced warning. *Do not wait* to get professionals involved until *after* the media express interest. The reporters have already formed opinions and are just calling to fill in some blanks. They will have determined who the good and bad guys are. You will have lost the opportunity to shape the first news stories that will set the foundation for all future impressions.

(2) *No "No Comments"*: Having a source say "no comment" to a reporter is a fine way to concede the entire story to the opposing point of view. Once journalists have decided something is newsworthy, sim-

ply ignoring it will not make it go away. If you are unprepared when the reporter calls, say you will get back to him or her before deadline. Return reporters' calls. Dodging calls will only ensure your role as a "bad actor."

(3) *You Can Negotiate*: When negotiating with reporters for more time, or to modify the story angle, understand that most reporters do want to report accurate facts. However, their news judgment is sometimes influenced by deadlines or a competitive situation—or, in the case of broadcast media, the need to entertain. Their instinct for the truth, even if buried, is still a tool in your arsenal. As such, you can generally advance your interest by urging that the story needs your input for balance and veracity.

(4) *You Can Live with a Bad-News Day*: Sometimes the story is just going to be bad. Minimize it if you can, but do not make it worse. If you have a bad story, gather all the facts and work with your media team in determining how best to release the information and to whom. In some cases, an exclusive to one reporter builds trust and minimizes the negative aspects. It is human nature to try and help those who reveal their warts. Release bad news all at once. If you trickle it out, you will have extended the life of the story and obliterated trust with reporters, inviting more scrutiny and coverage.

(5) *It Is Always about the Individual*: Funnel all media activity through a central source to eliminate multiple—and possibly contradictory—spokespersons. "Crisis media" is about the believability of the spokesperson. If audiences trust your spokesperson, they will be fair, and perhaps more favorable, to the company.

(6) *Speak in "Pictures"*: High-profile matters are won or lost in the minds of the public on a single mental picture, such as the U.S. Florida election recount picture of hanging chads. Your spokesperson must develop a *word* picture that unequivocally gives a snapshot of your position.

(7) *Develop Message Points*: Message points are the short, on-point answers that address any and all questions likely to be asked by reporters. Training spokespersons gives you the chance to help them "bridge" from any question back to an appropriate answer. No question should ever be answered "spontaneously."

(8) *Prepare the Release Materials*: Depending upon the crisis, you may want to prepare written press materials. They have a short shelf life, however. Having them developed largely in advance will be the only way to meet reporters' deadlines.

(9) *Contact Talking Heads*: If a story extends beyond "Day One" coverage, local media will look for fresh angles. For that, they will go to

new sources. It is imperative to identify the most likely of those sources and, if they are friendly, to be sure they are comfortable being interviewed. When third parties are supportive, it reinforces your position.

(10) *Going Proactive*: In stories with a lot of media coverage, there is, mercifully, a point at which the media grow tired of beating up the company. Sometimes there is also a short period between the negative reports and the positive. In the very earliest days of a crisis, identify positive messages so they can be incorporated from the get-go.

TIPS FOR TALKING WITH REPORTERS: WHAT DO YOU DO WHEN YOU ARE ON THE RECORD?

A key reporter is interested in having lunch with you. You have been misquoted before and now fear most media interviews and reporters. With a little nudging from your PR professional, you accept the invitation under the condition that she or he prepare you for what may transpire. Here are tips to help you survive and maybe even live through dessert:

(1) *Background Check*: Obtain copies of the reporter's most recent stories to review and discuss before the interview. Most reporters will be flattered and impressed. Usually, when people meet a reporter for the first time, they ask, "So what do you cover, anyway?" If you do not know the reporter and want to do a background check, call the publication's offices and ask the librarian to fax the reporter's four or five most recent stories. Then call sources quoted in the story, explain that you will be interviewed by the same reporter, and see what they tell you. Ask about any problems with inaccuracies or misquoting.

(2) *Comfort Zone*: Consider asking the reporter to meet at your office. Your may feel more comfortable starting out on your own turf. It will also give you a chance to offer the reporter a ten-minute tour before leaving for the restaurant.

(3) *Preparation and Background*: You should always go into a media session with three key message points, even if it is an informal "getting to know you" session. Better to err on the side of being too formal and prepared, than too informal and unprepared. Take a media kit or background information and offer it at the beginning of the lunch without a lot of explanation or fanfare.

(4) *Unobtrusive Expertise*: Let the reporter ask the questions and guide the discussion. If it seems to be going nowhere, then take charge. Identify new trends you see in your industry. Let the reporter know all the areas in which you are an expert.

(5) *Trust, with Caution*: Do not talk off the record to a reporter whom you have just met. Reporters are typically not bad people, but there is no need to take any chances. Always speak on the record, and address only the question that is asked.

(6) *Helpful Inquiries*: Ask, "How else can I help you?" Inquire about other subjects the reporter covers. You might know someone who can be a helpful source. Pass along the names of two or three other colleagues or people you know who would make good contacts.

(7) *Easy Communication*: Exchange business cards. Respond to the reporter's phone calls quickly. Keep in touch regularly. Offer constructive feedback on stories. Fax helpful articles about the reporter's area of expertise or hobbies. Share news tips and story ideas. Let the reporter know you care and he or she will care about what you know.

(8) *The Twenty-Four-Hour Deadline*: Keep any promises of sending additional materials to the reporter, and do it within twenty-four hours.

(9) *Keep the Peace*: If you have answered a question and you find yourself staring into the eyes of the reporter, do not let the silence frighten you. Sometimes this is a way to get you to say more. If you are uncomfortable with the silence, ask the reporter if you have provided the answer he or she was looking for. Get clarification, but do not continue speaking out of discomfort.

(10) *Reach and Repetition*: Do lunch again in four to six months.

Developing Your Visual Image 5

Burkey Belser

For hundreds of years, lawyers have adopted uniformity in their dress and in the materials they produce for courts. It is no wonder they have difficulty understanding the value of appearing unique. And yet, in today's swiftly changing and highly competitive marketplace, unique is exactly what they now are being asked to be. In this chapter, you will learn the following:

- the real goal of marketing communications
- how people find and choose their lawyers, and what they want to learn from you
- how often those people want to hear from you
- what works, and why and how it works

The Real Goal of Marketing Communications

Advertising, brochures, and Web sites do not sell professional services. The right person with the right service in front of the right audience at the right time sells legal services. Selling in the legal industry, like no other industry, is a relationship business. However, well-done marketing communications do serve two important functions: They *condition* the sale before you meet your prospect, and they *reinforce* the sale after you succeed. This happens by establishing a corporate personality—a visible persona that is the law firm in the minds of its various publics.

Law (like engineering and science) concerns itself with substance and scorns preoccupation with form. But, if only substance were important, magazines would publish typewritten articles, and in-house counsel would choose the unattractive and unlikable lawyer as easily as the attractive and likable lawyer. Buyers—even lawyers who buy legal services—are not immune to the form. Good design adds substance. And, whether we like it or not, people make buying decisions in part based on form. In this chapter, you will learn how to bring form under your control. Form does not rule over substance; neither does substance rule over form. Use them both!

How People Find and Choose Their Lawyers

All buyers (regardless of sophistication, and whether they are buying candy bars, cars, or legal services) go through distinct stages in the buying process. You need to address them all.

Finding Lawyers

The "finding" or "information-gathering" phase begins before people decide to hire outside counsel. Most buyers start by calling people they trust. Our research shows they are equally likely to ask someone inside their company for referrals (42 percent begin this way) as they are to ask someone in an outside firm (41 percent). Only 21 percent of sophisticated legal buyers resort to legal directories. With them, *Martindale-Hubbell* is still by far the most popular—whether on-line or in print. To find the "right" lawyer, buyers also attend seminars, read ads, search the Web, and look for articles authored by individual lawyers—in firm-sponsored newsletters or independent media.

The list of candidates usually narrows to no more than three or four, though the shortlist may double if the matter is of "bet-your-company" status. However, once the shortlist is created, all candidates are functionally equal; that is, one candidate may have more appropriate experience, but the other may be more likable. One may have international offices, but another more industry experience. The finding or information-gathering process is predominately intellectual, but once all the variables are weighed and valued, the process becomes predominately emotional.

Research shows the most important factors in the finding process are:

(1) expertise (prior experience with the same type of matter with positive results),
(2) cost (not the lowest hourly rate, but the best *value* when all factors are considered),
(3) the individual lawyer's reputation, and

(4) innovation (a fresh way of treating a routine matter, or an innovative approach to a complex one).

Other factors that buyers consider, which may be more or less important, include knowledge of the buyer's industry and company, chemistry, firm reputation, billing practices, and client orientation. Some of these factors can be learned through brochures, newsletters, or other communications, while others require in-person meetings.

Choosing Lawyers

Typically, people make decisions only because they *run out of time*—the matter is urgent, supplies have run out, or the car is waiting. Think about your own decision-making behavior. At the decision point, because choices cannot usually be measured on the same scale and are therefore roughly equal, the buyer must make a predominately emotional decision. *This important fact of buyer behavior is at the heart of all advertising and other marketing communication tools.* You must make the buyer feel good about the decision he or she is about to make and feel good afterward. (You will learn how to achieve that in the section entitled, "What Works, and Why and How It Works.")

Two factors dominate the process of finding and choosing a law firm: expertise in the pertinent area of law is usually the top criterion, and cost/value considerations rank second, becoming relatively more important in the selection stage. However, as the list of possible firms narrows, personal chemistry and law firm reputation move up the ladder of importance. In our research, the reputation of the firm became the most important factor for some (19 percent). That is not surprising, because those who regularly buy legal services often must justify their choices upstream to management. A strong firm reputation makes that chore decidedly easier.

Other important factors include individual lawyer reputation, knowledge of the buyer's industry, firm location, billing practices, responsiveness, and prior experience with the firm. Notice that the factors are slightly different—and in a slightly different order—than in the *finding* stage. Some are surprised to learn that responsiveness is so far down the list. But responsiveness is, in marketing jargon, a "post-purchase evaluation"—something that cannot be measured until the service relationship begins. Studies show that prospective buyers consider lawyers responsive if they deliver brochures or other materials within forty-eight hours. To prove you are responsive, start *being* responsive right away. But beware of building a market position premised upon "responsiveness," for two reasons: (1) every firm promises responsiveness, so the claim rings hollow, and (2) until you can control the behavior of every lawyer in the firm and are willing to punish unresponsive behavior, your claim remains at risk. Better never to make a promise that cannot be kept than to promise and fail.

Prior experience with the firm is also near the bottom of the list in choosing lawyers. That should terrify every lawyer—and with good reason. On average, companies with revenues between $100 million and $1 billion use fifteen firms, and those with revenues in excess of $1 billion use sixty-six firms! Your firm will always be competing with others who have a piece of the same business. So, marketers, remember that the best defense is a good offense: Keep in touch with clients through regular communication, preferably phone calls and letters, or newsletters and other communications.

Buyer's Remorse

Anticipating the buyer's emotions immediately after the sale is as important as understanding the emotions immediately before the sale. "Buyer's remorse" is that sinking feeling in the pit of your stomach—the fear that you made the wrong decision. Everyone goes through this stage, just as certainly as everyone goes through confusion in the finding and choosing stages. You can address this issue through reassurance programs. For example, soon after buying a car, you may have received a communication with some reassuring message such as, "Hope you're liking your new Jeep Grand Cherokee. Come in after three months and get a free oil change." This message really says, "You were smart to buy from us." Sellers of legal services can benefit from programs like this as well. The reassurance can be simple, such as a letter or useful gift (perhaps a booklet with the direct-dial numbers for all the lawyers in the firm).

Why is all this detail about buying patterns important to the law firm marketer? Imagine your brochure to be a hammer and your ads a power sprayer. Imagine your newsletter to be a drill and your announcements, saws. Each tool has a defined use and does poorly at the job designed for another. Understanding buyers' minds and habits allows you to understand and use your tools efficiently and precisely. For example, if you understand all the strategic uses of a firm brochure, you will recognize that many different brochures are possible—as many as there are types of hammers! Other businesses have known this for years and are sophisticated users of marketing tools. Lawyers are quick studies for learning the rules, but still far behind corporate America in both understanding and measuring their efforts.

What Works, and Why and How It Works

Let's examine each marketing tool to understand its precise role in the sales process. You need not simply believe this author; test these thoughts against your own experience for confirmation.

The Firm Brochure

The granddaddy of law firm marketing communications is the brochure. Firms spend thousands (or tens of thousands) of dollars each year writing, printing, and distributing firm brochures in hopes of catching the attention of potential clients. But most lawyers have heard in-house counsel claim that the brochures that cross their desks often land in the trash—without anyone taking even a few seconds to glance through them. How did brochures get such a bad reputation?

First, many firms develop bad brochures. And second, good brochures are often used in bad ways. Research shows that 56 percent of in-house counsel request brochures, and two-thirds of corporations with revenues above $500 million ask for brochures. Although lawyers increasingly recognize that brochures are essential, they often still treat them as a necessary evil—something like expanded business cards. For these lawyers, the firm brochure is a wasted opportunity.

What can a firm brochure do? It can tell your story in an organized way, arguing your case from beginning to end. It can speak for you after you leave a meeting, when the decision to hire is made. The best brochures can even act as scripts for sales calls—when you make the same points in both a meeting and the brochure, the brochure serves as a powerful aid to memory. Brochures can institutionalize cross-selling by telling existing clients about your firm's other capabilities. They can correct an outdated image and give the firm a personality—a visible persona in the marketplace. Brochures can also help clients "self-select." Because lawyers are afraid to turn away any potential client, they are unwilling to make the hard decisions necessary to locate the *right* clients. A brochure can help do that.

Law Firm Brochures

The first firm brochures were hardly more than catalogs of services—A-to-Z lists that began with Antitrust and ended with Zoning. Though these brochures succeeded in defining the scope of services, they utterly failed to sell those services. (After all, what can you tell in-house counsel about antitrust law in one or two paragraphs that he or she is unlikely to know already?) Moreover, a catalog fails to reveal a firm's personality and how the firm defines value in legal services in the marketplace—the primary goal of a firm brochure.

As a practical matter, these brochures are obsolete the moment they come off the presses. And finally, they are boring. These beginning efforts at the law firm brochure reflect a lack of understanding of its purpose. Your clients want information about you. They want to understand how you approach your work, and how you do business. If that is true, how do you create a really effective sales tool?

Before the Design Process Begins

A firm brochure should be a mirror through which lawyers see the firm as a whole. For some in the firm, the reflection might be unexpected. Because brochures should have a long shelf life, the mirror should reflect the future, not the past. Matching present-day reality with a vision of the future is difficult for any business. First you must "know thyself," and then, "know thy dream." And, even if the story of the firm exists in a business and marketing plan, actualizing that plan through a brochure is a challenge. That is when substance becomes form, and form, substance. This is hard work, but delightful when breakthroughs come.

An effective brochure is possible *only if you establish a design goal that reflects your positioning strategy.* But firms often begin developing brochures without plans—"because we need one!" And so, the resulting bad brochure begets the bad reputation brochures enjoy. Ask yourself: How hard is it to develop a winning case? How much creativity and thought does it require? How do I stage my presentation? Why should brochures be any different?

Identify the Key Messages

Every firm is unique. The mix of lawyers—with their various experiences, diversity, and talents—makes a sound that can be tuned into a single note. Lawyers who are uncomfortable with self-promotion can take some solace in the fact that the note will never sound true if it is dishonest. The message that overrides every other must be accurate about the firm's vision of itself, and must be accepted by the partnership and understood by the entire firm. (Therefore, the development process should include giving everyone the opportunity to hear that the firm's management believes the message is genuine.)

Behind a key message are other themes you should develop. For example, your network of offices might make you uniquely positioned to offer international, national, or regional coverage that others cannot match. Your deep experience in two or three industries gives clients a head start when you take the case. Your open culture gives clients access to teams of the best talent the firm has to offer. There are dozens of other themes you could explore. There are very few that fit your firm. Those that do become your "voice."

What Is a Design Strategy?

To you, your practice area is the most important feature of the firm's brochure. But that is *your* point of view, not necessarily your client's. Sellers focus upon their needs, but marketers focus upon client needs. The center of your client's world is not you, sad to say. It is a different "me."

Put on your client's shoes and you will realize there are many organizational schemes for a law firm brochure. They can also be combined with different levels of emphasis. For example, you could organize your brochure around case studies to group practice areas from a *business's* point of view. You could focus upon characteristics of service (such as speed, innovation, or multilingual capabilities). You could focus upon geography, laying claim to a region or state or area of the world. This is strategy.

You could illustrate your case studies with photographs or drawings. You could present your service characteristics with solid colors. You could tell the story of your South American experience by turning the globe upside down. This is design in service of strategy. Design animates strategy, brings it to life, and, if creatively done, makes people respond.

Client Focus

Some of us forget to ask others about themselves, so focused are we upon ourselves. Most brochures exhibit similar bad manners. They focus upon the firm, not upon clients' needs or concerns. Few things are more difficult than turning away from the gravitational pull of your busy workday and toward your clients' concerns. Understanding clients' needs—telling your story from their point of view—wins just as many clients as asking about others wins friends. In fact, consider the marketplace as a holiday party: Those companies that seem to care about their customers or clients, like people, seem to be the best liked and most successful.

Readers Do Not Read, They Scan

You should design brochures based upon the way readers behave, not upon the way you want them to behave. Readers rarely read according to your table of contents. Instead, they skip around and read the most accessible material on each page. As readers scan, they constantly make "reading" decisions; then, if they choose to read, they constantly assess whether they should go back to the scanning level. Studies of readers' eye movements confirm this. (If you do not believe this, study your own reading patterns and you will find a close parallel with the reading patterns of most people.) Therefore, your brochure should be designed for scanning readers. Tell your story in headlines, subheads, pictures or illustrations, and captions. Use bullet points. Keep copy brief. Do anything scanning readers want, because the more time they spend with your materials, the more likely you are to gain their trust and precondition the sale.

A Purpose for Every Page

Be rigorously goal oriented. Define the overall goal for your brochure, and then the key message for every page. These goals are always informational *and* emotional. They may be achieved through headlines, color, images, or any of a dozen other tools in the designer's toolbox. But the designer and the law firm should be clear about the key messages and should carefully study the developing brochure to confirm these goals have been achieved.

Enhancing Memory

Many factors encourage and enhance memory. Not all of them are known. What *is* known is that memorability increases if we burn multiple pathways into the brain—sound, sight, touch, and smell. Memory must be reinforced if we want material retained in short-term memory to transfer to long-term memory.

The Importance of a Name

The first memory to establish is your firm's name. Short names, no more than three or four syllables, stand a better chance of being remembered than longer ones (which are always reduced to shorter monikers anyway: Ford Motor Company becomes Ford, International Business Machines becomes IBM, the Food and Drug Administration becomes the FDA, and so on). Memory has little room for polysyllabic handles, so compression constantly occurs. Because smart marketers recognize this, an entire industry has grown around naming products and services.

Law firms often carry unmemorable names, but fortunately, the public is there to help reduce Skadden, Arps, Slate, Meagher & Flom to Skadden Arps or, even better, Skadden. A few firms market services under a "street name" (like Jones Day), but retain an official name of the partnership (Jones Day Reavis & Pogue). Other firms, like Proskauer Rose, have taken the plunge and simply shortened their firm names.

A slogan (which marketers call a *positioning statement*) reinforces memory by attaching an association to a name. An example is "Federal Express: absolutely, positively, overnight." The benefit of the company's service is directly linked to the company's name. Law firms trying to stake a clear market position have followed that model, as shown in this classic example: "Howrey & Simon: In Court Every Day."

The Importance of Visual Identity

Corporate identity has been defined as the "communicated essence" of a corporation. A visual identity attempts to project what makes a firm unique. And it provides a visual pathway for memory.

Visual Pathways

The development of marketing tools is solidly rooted in the history of our cultures. In fact, the development of logos—the modern equivalent of heraldry—parallels the rise of capitalism. Throughout time, no one has doubted the power of the image. Before humans could read, they could understand symbols, learning to love them or fear them, hate them or laugh at them. On that foundation, that basic activity of memory, rests the tradition of the corporate logo. *Logo* has come to mean the graphic associated with a company, product, or service.

What Is a Law Firm's Visual Identity?
Of course, the logo is just one visual element in the identity scheme. Though it is the cornerstone of the identity program, only the consistent application of that logo, coupled with a family of colors and selected type styles, gives your clients a memorable vision of the firm. Inconsistent messages are confusing. Consistency, the spirit of effective communication, cannot be overdone. Most businesses have too few opportunities in front of clients to waste them with more than one message.

The style of illustration or photography you choose—even the shape of your materials and the paper choices—influence memory and affect the impression your audience retains about your firm. Why? Legal services are intangible, and therefore their quality and reliability cannot be felt or seen or heard. So, consumers place inordinate emphasis upon any tangible indicia of you and your work—such as your letterhead, your business card, your fax form, and your brochure.

Chemistry is so important in business relationships—and what influences chemistry? Your appearance, posture, tone of voice, conversational style—and your printed materials. This is nothing other than your *personal* visual identity! Extrapolate this to the entire firm and you will understand the idea: Visual identity attempts to create a firmwide chemistry.

Consider IBM and Apple Computer, or CBS and NBC. Each has a distinct personality, but they provide look-alike services. Consumers understand what each has to offer because the companies have communicated their unique personalities (their corporate identities) through words, images, and music—all your senses they can reach. A law firm should communicate its visual identity—its image and personality—in all printed materials, from letterheads to labels, from brochures to wills. Most firms still fail to communicate their personalities to their publics. In the past, letterheads came straight from stationers, treated as office supplies rather than the most important indicator of a firm's presence. Those days are over. Our most recent survey shows that 79 of the AmLaw 100 have engaged designers to create letterheads that are integrated into all firm marketing materials. This is a stunning victory for law firm marketing. At the heart of marketing is a strong identity.

What a Visual Identity Can Do for Your Firm
A clear, distinctive identity gives a firm a platform for doing business. A well-managed identity can become the basis for building relationships:

(1) *Among Law Firm Partners*: Building consensus is difficult when individuals have no allegiance greater than their individual goals. A clear identity requires shared values and shared goals. Building consensus is made easier by consistent, tangible expression of a firm's culture through an identity program.

(2) *In Newly Merged Firms*: A clear identity can guide and motivate a firm in transition. And it can also make a firm being acquired appear more valuable.

(3) *Among Recruits*: New lawyers want to join a firm they understand. Studies prove that recruiting the best lawyers, and retaining them, are critical factors in profitability. A firm must present prospective lawyers with a clear definition of itself. A visual identity, properly developed and implemented, communicates stability, as well as the firm's philosophy, energy, and market position.

(4) *Among Clients*: Clients deserve the same succinct definition. A strong firm identity signals for clients a law firm's clear position in the industry and the marketplace, and that the firm knows who its clients are and why it is in business.

(5) *Among Employees*: Employees like being left out of the picture even less than they like being underpaid. If they understand the firm's objectives, and where their work fits in, their satisfaction increases. A shared identity helps employees understand these qualities, and it can motivate superior performance and develop emissaries for the marketing effort.

(6) *With Firm Administrators*: Poorly coordinated identity systems cost firms thousands of dollars each year through waste and inefficiency. Thirty-two percent of all printed materials are thrown away because they become outdated. A well-designed identity system often pays for itself in savings.

Consistency Is the Goal

Very few companies have the opportunity to reinforce their visual identities with the entire American public every day. To achieve that level of awareness, those companies spend hundreds of *millions* of dollars! To achieve more limited awareness, a few regional or local companies spend millions of dollars. All these companies understand that each impression has value, thus each presents a consistent impression to squeeze the most value from its advertising and promotional dollars.

For law firms, this idea is not always welcome. Some large firms still have as many as twenty-five designs for business cards, dozens of letter formats, or eighty fax designs. Many firms that coordinate a consistent look for all their promotional materials exempt the "holy" letterhead and business card, leaving their traditional stationery unchanged. Because a law firm has so few opportunities to make repeat impressions, valuable opportunities are wasted when letterheads and business cards (along with e-mail, the most common carrier of those impressions) are not included in the identity program. *Everything* published by the firm (with the exception of court documents) is an opportunity to remind viewers of the firm's consistent market position.

The Questionable Value of Firm Announcements

Firm announcements are a time-honored tradition of law firm marketing. They are, as one legal marketing consultant notes, "a venerable news release . . . gentle reminders of the firm's existence." Too gentle, perhaps. The changing tradition of the law is forcing the examination of traditional tools. Though firm announcements have undergone radical changes in format and design, budget-conscious marketers might ask whether they should be produced at all. The costs of engraving or printing, paper, postage, and handling should cause every "occasional mailing" of the firm to be scrutinized.

What Does Not Work

Rarely does an announcement hail a single lawyer. Usually, to save money, the announcement gangs two, three, or more names together on the same card or set of cards. The impression that a single name might have made on a more collegial community in years past has been diminished by today's crowded and competitive marketplace, which demands that large firms recruit dozens of new lawyers every year. Because of their cherished history, announcements will probably continue to be published. In the nearly forgotten world of etiquette, announcements acted upon the same set of sensibilities as cotillion balls. Today, some in-house counsel say they regard stacks of them almost with irritation. Instead of being helpful, they are nuisances in the daily mail. Listen up! Imagine that your new partner announcement could be regarded as a *nuisance*!

What Does Work

Continual contact with clients is critical. An announcement does remind the recipient that the firm is still in business. As repeated impressions are key to effective visual identity, announcements can play a part in the process. Morale is also important. Almost as a perk of partnership, an announcement signifies a formal welcoming into the society of lawyers that is a law firm, though the tradition may be more important for family and friends than for clients. An announcement is improved by adding a small biography of the new partner, which helps clients place the individual somewhere in their hierarchies of needs. Improved announcements also employ design, color, and innovative typography consistent with other firm identity materials, giving them personality and certainly improving their effectiveness as marketing tools.

If you cherish the tradition, then mail announcements to select lists. Include biographies. Add portraits. If you see this tradition as a "legacy system," then abandon it. Use the legal media to announce new partners. Publish "substantive" news of changes within the firm biannually or annually, giving information about the strategy behind those hiring decisions and your goals for the future.

Managing Change

The change from old to new is legitimately hard. It hurts to see a cherished way of doing things pass away. The introduction of a new visual identity, however, rarely causes the firestorm of protest that greeted new identities in the past. In fact, it seems more lawyers hunger for change than forbid it. Nevertheless, the success—or failure—of the process is in direct proportion to your ability to manage change. The following steps may be helpful.

Survey the Field

The dominance of tradition in the legal culture inevitably makes every lawyer's first question, "What are other firms doing?" So, the first step in designing a visual identity change is to collect as many examples of law firm identity programs as possible. Not many partners need it anymore, but the partners who need that reassurance need it badly. Check with the major engravers in the legal field. Ask lawyers in your own firm to collect letterheads that they like from other firms.

Show Process

Bitter experience encourages marketing partners and directors to make committees as small as possible. But keeping the design process confined to a small committee will be fatal in the development of a firm identity. Committee members learn quickly and, during the visual identity process, are not even aware of how much they have learned. They may consider solutions that would shock the rest of the firm. Rather than simply roll out a new identity program as a fait accompli, show partners how the process led to the conclusions. Teach the new viewers about typography, placement, design, and color so they understand and support the committee's decision.

Separate Issues of Change from Issues of Taste

Objections to a new design often are based upon emotional reactions to change, rather than the design itself. For example, "I prefer black ink" simply may be another way of saying, "I want my old letterhead back." Or, "I prefer the traditional typeface" is most often code for, "I like what I had, thank you." Lawyers find "traditional" to be that with which they are familiar. Be sympathetic. Lawyers were raised in the cathedral of logic. Visual "substance" may seem lightweight when compared with legal "substance." So attack with logic and seek to answer real objections, not straw men.

Yes, Your Clients Read Newsletters

The good news: 92 percent of in-house counsel read newsletters. Buyers of legal services like to be kept up-to-date on breaking issues that affect their businesses. The bad news: some in-house counsel receive as many as two hundred newsletters each month! Nevertheless, newsletters that are not too long (most readers prefer no more than four pages) and are packed with brief and usable information attract the attention of in-house counsel. To add to the difficulty, half want newsletters and alerts in print to read at their leisure on commuter trains or at home, and half want information via e-mail. Your job will be to learn which half want which.

Put News into Newsletters, But Do Not Give Away the Store

A newsletter worth reading may leave the client or prospect with just one new idea or one new piece of information. What kinds of ideas or topics are appropriate? Anything that is new and relevant can be "news"—new regulations, new laws, new services that benefit clients, new ways of doing business, strategies for new markets, or new opportunities.

News about the firm itself may also interest clients, when it is relevant to their businesses. The addition of a white-collar practice, the opening of a Paris office, or the introduction of extranets can be important developments to clients. And though firms typically use announcements to introduce new partners and associates, corporations typically use *newsletters* to introduce new employees, in greater depth than formal announcements allow.

Few of us have time to spare. A considerate editorial strategy would be to make news stories brief. Readers appreciate summaries of new laws and activities, no more than two paragraphs in length—or even shorter. Send readers to your Web site or offer a phone number for those who want more detail. If you believe the full story must be told, offer an executive summary at the beginning to allow readers to answer the question, "Does this story affect me?" Short summaries lead to (1) reduced lawyer resistance to writing articles, (2) better stories (Mark Twain—or if you are French, Pascal—once said, "If I had more time, I would have written a shorter letter."), (3) more interested and appreciative readers (test against your own behavior which items you are most likely to read in your favorite magazines or newsletters), and (4) the distinct possibility that the firm might publish on schedule.

Periodicals Should Be Published Periodically

In the magazine and newsletter publishing businesses, the worst sin is failing to publish on time. Yet law firms frequently announce quarterly newsletters with a grand splash in the first issue, and then get only one more issue out that year or, even worse, never publish again. If regular newsletters are part of your individual practice area marketing plans, then you must deliver on your promise. Otherwise, all your investment is wasted. A publication is a contract between the reader and the publisher. So, before you begin, answer the same questions you would before starting any business: What are our goals and strategies? What are our resources? Do we have management support? If any answers come up short, do not even start. There are other ways to keep in touch with your clients and prospects that might work better for your firm.

Develop a Voice—Your Voice

You may not even realize that your favorite publications keep your allegiance and command your affection because they have developed voices you admire or like. Consider *The New Yorker, Atlantic, Metropolitan Home, Vanity Fair,* or *Forbes*. Any magazine that leads its market does so with a strong editorial voice. Let your voice—your personality—come through. Have an opinion and a point of view. You will be read. Editing for clarity, power, and personality is what good publications do best.

The Designer's Art May Offer Your Only Chance to Be Read

As buyers, we remember only a few providers of products or services (usually only three or four) but we rank them in precise order in our minds, like rungs on a ladder. Typically, the three or four we remember are the market leaders, which have won the battle for our minds.

This theory about the organization of consumer memory is called "positioning," a concept as fundamental to marketing as gravity is to physics. Positioning is a theory about human memory applied to consumer behavior. Businesses study positioning to learn how to influence consumers' minds, not only to recall their products or services, but to remember them in a positive light. It is at the heart of advertising and all marketing communications. Physiological research confirms this theory. Studies suggest that the eye is a relentless hunter, always scanning the scene before it. As it scans, the eye is also continuously focusing and discriminating, separating figure from ground. The scanning eye sends signals to the brain, where decisions are made about whether to linger on an object. Studies show the eye lingers most often on complex or new images, as it tries to sort out the complex or identify the new.

Web Sites and Other New Media
The Pervasive Internet

In 2001, only 77 percent of law firms were online, although more than half (58 percent) of those got there after 1999. Today, all firms with more than 150 lawyers have Web sites. Astonishingly, many sole practitioners are not yet online. Shame on you. The Web is essential for doing business today.

Forget everything you *think* you know about the Internet. Your understanding of the Internet is probably out of date. For example, did you know that:

- The Internet is now universally used by law students to evaluate law firms; therefore, not having an effective Web site jeopardizes the future of your firm.
- Sixty-six percent of buyers of legal services search the Internet for lawyers and 38 percent surf the Net weekly—some more often. And those searches are growing!
- Sixty-five percent of searches begin by practice area, *not* by lawyer. In fact, more searches begin by office (36 percent) than by lawyer name (32 percent).
- The most important feature of your biography or practice area description is your experience in specific industries.
- As of this writing, 11 percent of corporate counsel have signed up to create custom pages on Westlaw's Corporate Counsel Marketplace where articles and ads from individual firms are *pushed* to them daily. That figure will probably seem silly before this book goes to press. Corporate counsel are beginning to understand it is your job to find them, not vice-versa.

But the Internet is not marketing's magic bullet. In effect, it doubles your marketing responsibilities because work that is published on your site often must also be published in hard-copy form. For example, half of corporate counsel want to receive newsletters via e-mail or e-mail notification of on-line information. Half still prefer to get paper copies they can read on trains or planes, or at home.

Let's explore how the Internet is really used and what you should do to stay at the cutting edge, especially considering 66 percent of buyers of legal services say that in deciding whether to try a new law firm, they are likely to be influenced by how effectively the firm uses all aspects of the Internet. Law firms have set the technology bar very low. Sharing documents via e-mail is not particularly impressive to sophisticated corporate buyers.

The Web: The Internet Made Visual

The Internet is home to the World Wide Web, a come-one-come-all global repository of words and pictures. The Web is the Net brought to life—with colors, sounds, and intuitive navigation. It is the most graphic-intensive region of the Net. And, because its ease of use has attracted millions, the Web is now responsible for most of the traffic (and congestion) on the Net. The growth in

Web use stuns the imagination. Your home may already be wired for broadband service. Your hotel must certainly be, or it risks losing business travelers to "smart" rooms in other hotels.

Practically every business uses the Web for e-mail connectivity, electronic banking, and research. Unfortunately, more and more companies of all sizes find the Web to be an inexpensive way to reach millions of potential customers via unwanted e-mail or spam. As little as one response per thousand makes spam a cost-effective marketing tool. Spam is marketing *push*; that is, like direct mail, the marketing message finds its way to your doorstep, whether you want it or not.

A Web site is a good example of marketing *pull*. If I can encourage you to visit my site through advertising or articles, I have, in effect, brought you into my "store." Our research shows that almost half the time (47 percent), visitors are "browsing" when they visit your site, just as they might do in a store. What are they looking for? A third are looking for information on opposing counsel! Another third are looking for articles or white papers on the latest developments in the law; so it makes sense to have an information-rich site with the shelves fully stocked. It also makes sense to create an easily navigable site—considering 28 percent of your visitors are searching for general information, you should make walking around your site easy and comfortable. The most successful high-end stores pay close attention to the decor that contributes to the experience of being in the store. Similarly, a well-designed Web site that promises a rich experience pays dividends for the firm.

Research tells us that in-house counsel are looking for more specific information about law firm capabilities than brochures typically provide, yet many law firm Web sites are still little more than on-line brochures. Simply transferring existing print materials to the Web is an understandable first step, but it ignores the potential—and the character—of the new medium. Not only can a Web site be a repository of a firm's skills and experience, it can also preview what it is like to work with the firm; that is, a Web site can reflect a firm's personality. Any tool that effectively *previews the actual experience of working with you* is a powerful marketing tool. (For more information about Web sites and their design and development, see Chapters 10 and 11.)

New Media

New media, in the broadest sense, are methods of presenting information digitally. Books, brochures, and newspapers are, by inference, *old* media, as are slides and overhead transparencies. PowerPoint presentations, multimedia techniques, CDs, interactive kiosks, and the Internet are new media.

Formal presentations are now a fixture of competing for legal business—particularly for complex projects such as multijurisdictional litigation. Thus, the need for media that enhance presentations and extend their impact has increased.

Outshine the Competition: Be Presentable

Improve your presentations by designing templates for software applications such as PowerPoint. In creating presentation screens, extend your firm's visual identity right through to the point of sale. Transfer key messages from the firm brochure to build a framework for the entire presentation—creating standard introductory and concluding screens, and style guidelines for text, lists, charts, and graphs.

For "low-tech" presentations, PowerPoint can help create complementary handouts. Handouts can add value by allowing you to provide more in-depth information than can be put on a single screen. The best handouts include information you may not have had time to cover. They remind your audience of salient points in the presentation. Moreover, your handouts reflect your firm. How they look gives a nonverbal message about you, your firm, and your firm's commitment to high quality.

DVDs, CD-ROMs, and Other Pressing Demands

Other digital tools are available for firms committed to technological presentations. For marketing purposes, CD-ROMs offer substantial storage. All newsletters, white papers, and practice descriptions can be delivered on one disk—with room to spare for full-motion video, audio, animation, and lush illustration. Compared with the Web, CD presentations are a static medium. Revision is expensive and far from immediate. But once the CD is in the hands of the client or potential client, the information is accessible to the buyer at any time. DVDs are no more difficult to prepare than CDs, and even have some advantages.

With those advantages, it is surprising that promotional disks are used so little in the business. But the "click-through rate" for CDs remains stalled at 4 to 8 percent, which means that few are willing to install or view a presentation. Why? Ask yourself. Your own behavior is probably typical. A somewhat dated survey shows that three out of every four executives prefer printed material. Undoubtedly that will change as comfort with the Internet soars, but old habits die hard. Paper still competes favorably as one of the cheapest, most flexible, and efficient media for information delivery. In spite of America's love affair with gadgets, simple and familiar solutions are often the best.

Section III

Implementing Marketing Strategies

Marketing with the Written Word

6

Roberta Montafia

Why Write?

The written word can be one of the most powerful marketing tools lawyers can use. For an individual lawyer, writing can be used to build credibility, raise a profile, and differentiate the lawyer in a highly competitive market. Writing is a logical first step in building a reputation, enhancing a résumé, developing name recognition, and establishing a lawyer as an expert in the eyes of peers, clients, prospects, and the media. Properly planned and executed, writing can be a cost-effective way to spend a portion of marketing time. Although nothing rivals face-to-face meetings for business development effectiveness, writing should be part of every lawyer's marketing mix, as it has the potential for reaching a large number of clients and prospects, in a meaningful way, with relatively little expenditure of money and time.

For firms, practice groups, law firm marketing departments, and industry-focused marketing initiatives, the written word can be used in a variety of ways, each of which is discussed below.

All lawyers and firms face the challenge of breaking out of a crowded market by demonstrating uniqueness or a special understanding of something that is important to clients and prospects. Marketing is not a "one size fits all" endeavor, and the written word can be a remarkably effective vehicle for achieving differentiation. A published article sends a message to the reader that the writer has experience. It also carries an implied endorsement by the publisher that this person or firm has credibility.

Perhaps the greatest attraction of writing as a marketing and business development tool is that even lawyers who are reluctant to "market" are generally comfortable with the activity—it is safe and familiar to them. Further, the variety of available formats and the flexibility of the medium allow lawyers and firms to present their legal strengths, business insights, and general competence in a way that readers seeking expertise will recognize. Even for a newly qualified lawyer, who may feel he or she has limited legal skills and experience, writing is a way to start building a reputation and relationships.

The key to success with the written word rests in strategy. Do not let yourself be lulled into a false sense of comfort simply because you are a good writer. Every time you write something for publication—whether it is a scholarly treatise, a one-page client advisory, or anything in between—it creates a marketing opportunity; each of these opportunities must be approached with care. To build a practice, you must create a connection in the prospect's mind between you and the prospect's needs. If you want to be in a buyer's consciousness, you first must get into the buyer's mind. Using written materials can be one of the least intimidating, yet effective, ways of achieving this goal. Nevertheless, you must have a plan, and you should approach a writing project with the same precision as you would a complex matter for a client. You must think long-term, and be prepared to devote the time and resources necessary to achieve success.

How to Begin

Once you decide to use the written word as a marketing tool, you must decide what to write, how to write, and where to publish. On the surface, the answer to these questions may appear simple. You should resist the temptation to "just jump in" and write for what might seem like the obvious choice (such as the publication you know best, or the one that is "easiest" to get into). The planning stage is often dismissed as unnecessary, or is neglected because it can be tedious and time-consuming. But without a clear sense of strategy and direction, even the most disciplined writer wastes time.

You must also avoid the mind-set that one bylined article will lead to business development success. Many a lawyer has written and published an article (usually at the prodding of someone else), and then sat back waiting for the telephone to ring. Such a singular effort is usually doomed to failure, as such expectations are hardly realistic. Any isolated marketing effort—

whether it is writing, speaking, or advertising—seldom achieves results. With writing, repetition is important; though there are exceptions, generally the quantity of exposure can be as important as the quality of the exposure. Marketing and business development are the cumulative effect of consistent efforts. Success takes time and energy. Therefore, an important first step in writing is to create a plan—one that is realistic, attainable, and sustainable, and one that complements your overall marketing plan. The plan can be as uncomplicated as submitting four articles to targeted publications in the coming year, or as elaborate as writing a series of books.

Steps in Creating a Plan

Initially, you must identify the best audience for your marketing efforts. Examine your current client base, or, if you are just starting, determine the type of clients you want to form your client base. To help you decide what to write, you might ask yourself the following questions:

- What type of work have I enjoyed the most?
- What type of work would I like to do more of?
- What type of work is, or would be, financially rewarding?
- Which clients have I enjoyed working with?
- What areas of business or my practice are growing?
- What areas of business or my practice are declining?
- What type of clients will I need to have in the next three to five years to attain my goals?
- What trends can be detected in the legal and industry sectors I serve that might affect the growth or decline of my practice?

Additionally, you should examine the referral sources for each of the types of clients you want to attract, as you might want to target your writing to them. It is helpful to analyze referrals in a variety of ways, such as by geographical region, by industry, and by source (such as other lawyers or accountants, or existing clients or in-house counsel). By categorizing your desired client base, you can segment and group clients by common characteristics. Generally, clients who share common characteristics engage in related activities and have similar legal needs and interests.

Once you have gone through this exercise, you will have a clear picture of the makeup of your target audience. A critical element of effective marketing is knowing to whom you are communicating. You can then turn your attention to what to write, how to write it, and where to appear in print.

What to Write

You have identified your audience and are ready to put pen to paper, but you need a topic. The obvious and most appropriate approach is to write about what is important to the target audience. Ideally, what your audience needs overlaps with subjects about which you have strong knowledge and interest. Your own work product can also be a good source of ideas and may be an excellent starting point. If you have done a research memo or produced material for a seminar or speech, it often can be turned into an article with relatively little effort. Leveraging your existing work product is clearly a good way to get more out of your marketing time. Similarly, once you have written an article, you can leverage that effort through future rewrites and updates. Previous articles can also be used to create a series or to form the basis for new articles tracing trends and examining patterns in developing areas.

Probably the most fertile and relevant ground for ideas can be found with your clients and business contacts. Who better to ask about what issues are important to them? If a client has asked you a particular question, or if there has been an unusual issue raised in a transaction, there is a good chance that an article or advisory about the issue will interest other people in similar circumstances.

One lawyer I know keeps an "idea" folder. When she has an idea for an article, she makes a few notes and puts them in a file. Then, when she finds additional pieces of relevant information from various sources, she adds them to her file. By the time she starts writing, she has accumulated most of her research and can eliminate the time-consuming research process. What began as a conscious effort for this lawyer is now an unconscious act—a habit. She benefits by being prepared when a writing opportunity arises and often finds herself with enough material for several articles.

Once you select a topic, take care to ensure that your writing is framed in terms of benefits to the audience. Though people perceive benefits in different ways, it is essential to focus your writing on the benefits to your selected group. There will always be issues that are client- or case-specific, but, by categorizing your clients, you can address at least some common concerns.

The process of analyzing your client base, targeting a market segment, and focusing your efforts can be demanding and time-consuming. It is easy to see why many lawyers want to forgo this exercise. Yet the process results in a strategic assessment, without which your marketing endeavor will probably be of little value.

How to Write—Your Style

Legal writing should be clear, concise, persuasive, and precise. But, in reality, much of it is strangled by using the "legalese" presented to lawyers throughout law school. To avoid confusing or alienating your readers, you should strive to simplify your writing and avoid using obscure phrases, terms of art, and weighty sentences.

Most of lawyers' writing is intended to persuade. To be persuaded and convinced, the reader must understand your point of view. To be persuasive and convincing, you must organize and present issues in a logical fashion. The writing need not necessarily mirror a chronological sequence of events, but it should run with a logical flow of ideas.

The constructive and informed use of metaphors, case studies, or anecdotes from your audiences' industries can be powerful tools of persuasion if applied sensitively. Clients generally warm to the "familiar"; it increases their comfort and allows them to "own" the ideas you try to sell. Clients may even take your ideas further and discover additional applications that, in turn, become business opportunities for you. Good legal writing is an art that must be cultivated, and because words are our primary method of communication, the development of that art is critical. But it is also critical to understand that the writing style needed for a business audience is not the same style used in a brief or legal memorandum. You should not start any business article (or most law articles) with an exhaustive recitation of legislative history, statutes, or cases. The goal of the written piece is to share insights and information that can be useful to your readers, not to provide them with a document that can be filed in court. If you write with clarity and relevance, your piece will be copied and circulated throughout a company. If you write a lengthy, technical, lawyerlike piece, it may not even be read.

Where to Publish
Using Research to Choose Publications

With the proliferation of newspapers, newsletters, trade journals, and electronic media, there is an inexhaustible supply of publishing opportunities from which to choose. For those who already know the publications their clients or target audiences read, selecting a publication may be an easy task. For others, it will involve research.

Here, again, your clients can help. One of the most cost-effective and foolproof research methods is to ask your clients which publications they regard as necessary reading for their industries. This request has the added benefit of demonstrating to clients that you are interested in their businesses and value their input. Trade journals are one of the best places to consider for publishing articles. Virtually every industry relies upon certain trade journals that are viewed as "must-reads" by people who work in the industry. Because the journals are dedicated to providing education and information to a particular industry, appearance in them carries great weight with readers.

If you are just beginning to build a client base or target a new market, it is essential that you do some research. It is not unusual for lawyers to begin writing without specific outlets for their products in mind. Generally speaking, this is not a good idea. By targeting a specific publication, you have the advantage of reviewing previous editions and requesting a media kit, which will provide you with the publication's circulation numbers, demographics, advertising rates, editorial calendar, and additional relevant information.

Reviewing previous issues of a publication allows you to see the style, format, and typical length of the articles. Also, do not overlook evaluating the quality of advertisers in a particular journal. Would the audience you are attempting to reach be consumers of the goods and services being offered in this publication? Are the advertisers leaders in their fields? Remember, organizations do not typically allocate advertising dollars to a publication that does not get results. And, finally, is this a publication with which you want your name associated?

Moreover, learning about a particular publication not only helps you select the best vehicle for your message, but also increases your chances of getting published. You would not want to devote your valuable marketing time to a written piece only to discover that you selected a publication that does not accept submissions from outside sources, or that has just published a similar story.

For those whose search requires a broader scope, there are media directories that provide excellent references. They can be great time-savers, as they collect information from a wide variety of sources and produce it in a concise and easy-to-reference manner. They typically provide information on publications, trade shows, conventions, and mailing lists, as well as editorial profiles—all the information you need to help you target appropriate publications.

Convincing the Editor to Accept Your Article

Once you are satisfied that a particular publication is appropriate to pursue, you must persuade the editor that your article is worthy of publication. Write a clear, concise letter introducing yourself and outlining your proposed article. Make sure you provide sufficient information about your background and expertise, as well as the benefits the readers will gain from your article, so the editor can make an informed decision. Be mindful that editors are very busy people—keep the communication as short as possible and to the point. You should also follow up with a phone call. You run the risk of reaching a harried editor scrambling to make a deadline, but you also may get the opportunity to "close the sale." Many firms rely upon professional public-relations specialists to assist them in this effort.

One comment about paying for placement of an article: *Don't*. It is not necessary, and you certainly will not get good value for the expenditure. There are plenty of reputable outlets for your work that do not charge for placement and are appreciative of fresh ideas and well-written articles. This is particularly true for professional and industry trade journals, which depend heavily upon outside sources for editorial content.

Even if your article is turned down by your first-choice publication, do not assume the article would not be attractive to someone else. Sometimes you simply did not fit within the editorial calendar or guidelines of the publication you approached.

It is always good to remember your manners, as well. Write a thank-you note to the editor after the article is published. It is yet another opportunity to put your name in front of the editor, and, because it is not something most authors do, it serves as another means of differentiation.

Leverage

Every time you complete a marketing exercise, you should look for ways to maximize the value of the effort. An article that has been published has by no means outlived its usefulness. You spent effort producing the initial publication—now capitalize on that effort by looking for additional audiences. How else can the article be used? The first consideration should be whether the same article could be offered, in whole or in part, to other publications. (A note of caution: Policies regarding the assignment of copyright vary among publications. Make sure you have a clear understanding of who retains the copyright.)

Reprints of articles will usually be supplied by, or can be purchased from, the publisher. If not, with the publisher's permission, you can have them produced at a local print shop or in house with a desktop publishing program. Reprints can be used in a variety of ways and generally have a long shelf life. They are a wonderful means of increasing exposure for little additional expense, which is typically just postage and copying. In the first instance, they should be sent to your clients with short notes. They should also be circulated throughout your firm—ask your colleagues to distribute the article to their clients. The article can be mentioned in a general firm newsletter, with an offer to send a reprint to interested readers. Articles can also be reproduced on your Web site, or you can link to the article on the publisher's Web site. Reprints should be available in firm "waiting areas" or at firm conferences and seminars. They can be added to your portfolio as you progress through your career, and used as part of an introductory package when someone asks for information about your services.

Reprints are also excellent sources of writing samples. Being published in a reputable journal buys a level of credibility that can prove useful in "selling" yourself to another editor; your collection of prior articles can do the selling for you. They are an instant demonstration of your credibility and expertise.

Electronic media is a developing area—one that deserves its own space and is addressed more extensively elsewhere in this book. Do not neglect it as a potential outlet for your work.

Other Forms of Writing for Lawyers

Letters and Notes

Letters, both personal and business, can be an efficient and effective marketing tool, yet their impact is not widely appreciated in the era of e-mail. Letters are particularly beneficial as supplements to more formal client communications, such as newsletters. If you take the time to know your clients and their businesses, you can use letters to capitalize upon opportunities to demonstrate your interest and strengthen client relationships. When you see an article that a particular client might find interesting, take the time to write a short letter or note and send it along with the article to the client. Such communications keep your name in front of clients and demonstrate that they and their businesses are important to you.

You should make it a habit to review your local and regional newspapers, as well as industry trade journals, for news regarding your clients and prepare to follow up with a note. Regardless of whether the note is sent in relation to a business matter or a personal matter (such as a congratulatory note for receiving a community or business award), it has the potential for advancing the relationship and getting more business. At the very least, a personal note sends a message that you care. All lawyers should keep good-quality note cards in their desks, and develop the habit of handwriting brief personal notes.

Letters to the Editor and Op-Ed Pieces

Too busy to write an article? Then consider writing a letter to the editor—a simple, efficient, and effective variation of the personal letter. Lawyers often have strong opinions or questions about some of the issues discussed in publications they read. A well-considered letter that persuasively sets forth an opinion or adds substance to a particular topic will generally find placement.

Similarly, an opinion piece that is placed opposite or near the publication's editorial page (hence, "op-ed") can provide good exposure. These pieces are typically short, and can be written reasonably quickly. However, they generally address current issues, which makes them time-sensitive, and they are highly sought-after opportunities. You will have a much better chance of getting an op-ed piece placed in a local or regional publication than in a national publication, where intense competition for placement leaves editors with the luxury of publishing mostly by invitation only.

The same rules of research discussed in connection with bylined articles apply to op-ed pieces. Study previous pieces to discover their common elements, and then structure your piece accordingly. The best op-ed writings cover a substantive issue in a timely and somewhat (but not too) provocative manner, and then provide possible solutions.

Firm Brochures and Collateral Materials

It is expected that all law firms will produce printed brochures describing the firm's practice. Most law firms conclude they need brochures because other firms have them and clients expect them. The first brochures were mostly dry recitals of the practice, with the text chosen by committee and compromise. This resulted in brochures that were too predictable, too broad, and too generic to have real marketing value. Although a brochure has a definite role to play in the marketing of a firm or practice, it will have relatively little value if it is an unfocused, stand-alone piece written in an attempt to reach every audience.

The brochure is the most expensive, visible, and widely distributed communications document used by most firms—but of all the things lawyers can write, it is probably the least read. To have the most impact, it should flow from a uniform firm signature, created as a result of the firm's image and not in a vacuum. It should be written by a professional who has the experience and talent to translate the firm's philosophy in a manner that celebrates the firm's uniqueness and understanding of what is important to clients. The task of developing a firm brochure is not simply a writing exercise; it is a process that should articulate the firm's strategic position. If well written and produced with care as part of a larger marketing effort, a brochure can capture and convey the culture and vitality of a firm, communicate the benefits the firm brings to clients, and serve as the key tool for presenting an overall picture of the firm's capabilities. Even with the increasingly sophisticated use and importance of Web-based publications, the printed brochure has not outlived its usefulness. (See more on the development of firm brochures in Chapter 5.)

Individual brochures for practice groups, departments, or industry groups are an essential complement to the general firm brochure. They are particularly useful for providing specific information about a firm's experience in multiple practice areas. A good practice brochure should have a narrow focus, describing the services and capabilities of the area in detail, stressing competitive advantages, and providing adequate information to assist in the buying decision. The practice brochure can be used in concert with a firm brochure, yet should contain sufficient substance and information about the particular practice experience to be used as a stand-alone piece.

Fortunately, law firms have matured in their designs and uses of brochures. Today you can see any number of brochures that convey distinct images of firms. Many firms follow the practice of other industries and produce pieces similar to "annual reports," providing information that answers the question, "Just what exactly does your law firm do and what does it mean to me?" The brochures effectively communicate firm strengths, range of services, past successes, current issues and projects, and short- and long-term plans. Law firm marketers understand that the use of vignettes and "mini" case studies can have memorable, illustrative value.

The objective of the brochure is to convey the message that this is a successful, dynamic, forward-looking, and innovative law firm with which the client or prospect should be working. If you decide to produce an "annual report" to clients, make sure you have the resources and support to commit to yearly production. Consistency greatly enhances effectiveness.

Résumés and Biographies

The last time you gave your résumé serious thought was probably when you were looking for a job. Though this is not uncommon, keep in mind that a résumé is a good marketing vehicle that should be approached as a sales tool. The intent is to generate a response from the reader. To be most effective, a résumé—like all other written pieces—must be drafted with the audience in mind. Before distributing your résumé, you must customize it for the intended purpose. Is it going to a potential buyer of your services? To an editor of a journal you are targeting for publication? To a conference organizer to promote yourself as a potential speaker? Most lawyers should have multiple biographies and résumés for different settings.

Before you begin drafting, ask yourself, "What information must I include to make myself more attractive for marketing or business development purposes?" If you create your résumé in sections, it can be easily accessed and customized for a particular need. This also allows you to store up-to-date information about your publications, speaking engagements, community involvement, associations, and memberships.

A good résumé is not merely a list of positions and experiences. Instead, it includes language that connects your skills with the readers' needs. What about the inclusion of personal information and photographs? For those who believe you should include only results-oriented elements and professional-accomplishment material, and save the personal information for the cocktail hour, an exception should be made if the information demonstrates a unique skill, attribute, or experience that would be attractive to the audience, especially if the message is not otherwise apparent.

Some general guidelines apply. If the résumé is to be included as part of a proposal, you should highlight "like-kind" transactions with which you have been involved, as you want the résumé to be a showcase for your professional experience and expertise. If you are marketing to a prospect and the purpose is introductory, you should emphasize previous industry experience and the types of services the target may require. You also should ask yourself, "What else would a prospective client need to know?" Here is where more personal information might be beneficial. It could be used to describe yourself beyond the terms of your practice.

Providing information about personal achievements and community involvement can be effective. If you have raised a significant amount of money for a charity, or run an ultra-marathon, consider how including that information might demonstrate your level of perseverance, commitment, ability to focus, and character, all of which could be very attractive to potential clients. You should also consider adding personal information if you are using your résumé to promote yourself as a speaker, or are attempting to sell an editor on a particular story.

Newsletters and Advisories

A good newsletter can be a useful practice development tool; done right, a newsletter can improve relations with existing clients, stimulate referrals of new business, build and maintain name recognition, and provide a forum in which lawyers demonstrate special expertise. As with other nonbillable activities, the pressures of practicing law often make it difficult for firms to produce client newsletters in a consistent and timely fashion. Unfortunately, the effectiveness of a newsletter is greatly diminished if it is not produced on a regular basis.

To avoid the problems of production, some firms and lawyers have turned to outsourcing. The marketplace contains many organizations and consultants that provide production services for newsletters. They offer services with varying degrees of firm participation and control, thereby allowing the firm to structure a program with which it can be comfortable. If you want to take advantage of the benefits of outsourcing, you must decide what type of service will work best for your practice.

Some newsletter production companies hire staff lawyers to produce articles, which can then be mixed with some of the firm's copy. At the other end of the spectrum are organizations that provide completely prepackaged pieces. They may simply put the firm's logo on the top and retain complete control of every detail, from inception to mailing. Be aware, however, that with canned newsletters you run the risk of your clients getting the same articles in a newsletter from another lawyer or firm. If you choose to use a canned newsletter service, make sure you get an agreement giving you geographic exclusivity, and make sure you are familiar with all the content of the newsletter, as clients may present you with questions at a later date.

You might also consider using freelance writers to help produce newsletters. Good freelancers can convert drafts of articles into publication-ready pieces. They can also interview lawyers regarding particular issues, and write articles from scratch.

A newsletter should be created only if it is written as a service to the firm's clients. There is a wide range of attitudes among clients about the value of newsletters—some clients appreciate personnel and firm information, while others expect strictly business. It is essential, however, that the content be manageable, navigable, and understandable. Ideally, the recipient can pass the newsletter to other executives and colleagues, both inside and outside the company. Many firms have successfully utilized Internet-based newsletters, which offer the advantages of no postage or printing costs, easier mailing-list management, and shorter turnaround times between writing and publication.

Although mailing-list management might be viewed as just another mundane administrative process, a well-populated and well-maintained mailing list is critical to the success of many marketing efforts. If you are going to spend valuable time and resources producing a good newsletter, you should not then waste the effort by having a mailing list that is untargeted, incomplete, or out-of-date. There are many good, inexpensive software packages available that provide the tools for managing mailing lists.

Clients typically prefer advisories, alerts, or bulletins as alternatives (or supplements) to newsletters. A good advisory is a one-page document, dealing with a very focused issue, which is sent to a targeted audience for whom the information is immediately relevant. The brevity and relevance of the advisory means it is more likely to be read than a newsletter. Using good technology, the advisory format allows quick and efficient production, so lawyers can deal with breaking news—which may have a profound impact upon a segment of clients—in a timely manner. Advisories can also help establish lawyers as experts in given fields. Frankly, the advisory is not really an optional tool in most clients' minds. Clients *expect* to hear from their lawyers whenever important issues arise, and to be alerted to issues *before* they could negatively affect their businesses. An upcoming change in legislation or regulations that will affect an industry sector is an excellent example of when to use a client alert.

Announcements

Law firms often send costly announcements about new partners. If you believe they are essential, then at least get some value by sending them only to people who might have an interest, and by giving the recipients some additional information that might be beneficial to *them*. You can do this by describing the uniqueness of the partner or the service that he or she offers to clients, especially if it is the addition of special expertise or the creation of a new practice area.

Press Releases

Press releases are often considered by lawyers to be the most efficient and effective means of communication with the media. However, they are also the most frequently misused communication. They have their limitations and should be used cautiously, but, if used correctly, can be powerful.

Press releases have a definite place in the marketing mix, and can be effective if they deal with subjects that are newsworthy and appealing to a wide audience. For example, a press release could be used as an alert to the community regarding a change in the law that might have an adverse impact on a segment of society or business, or as an announcement of a firm's involvement in the formation of a much-needed new practice or an industrial development project.

One very important point: a press release is a discretionary matter. Before you write a press release, ask, "Is this something that would interest anyone else? If yes, then who?" Send it only to a targeted audience. And, do not let your ego get in the way. Take an honest look at whether dissemination of the information benefits the reader, enhances your reputation, raises your profile, and generally reflects upon you in a positive manner. If it does not meet those criteria, then do not issue the release.

If you determine the press release will contribute to your business development efforts, then you must develop relationships with members of the "press." Editors and journalists are bombarded with press releases and press space is finite. You must give them a reason to accept your release. Decide which journals you want to target, and then assess the journalists to learn who writes about what, and who covers which industries. Call and introduce yourself. Work toward establishing relationships and building credibility with the journalists, so when they see a release you sent, they will be inclined to give it consideration. Building good relationships also means the journalists will be more apt to call you when they have questions, need background information, or want to add quotes on given topics.

A press release can give you an element of control and be particularly effective in dealing with an event that might receive negative publicity. For example, if your firm has a seemingly sudden departure of a group of lawyers, or if you have a client who lost a particularly controversial case, a press release offers an opportunity to structure the story in a way that lessens negative speculation.

An accepted "rule" is that a press release should never exceed two pages. To grab readers' attention, the first paragraph should contain the relevant information, and the release must tell a complete story. Write in clear, concise language; stay away from sophisticated legal terms or you will lose your readers. And, it is often a good idea to mail copies to your clients.

As with bylined articles, remember that different publications have different audiences. To maximize the attractiveness of the press release, tailor it to the individual audience. Though a press release may go to a number of sources, it need not be identical for each source. Many firms employ a professional public-relations firm or individual to assist with press release placement and strategy.

Putting It All Together—One Lawyer's Story

Michael C. Fondo is a tax lawyer in Boston. He clearly understands the business development benefits of the written word, and has used writing to his advantage as part of his overall marketing efforts. Mike is also an avid golfer. While reading an issue of *Golf Digest* magazine, he came across a blurb about the Internal Revenue Service (IRS) and its proposed treatment of caddies as employees and not independent contractors. Mike was familiar with the issue of independent contractors, and believed the IRS was wrong. A little research proved not only that the IRS was wrong, but also that it had issued a revenue ruling about thirty years ago that looked at the issue and concluded that caddies were independent contractors. Mike was indignant that the IRS could now take a position against the taxpayer, contrary to its own publicly announced position.

Mike immediately thought the *Wall Street Journal* (*WSJ*) might be an appropriate outlet to express his views. He was astute enough to recognize that the issue was timely, as it was the beginning of golf season and shortly before the U.S. Open Golf Championship. Though he viewed this as principally a marketing effort, Mike also had genuine underlying concern and empathy for the caddies—the majority of them were teenagers just trying to make a few dollars.

Mike began his research by contacting the Western Golf Association to get some background information on caddies in the United States. He then drafted a piece and sent it by e-mail to the *WSJ* editor, asking if this was something the *WSJ* would consider publishing. The *WSJ* jumped on the story, immediately contacting Mike and asking if he could have it ready to run for the next day. He spent some time working with the *WSJ* copy editor, and an article entitled, "IRS Bogey-Man Threatens Caddies," by Michael C. Fondo, was published the next day. Mike's efforts, from research and writing to dealing with the editor, took about five hours—a small investment for a very large return.

On the day the story ran, Mike received about a half-dozen telephone calls from people who shared his concern. One of the calls was from an organization that lobbies on behalf of golf clubs. It had been disturbed by the issue and had already been working with Congress, trying to get the relevant IRS Code section amended. The organization was thrilled, as Mike's article focused national attention on the issue and was a huge boost to its effort.

The story was quickly picked up by Bill Littlefield of National Public Radio for his *It's Only a Game* broadcast, for which Mike was interviewed. CNN also interviewed Mike for background information on a story it was running. The print media responded as well, as *Sports Illustrated* asked him to write a column, which resulted in a similar request from *Golf Journal*.

However, the most significant contact came from Congressperson Dan Burton. He saw the *WSJ* story and as a direct result introduced H.R. 2321, the Caddie Relief Act of 1997, to amend the Internal Revenue Code to provide that nontouring caddies are independent contractors and not employees. In a press release announcing the filing of the bill, Congressperson Burton noted that he became aware of the IRS's efforts to reclassify caddies after reading Mike Fondo's column in the *WSJ*.

The name recognition and business contacts that Mike received as a result of this effort are immeasurable. The National Association of Touring Caddies, as well as several prominent business people, contacted him. The article has been distributed to the boards of various caddie scholarship funds, all of which are large organizations with very impressive board members. And the benefits kept coming. Mike was featured as one of the up-and-coming lawyers in his home state of Massachusetts by *Mass Lawyers Weekly*. He credits the article as being an instrumental factor in his selection. He has also received some very positive feedback from existing clients. A published article goes a long way toward legitimizing you in the eyes of your clients. This is particularly true when you write for a well-recognized and respected publication such as the *WSJ*.

What did Mike do right? Just about everything. He recognized an issue of importance, did his research, targeted a publication, knew his audience, wrote about it with passion, leveraged the work, and provided a valuable service to a distinct business sector. What were the benefits he received? He increased his profile both inside and outside the legal community, gained name recognition, significantly added to his business contacts, enhanced his reputation with his peers, and has the satisfaction of knowing he helped thousands of caddies. A lot of benefit for five hours of work—not a bad return on the investment of time. Any lawyer who could not turn this level of exposure and credibility into business probably needs to be doing more than reading this book!

Conclusion

Building a career in the law used to be a great deal simpler. Whether you were pursuing a career as a sole practitioner, within a law firm, as an in-house lawyer, in government service, or in academia, the various paths to success were well known. If you worked hard and became a good legal technician, you could reasonably expect to prosper and remain in your selected profession for your entire career. It is not that simple anymore. Today lawyers face increased competition and are entering a more diverse, complex, and global environment than ever before. There can be no doubt that hard work and legal competence remain critical elements of success, but they constitute only the foundation. To shore up that foundation, lawyers must develop other talents that will help them stand out in a crowded marketplace. The written word is an effective, user-friendly, business development tool that can be used to impress, assist, and differentiate.

Marketing Through the Spoken Word: Conversations and Public Speaking

Robert N. Kohn
Lawrence M. Kohn

The vast majority of your marketing efforts depend upon the spoken word. Though the written word plays an essential part, the spoken word has many distinguishing qualities. First is its interactive nature: Conversations provide opportunities to receive immediate feedback. Prospects can ask questions and express concerns, and lawyers can immediately respond. This rapid exchange of information expedites the sales cycle. The spoken word also is multisensory: It allows lawyers to use body language, intonation, volume, rhythm, and energy. These added qualities help give depth, meaning, and motivation to marketing communications.

Marketing through the spoken word comprises two components: sales dialogue and public speaking.

Sales Dialogue for Lawyers

Most lawyers feel uncomfortable with—and even hostile toward—the idea of sales dialogue. There is a strong anti-sales sentiment, which is constantly reinforced by exposure to obnoxious, pushy, and unknowledgeable salespeople. This negative stereotype of selling is prevalent in industries where the consummation of a sale represents the *end* of the interaction. For example, when someone buys a car, the salesperson does not handle the ongoing service. By contrast, for most lawyers, closing the sale means *continuing* the relationship. Pushy, abusive sales dialogue cannot work for lawyers, whose clients expect trusting, supportive, and loyal service. This chapter's goal is to prove that sales dialogue can be appropriate and effective. In fact, after exposure to the techniques discussed in this chapter, many lawyers learn to appreciate that sales dialogue is emotionally gratifying, in that it develops friendships and financial security, and intellectually stimulating, in that it requires clear thinking and sophisticated strategies.

Some types of sales dialogue are more comfortable than others. Most lawyers feel relatively comfortable when explaining their services to prospects who have expressed needs, but much more uneasy when initiating conversations with prospects who have not yet expressed needs. In many states, there are ethical restrictions on initiating sales dialogue. Also, initiating sales dialogue exposes lawyers to the risk of feeling rejected and embarrassed, and of being perceived as pushy or needy. As a result, many lawyers simply prefer to wait until business comes in the door. But this approach may be too slow. You may want to be more proactive in pursuing new prospects.

There are two groups of prospects you can pursue: people you know, and strangers. Your most immediate marketing opportunities are probably with people you already know—your clients, friends, family, and business and social acquaintances. You have greater access to these contacts. And, depending upon the state where you are licensed, there may be fewer ethical limitations in pursuing preexisting relationships.

Sales Dialogue with Clients

Obviously, your best marketing opportunities are with your existing clients. Satisfied clients can give you more work and they can introduce you to their contacts. However, your clients may not be thinking about these issues, in which case you must initiate the subject.

Expanding Client Relationships

You may have clients with needs that could be served by either you or other members of your firm. The key to feeling comfortable in discussing additional services with a client is confirming that a need exists. If in fact there is a need, then initiating the subject is not only appropriate, it is obligatory.

However, if you cannot anticipate client needs, there are two techniques for doing research. (See Chapter 3, as well as the Appendix, regarding research strategies.) One is the client survey. A survey can be informal, such as asking for feedback on the work you are doing, or it can be a formal questionnaire. In either case, you could ask the question, "Do you have other legal needs where the firm can assist you?" Another approach is to provide a detailed list of services so clients can learn what is available.

The other technique for identifying client needs is an annual legal review. The purpose of the review is to help your clients look into the future. Ask them about future plans and other issues about which you may be unaware. As you help clients look into the future, you may identify areas where you can assist them.

Leveraging Relationships

Another marketing opportunity clients offer is their ability to introduce you to their contacts. For example, you should consider meeting their accountants, bankers, and other advisors. This is not a problem if you meet them in the normal course of your work. But, if your work does not provide easy entrée to clients' contacts, it is a good idea to request an introduction. Another technique for meeting client contacts is to ask clients about the organizations they support, such as trade organizations or charities. Getting involved in these organizations is a way of becoming familiar with issues that affect clients' lives, and it will help you meet their contacts.

As you initiate sales dialogue with clients, be sensitive to the concern of selling when you are practicing law. You do not want to upset clients by selling to them on billable time.

Sales Dialogue with Friends

Another group of potential prospects are friends (and family). However, many lawyers feel uncomfortable discussing the availability of their legal services with friends. One concern is the risk of losing the relationship by either imposing on it or failing to meet expectations. Another problem is not wanting to discuss sensitive personal matters. Though these are valid concerns, it would be unfortunate if you categorically dismissed the opportunity of doing business with friends, as they can be a significant marketing resource. Many lawyers regularly represent and receive referrals from their friends. In fact, some friendships are significantly enhanced by a business relationship. You should analyze each friendship individually, carefully looking at the opportunities and risks. You may discover that doing business with a select group is the most appropriate choice. Once a friend is identified as a prospect, the next question is how you appropriately raise the subject of providing legal services. Some indirect and direct methods follow.

Describing Daily Activities

One indirect method is to increase your dialogue about the daily activities in your practice. For example, a common lost opportunity may be your response to the question, "What's new?" Instead of saying, "Not much; what's new with you?," consider talking about an interesting case or legal issue. You might also encourage your friends to discuss their own concerns, and then discuss your work, if it is relevant.

You can also transition from social dialogue to business dialogue by identifying issues appearing in current events that also appear in your practice. For example, in talking about a current issue, you could say, "I experienced something like that in my practice." Another technique is to invite your friends to law-related programs they might find interesting. When using any of these techniques, focus upon whether the friend would generally be interested in the matter. All these indirect techniques help paint a picture of you as a lawyer, as well as a friend.

"Full-Disclosure" Technique

A much more direct approach for initiating the subject of business with friends is a technique we call "full disclosure." Full disclosure is the process of introducing a sensitive topic by first fully disclosing your feelings and concerns.

For example, assume you have a close friend who owns a business, and you think you could do a good job as the friend's lawyer. But you are uncomfortable suggesting it, because you worry that it might be perceived as an unwelcome offer. You could say something along the following lines: "I'd like to discuss a business issue that is really important to me. I think it would be of great value to both of us. But before bringing it up, I want you to know that I feel a little uncomfortable mentioning it. I really value our friendship and I don't want you to feel that I'm imposing on it in any way. If you are not comfortable with my suggestion, just let me know and I won't bring it up again. With that in mind, I'd like to express my interest in the possibility of becoming your lawyer." This dialogue allows you to raise a sensitive issue without placing your friend in an awkward position.

Of course, doing business with friends is a personal decision. Friendships are too valuable to be taken lightly. But make sure your concern about doing business with friends does not eliminate the possibility of harvesting this potentially valuable resource. In fact, you may find it helpful to remember the following poem:

Business with Friends

Business with friends offers great dividends.
In addition to cash, it's relaxing.
Dinner out is a night off, as well as a write-off.
That's why business with friends is less taxing.

—Lawrence M. Kohn, 1985

Sales Dialogue with Strangers

Though much business comes from people you already know, you may not know enough people to build your practice. This means you need to initiate dialogue with strangers.

A common opportunity for initiating sales dialogue with strangers is at a social gathering, such as a wedding or cocktail party. You learn that the person you just met is a good-quality prospect. The question is whether it is appropriate to talk about your practice. And, if so, how do you bring up the subject?

A rule of thumb is to refrain from discussing your practice until someone asks you what you do for a living. Once you have been asked, it is socially appropriate to respond. However, it may be a long time, if ever, before you are asked that question. So, if prospects fail to ask what you do, ask what *they* do. Raise questions about their industries. Ask how the economy or technology has affected their businesses and their clients' businesses. Generally, if given an opportunity to describe their own businesses, prospects will return the favor. If they still fail to ask what you do, comment on how the issues they describe in their businesses apply to your practice as well.

Goals When Networking in a Business Environment

In the process of marketing, lawyers inevitably find themselves at social functions designed specifically for the purpose of meeting prospects. Although these events—if well targeted—are extremely beneficial, lawyers may find them to be distasteful experiences. It is common to feel insecure in a room filled with strangers. The solution for many is to look for a familiar face, and then visit with that person for the rest of the meeting. Following are some techniques that will minimize the unpleasantness and maximize the effectiveness of "working a room."

One of the reasons lawyers find "working a room" so distasteful is that they often do not have clear understandings of their goals. They make the mistake of assuming the goal is to be entertaining, providing witty remarks and quick repartee. This myth imposes pressure on lawyers who feel shy. Another mistake is desiring to close deals in the first meeting. Meeting someone for the first time and convincing that person to hire you on the spot is unrealistic. Potential prospects may not have immediate needs for your services, or they may already have relationships with other lawyers. When lawyers "go for the close" too quickly, they come across as being pushy.

At networking events, focus upon the following goals: (1) meeting as many new people as possible, (2) qualifying them, (3) maintaining open lines of communication, and (4) creating opportunities for follow-through.

Meeting New People

When you go to an event and find yourself in a sea of strangers, follow these tips to navigate the situation. First, arrive early. You will find it much easier to make acquaintances when the room is relatively empty. Meeting people after they have already formed small groups is more difficult. Furthermore, if you arrive late, you may miss valuable marketing opportunities. Next, upon arrival, introduce yourself to the organization's staff persons. They will know many of the organization's members and will gladly introduce you to appropriate contacts.

Another tip for meeting new prospects is to go with a friend, which can ease the pressure of being alone in a room full of strangers. You can work as a team to meet people, but avoid the temptation of sticking together. If the function involves a meal, do not sit at the same table. Your goal is to meet others, not socialize with your teammate. (With this concept in mind, it is fascinating that some law firms reserve whole tables at networking events and stick together the entire time!)

One of the difficulties lawyers have with working a room, especially those who are new to networking, is the fear of introducing themselves to complete strangers. One technique for overcoming this obstacle is to realize that many people at the networking activities share the same fear, and that you do them a favor by taking the initiative to introduce yourself.

Begin by establishing eye contact. This helps you determine whether someone is approachable. The easiest technique for breaking the ice is simply to ask, "Hello, may I introduce myself?" You can then talk about the organization sponsoring the event. For example, you could say, "I'm new to this group. Are you active in this organization?" Your goal at this early stage is merely to establish enough rapport to begin qualifying the person as a potential prospect.

Qualifying Prospects

After establishing some rapport, your next objective is to determine whether the person is a *qualified* prospect. This requires asking in-depth questions. Instead of engaging in small talk, ask questions that invite answers that help you in the selling process. Some samples follow:

- "What do you do for a living?" This is one of the first questions to ask, as it helps you determine whether the person fits your client demographic.
- "Who are the kinds of people you do business with?" This helps you discover whether the person is a potential referral source.
- "What obstacles does your industry face?" and "How are you planning to deal with those obstacles?" These questions reveal something about the person's needs.

- "What trade organizations are you involved with?" This helps you explore other marketing opportunities.

The answers to these questions help you determine whether a prospect is worthy of your marketing attention. If so, then your next goal is to make sure you have the ability to maintain an open line of communication.

Maintaining Open Lines of Communication

One technique for maintaining open lines of communication is to send the message that you have some things in common, such as interests, values, or contacts. These similarities are called "connectables," because they create connections between you and your prospects. The technique for verbalizing connectables is to listen for similarities and then point them out. For example, try to identify common interests, such as hobbies or organizations, or similar values, such as the importance of family and charity. Look for common experiences in your past, such as having gone to the same school or lived in the same city. Identifying connectables will increase the feeling of safety in working with you, create a bond between you and your prospect, build trust, and create opportunities for doing things together.

Another technique is to respond effectively to the question, "What do you do for a living?" Keep in mind that when someone asks this question, he or she is really asking, "How can you help me?" Instead of simply answering, "I'm a lawyer. What do you do?," structure the answer to respond to the underlying value you offer. For example, a tax lawyer ultimately will help a client save tax dollars. Therefore, the answer to the question should be, "I help people save tax dollars—I'm a tax lawyer." The goal is to keep the door open by quickly communicating that there is a *reason* to build the relationship. However, keeping in mind that telling prospects what you do for a living is not nearly as important as learning whether you can help *them,* *you* should quickly shift the focus back to them after explaining what you do. As you learn about their needs, you will be in a better position to describe how your services can help them.

Creating Opportunities for Follow-Through

Always request the prospect's business card. Often, instead of asking for a card, lawyers say, "Here is my card. Give me a call." The problem with this approach is that the prospect may lose your card or forget to call you. If *you* get the *prospect's* card, then you are in control of the ability to further the relationship. Also, even when lawyers ask for business cards, they often intend to follow up but never do. To ensure follow-through, you should—as you engage in the conversation—make a commitment to implement some future activity. This technique is called "marketing at the moment." For example, making a commitment to mail something or to call and schedule a future meeting forces you to take action and further the relationship. Write your commitment on the prospect's business card so you will remember it later. Add the information to your database or contacts-management program. Then, when you do follow through, it will demonstrate to your prospect that you are someone who honors commitments.

After you leave an event, take a moment to review the cards you collected. On each card, write whatever you can remember about each good contact and make sure that person gets added to your mailing list. Remember, your goal is to build relationships. If you fail to put a prospect on your mailing list for follow-up, you have rendered the effort of meeting people virtually meaningless.

Ending the Conversation with a Nonqualified Prospect

One of the challenges at networking events is not knowing how to extricate yourself tactfully from a conversation with a nonqualified prospect. One universal signal that brings closure to a conversation is the question, "May I have your card?" Another technique is to spot someone else in the room you want to meet and say, "I hope you don't mind, but I see someone over there I'd like to visit." Always comment that you enjoyed meeting the person before you leave—*never burn bridges.*

Sales Dialogue with Qualified Prospects

As you follow through with qualified prospects, it is important to understand that prospects use varying criteria in deciding whom they should hire. Some have only a few requirements, such as adequate skills and affordable fees. Others have more elaborate criteria, such as graduation from a particular school or connection to a certain social group. Before attempting to close the sale, you should make certain you understand your prospect's criteria. This requires active listening. You then need to communicate that you can satisfy those criteria (that is, reveal your worth), discuss fees, and accelerate the "close." Finally, you can use voice mail and e-mail as effective tools in furthering your relationships with your prospect. A discussion of these steps follows.

Active Listening

Active listening means focusing on the statements of your prospects and encouraging their continued communication. Asking meaningful and insightful questions can help stimulate conversation. Obviously, you should ask questions concerning legal needs. In addition, however, you should ask prospects about any past experiences with lawyers, their expectations in working with you, and, if possible, their interests and personal background. The more you know about your prospects, the easier it will be to satisfy their criteria.

Make sure you maintain consistent eye contact. Wandering eyes communicate boredom and disrespect. If you are uncomfortable with maintaining eye contact, try looking at the speaker's mouth or the bridge of his or her nose. You can also provide supportive sounds and gestures such as, "Uh huh," or "Hmm," as you nod your head and smile, and use supportive words such as, "That's interesting," or "I hear what you're saying." It is no secret that people enjoy talking about themselves, and will do it freely if you show genuine interest in what they are saying.

Finally, confirm your understanding of what the person has said. Ask questions such as, "Are we on target regarding your needs?," and wait for a response. Do not assume you understand the situation until the prospect acknowledges that you do.

Revealing Worth

Once you understand your prospect's criteria, the next step is revealing that you possess the qualities that satisfy those criteria. These usually include expertise, quality of service, and personality.

Expertise

Most prospects want to be convinced you have the expertise to handle their matters, so you must be able to discuss your knowledge, skills, and experience. Though you could simply give prospects brochures or biographies, do not be surprised if they never read them. And because many prospects will not know how to interview you, they may not ask necessary and specific questions. To communicate your expertise during conversations with prospects, make sure you weave in facts about your background and credentials, such as the law school you attended, awards or honors you may have received, articles you have written, and speeches you have given. Describe bar association committees on which you have participated, and other important legal organizations in which you are involved. When you are discussing a particular problem, cite cases that support your position and explain your track record with similar situations. And, if possible, provide the names of satisfied clients.

Quality of Service

Sales dialogue about the quality of your service involves information about your responsiveness, fees, procedures, partners, support staff, and other valuable resources. Most lawyers say they offer good service. But claiming to offer good service has little impact on prospects, because every lawyer claims the same thing. Merely saying you offer good service has no meaning unless you can *support* it. One way to do that is to mention specific details about your practice, such as these: "I carry a beeper." "We always return phone calls by 5:00." "We offer to take calls at home." "We are acquainted with contacts who would be valuable for you to meet." (Of course, you must be careful about name-dropping; mention only those people who will unquestionably take your call.)

Personality

Another important goal in sales dialogue is differentiating yourself from the competition. Legal expertise and quality of service alone are often not enough to position you as unique. In fact, many prospects are not sufficiently knowledgeable about legal issues to even appreciate expertise or service. One of the most important qualities that will distinguish you from the competition is your personality. The following list identifies several personality traits; take a moment to consider which traits will be important for you to reveal to your prospects:

Aggressive	Intelligent
Conscientious	Loyal
Courageous	Patient
Creative	Persistent
Empathic	Reasonable
Energetic	Responsible
Enthusiastic	Self-confident
Ethical	Supportive
Honest	Trustworthy

Although these personality traits are some of the most important criteria prospects rely upon in hiring lawyers, they can also be the most difficult qualities to reveal. For example, let's say you are proud of your creativity. Saying that you are creative may seem like bragging. And also, as with describing the quality of your practice, simply stating it has little meaning unless you can support it. The solution to revealing positive personality traits effectively is finding indirect methods of communicating that you possess them.

Examples and War Stories

One way of indirectly revealing personality traits is by giving examples or telling stories in which these qualities were operative. Some call these "war stories," because they often are depicted in environments of conflict. For example, if you wanted to reveal your creativity indirectly, you could tell a story about a personal experience in which you faced a significant obstacle, but then came up with a creative solution. Or, let's say you wanted to show that you are reasonable. You could give an example of a transaction in which you were able to balance the business needs of the client with your legal concerns and still close the deal. Using the above list, or other traits you would like to reveal, think of examples or war stories in which those characteristics were operative. This will give you the ability to plan in advance, so you will be more likely to incorporate these stories in your sales dialogue.

How to Avoid Revealing Negative Qualities
If you do not make an effort to reveal specific personality traits, the risk is great that your prospects will not perceive or appreciate those qualities. If you are not clear about your personal qualities, an even greater risk is that you may inadvertently reveal qualities that make you *undesirable*.

Lawyers regularly speak in ways that do not accurately reflect their true personalities. We once coached a lawyer who consistently decorated his dialogue with phrases like, "Sort of . . .," "Kind of . . .," "I'm not sure, but . . .," and, "I'm afraid that . . . ." Interestingly enough, he thought of himself as being decisive and self-assured. Yet his dialogue made him appear apologetic and insecure. Some other common mistakes to avoid:

- Do not deliver too much technical information during a social conversation. An overabundance of it will be boring and position you as an intellectual elitist.
- Eliminate off-color jokes and cultural slurs. Though this should be obvious, people regularly make these mistakes. Be aware of bad habits that may be acceptable in your social dialogue, but disastrous with prospects. Even minor infractions of this rule can be incredibly insulting.
- Be careful not to show disrespect for clients. Lawyers sometimes forget their clients are not supposed to know legal issues, and they make light of the clients' lack of knowledge. This hurts you in your sales dialogue because your prospects logically assume you feel the same way toward them.

There are, of course, many more negative qualities you should be careful to avoid projecting. Maintain constant vigilance to reveal characteristics that position you positively.

Talking about Money
Once you are satisfied that you understand your prospect's criteria and adequately communicated your worth, you need to discuss your fees. It is important not to be defensive about any aspect of your terms. A lack of confidence in discussing your fees could easily be misinterpreted as a lack of confidence in your legal skills.

Obstacles to Talking about Money
One reason many lawyers lack confidence in discussing their fees is that they are defensive about the subject of money. It is interesting that lawyers can be

so effective in discussing the financial needs of their clients, but when it comes to talking about money for themselves, they feel uncomfortable. This attitude may stem from prevalent beliefs that money is tainted. After all, a well-known proverb holds that "the love of money is the root of all evil." Negative attitudes about money may also stem from fear of being greedy, lack of confidence in self-worth, and lack of familiarity with the competition. Some ideas for alleviating this anxiety follow.

Remember That Law Is a Business

Talking about money requires that you look at law as a business. You should have a clear understanding of all the costs of doing business, including depreciation, write-offs, and marketing. Similarly, you should be aware of what your competitors charge. Thinking of your practice as a business will help you quote fees with confidence.

Focus upon Benefits in Comparison with Fees

Another technique is to remain mindful of all the benefits you bring to your prospects. Most lawyers underestimate their value, especially those who feel they do not live up to their own standards. Regardless of their talents, some lawyers minimize their worth by judging themselves too harshly.

When you quote your rates, always do so in relation to benefits. The first type of benefit is your ability to help your prospects make more money. Virtually every transaction makes money by either increasing the client's profits or minimizing liabilities. In quoting fees, you should explain to your prospects the financial impact of your services. It is easier to quote fees when they are smaller than the benefits. Also, remember all the other ways you bring value to your prospects, such as your ability to reduce their anxiety and introduce them to other contacts. Though these qualities may be difficult to appraise, an awareness of them makes it easier for you to quote—and for your prospects to appreciate—your fees.

Accelerating the Close

The goal in sales dialogue is to receive and reveal enough information that prospects will ask to get started. If they do not ask, and you believe you invested enough time in the process, it is time to accelerate the close.

For certain prospects, such as large institutions that are accustomed to using many lawyers, an effective approach is to ask, "What are the procedures for becoming an approved provider?" Usually, a large institution has written procedures for becoming part of its approved-provider list. For prospects without written procedures, the best way to accelerate the close is simply to start solving the prospect's problems and begin doing the work. For example, you might offer to do some research or make a phone call on the prospect's behalf. By starting, you "assume the close," and hopefully the prospect will consider the relationship established.

If you just cannot get started, the second-best technique for accelerating the close is to be forthright and state, "I'd like very much to represent you. Are you ready to proceed?" If the prospect is not ready, then you must discover and address the prospect's objections.

Overcoming Objections

When prospects express objections, do not respond negatively or defensively. You want to avoid confrontation or weakness with prospects. Negative communication about one small point could cloud the entire sales process. Instead, try using a technique called "agree and clarify." This technique requires that you find some aspect of the objection with which you can agree. For example, if a prospect objects to your fees, you can agree that it is important to be cost-conscious. Then, you can clarify your position by explaining the value you offer.

Do not be surprised if it takes a long time to win a client. Many lawyers give up too easily when prospects are slow to hire them. Keep in mind that in sales, a "No" really means "No, not now." Just because you are unable to close prospects today does not necessarily mean they are no longer prospects. The key in sales dialogue is follow-through. The goal is to maintain a positive presence in the lives of your prospects until they ultimately need your services. As stated before, never burn bridges. Circumstances can change dramatically. There are many amazing stories of nonprospects who convert to clients!

Using Voice Mail

In furthering relationships, you will inevitably swap voice mail messages with prospects. It is often difficult to reach people during the day, and voice mail is an effective communication tool. Without it, busy schedules could result in weeks of missed calls. Although some lawyers see voice mail as a barrier to the sales process, others see it as an advantage. Using voice mail is superior to leaving messages with secretaries or receptionists; humans are rushed, and they make mistakes. And others cannot deliver your message with the same power and authority that can be communicated through your own voice. Following are some techniques for using voice mail to further relationships.

Use Helpful Outgoing Messages

First, make it easy for prospects to leave messages. Make your outgoing message brief, and leave good instructions for getting the caller's name and phone number. Also, if you have a voice mail system that allows callers to press the "pound" key at any time to leave a message, make sure you say so at the *beginning* of your outgoing message. Prospects may become very annoyed if they must listen to lengthy messages before learning they could press the pound key to stop your message and begin recording.

Leave Voice Mail Messages That Invite Response

Lawyers regularly complain that their messages to prospects are not returned. To encourage a return call, you must leave a message that invites a response. For example, if you have something of value to communicate, leave a message that says, "Please call me when you get a chance. I have something that I believe will be helpful to you." If you want to have lunch, leave a message suggesting it, and offer some potential dates. Then ask the person to get back to you as soon as possible, either selecting one of the dates you offered or suggesting alternatives. This approach allows you to schedule a meeting without having live contact. Or, you may want to schedule a telephone appointment instead of a face-to-face meeting. If so, leave a message saying that you are going to call on a certain date and time, and if that is not convenient, to please call with some alternatives. You can also use voice mail to invite people to events, asking them to respond by a certain date.

If you want to use voice mail to communicate with the press, you can call editors and reporters and pitch your ideas for articles or offer your expertise as a quotable source right on their voice mail systems. Many editors and reporters respond promptly.

Use E-Mail in Conjunction with Voice Mail

Although the purpose of this chapter is to focus upon the spoken word, it is worth mentioning that you might find it helpful to use voice mail and e-mail together. For example, you could leave a brief voice mail message, and follow it with a more detailed e-mail message on the same subject. We have learned that many prospects are more prone to respond to e-mail messages than voice mail messages. This is because e-mail is far more convenient, comfortable, and efficient.

Conclusion

As you understand and experiment with the foregoing sales dialogue techniques, you—like every other rainmaker—will learn that selling is not only appropriate (within ethical constraints), but also sophisticated, exciting, and fun. One limitation to sales dialogue is that it is usually restricted to small numbers of prospects at any given time. If you want to communicate with larger numbers, you should consider public speaking as a marketing technique.

Public Speaking as a Marketing Technique

Of all the marketing techniques available to lawyers, public speaking stands out as one of the most effective. Well-targeted public speaking provides exposure to large numbers of high-quality prospects and referral sources. Members of the audience, by virtue of attendance, have demonstrated an interest in the topic and are more likely to perceive the need for the speaker's services. Speaking to groups of lawyers can also be an excellent marketing opportunity, due to specialty areas or conflicts of interest. Another benefit of public speaking comes with the effort of *preparing* the speech. The research, organization, and scripting for a speech helps you clarify your thinking about a topic and thus creates not only the speech, but also valuable dialogue. Also, once implemented, a good-quality speech will increase your self-esteem and self-confidence. It will position you as a leader in your field and enhance your résumé.

Most lawyers think that the best way to use public speaking as a marketing technique is to educate the audience. This is based upon the belief that if the audience finds the information helpful, they will, in turn, be more inclined to hire the lawyer. However, though education is an important element of your speech, it is not enough. As with sales dialogue, you want to communicate to prospects that you are the right person to help them with their needs. You want to reveal the qualities that will help the audience feel connected to you. And, finally, you want to create opportunities for follow-through.

But, unlike sales dialogue, speeches are primarily monologues and so present additional challenges. Greater distance between you and the audience makes it more difficult to keep the audience's attention. Subtle expressions and gestures will not be noticed. There is less opportunity for eye contact. There is less opportunity to ask and respond to specific questions. There is uninterrupted speaking for a prolonged period of time. You have to be more general so you can appeal to a more diverse audience. Because of these differences, speeches require some additional selling techniques.

Meet the Audience

Before the program begins, try to meet members of the audience. Introduce yourself as the speaker and ask if they have any specific issues they would like you to address during your presentation. This allows you to personalize your presentation, which in turn will help you gain and keep the audience's attention.

Prepare Your Introduction for the Host

Often, the host's introduction of the speaker does not stimulate the audience, especially if the host simply recites material from the speaker's biography. Ideally, the host should prepare the audience in a way that generates optimism and enthusiasm about the upcoming presentation. You can help in this effort by preparing your introduction for the host. Consider the following example:

> *I'm pleased to introduce someone who is a close friend of our organization. Many of us already know him as a great asset to us. Here are a few of his achievements [from biography]. His topic today will help us in our ability to earn a living. Please join me in giving a warm welcome to [speaker].*

Additionally, you can ask the host to share a personal experience:

> *I have personally worked with [speaker], and found him to be very helpful.*

Prepare Your Speech

The more effort you put into the preparation and delivery of your speech, the greater the return. And although it is true that preparation is time-consuming, keep in mind that acquiring one good client as a result of your speech could more than compensate you for your efforts.

The Open

An important part of a speech is making a good first impression. Because you do not have a lot of time to make your first impression, everything you do and say in the first moments of your speech should position you as someone worthy of the audience's attention.

To help communicate self-confidence, be sure to have good posture, try to establish eye contact with as many people as you can, and smile. Remember the following phrase as you walk up to the lectern: "Tall, focused, and happy."

A common dilemma is not knowing whether to open with a joke. Because this can be very risky, you should not do it unless you are extremely skilled in telling jokes. Jokes are often insulting or not funny. In either of these cases, it takes a lot of time to recover, if you ever can. Similarly, you should be especially cautious about using self-deprecating humor. Although this may seem like a good way to entertain the audience, it usually positions the speaker as being weak or deficient in some area. We once coached a lawyer who wanted to prove to his audience that he was an exceptional negotiator. Unfortunately, he decorated his speech with self-deprecating stories and examples that inadvertently positioned him as being a poor negotiator. Though his comments made the audience laugh, his failure to communicate his worth was anything but funny.

An alternate method for starting a speech is to tell a story that has the same main point as your speech. A story makes the issue more interesting and memorable. It creates drama, and gives the speech direction. The story could be about the history of your topic, or about why you became interested. Personal stories are the easiest to tell, and audiences often relate well to them.

Another effective technique for opening a speech is to state your goals and objectives clearly. This helps the audience members pay attention, because they know how they will benefit from your speech.

Content

In our role as coaches in public-speaking skills, we have observed that some trainers focus primarily on delivery skills rather than content. Though delivery skills are important, we have found that superior content produces superior delivery. When you are confident that your speech contains valuable and easy-to-understand material, you will naturally be more expressive in your delivery. A simple technique to ensure your speech is informative and understandable is to provide lots of tips. Audiences regularly comment on how much they appreciate tips. In fact, we often hear comments such as, "If I can leave a program with one new tip, I'm satisfied the program was worthwhile." With this in mind, here is our tip: Offer a dozen.

Sound Bites

A technique for making points that are both understandable and memorable is using "sound bites." A sound bite is a small number of words revealing a great deal of meaning. An example in the advertising industry is the famous question, "Where's the beef?" This sound bite captures the concept of a competitor's inferiority, making it understandable and memorable. The strategy of using sound bites is appropriately and easily applied to legal issues.

Notes and Memorization

It is perfectly appropriate to use notes when you speak. Your audience will be pleased with useful information and not concerned that you did not memorize it. However, the risk in using notes is that you will refer to them too frequently and lose contact with the audience. Consider these tips for using notes:

- Try using notes as a reminder, not a script.
- Use a large font size, such as 20 points or more. A large font will help you see your notes, and still allow you to maintain contact with the audience.
- Use colored markers to identify important points.
- Write your notes in narrow columns, similar to a newspaper or magazine. By stacking the words in narrow columns, you can see the entire thought at a glance more easily than reading across a full page.

Memorizing material also has its benefits. If you are not dependent upon notes, you will find it easier to be animated and to focus on the audience. One technique is to memorize both the introductory and last sentences of each main point. This approach is similar to the structure of a joke. The opening line and punch line are delivered as written, while the rest of the content can be less structured. It is not necessary to remember the entire text, word-for-word, as long as you communicate the main ideas. Memorizing the closing statement guarantees delivering it with power.

Enhancements
A technique for improving a speech is to "decorate" the main points. This is done with examples, metaphors, stories, and quotes. Try to select these enhancements from unusual environments that may not directly relate to the topic at hand. For example, you could quote from a popular song, take an example from science, or tell a personal anecdote about your family. By drawing upon information outside the legal topic, you bring life to your presentation.

Audio/Visual Equipment
The purpose of audio/visual equipment is to increase interest and enhance meaning. However, most speakers who use it do so in a way that actually detracts from the presentation. Too often, using overhead projectors gives an audience the opportunity to daydream. And, if you turn down the lights, you might provide a nap-taking opportunity. Another risk in using this equipment is that it might not function. So, if you use audio/visual equipment, make sure it adds value to the presentation (which could even be accomplished with music, or a film clip), and be sure to either have a backup or be prepared to speak without it.

Handouts
According to conventional wisdom, speakers should provide the audience with reams of written material. Though in some cases this may be a requirement, such as for continuing education programs, extensive handouts do not necessarily serve your best interests. If the purpose of the speech is to sell yourself, you want the audience to focus upon you and not the written materials. Extensive materials create the impression that your entire content could be read at a later time. This allows the audience to be distracted. One of the best ways to increase interest and enhance learning is to use the "fill-in handout." Unlike conventional handouts, which provide printed information, fill-in handouts are predominantly blank, with spaces that allow audience members to take notes. The speaker provides verbal information and instructs the audience on how to fill in the blanks. This approach forces audiences to pay attention, and allows them to feel greater "ownership" of the material.

Audience Participation
Another way to improve your speech is to promote audience participation. Try to ask questions and stimulate discussion. This maintains interest. To

maximize the effectiveness of this approach, be sure that you are supportive of the audience's remarks. Be careful not to criticize or embarrass anyone. Even subtle negativity will discourage continued participation.

If you plan to ask questions to stimulate audience participation, make sure you ask questions the audience will be motivated to answer. A common mistake speakers make is asking questions that require a specific answer. It is a technique many of us learned from our teachers and professors. However, instead of stimulating a response, this approach actually inhibits audience participation. Audience members feel embarrassed for not knowing the answer, or worse, for giving the wrong answer. A superior approach is to ask about attitudes and experiences concerning the issues being discussed. Ask the audience members what problems they have encountered and how they solved them. If given the opportunity, audiences are enthusiastic about sharing feelings and opinions, and, in turn, you gain greater insight into their needs.

Timing

As you write your speech, make sure you identify specific time slots for your main points, and even annotate your notes with time markers. You do not want to make the mistake of focusing too long on one point, at the expense of the rest of the presentation. The timing issue becomes even more challenging when you encourage audience participation. Make sure you do not stray too far from the main point, and remember to check the time frequently. Consider putting a small clock on the lectern.

Opportunities for Follow-Through

Throughout the speech, one of your goals is to create mechanisms for furthering the relationship with prospects in the audience. The standard approach is to give information and hope someone will be motivated to hire you. The reality is that the sales cycle for closing a deal with someone in the audience could be years. Therefore, as with sales dialogue, you should be looking for ways to maintain communication with your prospects over an extended period of time. The following techniques will significantly increase the likelihood of your staying in touch.

Call to Action

One of the ways you open the door to future interaction with your prospects is to make a call to action. At the end of your speech, you can offer some activity in which you invite them to participate. For example, you could invite them to join organizations in which you are involved. You could enlist their assistance on some project you may be implementing. Or, you could suggest they participate in roundtables or brainstorming sessions you are coordinating. The more interesting the offer, the more likely you will find eager participants, which will enhance the likelihood of developing alliances and ultimately acquiring clients.

Request Business Cards

Another effective technique for furthering interaction is to motivate members of the audience to give you their business cards. During your speech, offer to add interested prospects to your mailing list by promising to send them newsletters, articles, surveys, reports, or other informative correspondence. Offer to send them invitations to programs such as seminars or workshops. Experience has demonstrated that after a speech, when members of the audience return to their offices, the pressures of their lives take over. Even if they intend to call you, they are likely to procrastinate or forget. A successful marketing speech always provides many reasons for prospects to give you their cards.

Practicing

Finish writing your speech well before the date of delivery. Busy lawyers often procrastinate and destroy opportunities to practice. As you practice, stand in front of a mirror. Repeat your introductory and closing sentences and sound bites dozens of times until they flow naturally. Try recording your speech on audio or video, and then review it to identify weaknesses in content and delivery.

Another helpful tip is to speak in front of audiences frequently. Not every speech you give must be in front of prospects. In fact, you might want to join a speakers group such as Toastmasters International. This well-known organization provides a network of individuals throughout the world who share the desire to practice and improve their public-speaking skills. Practicing not only improves delivery, it helps you overcome fears about speaking.

Overcoming the Fear of Public Speaking

Most people are remarkably uncomfortable with public speaking. However, it has been our experience that anyone can overcome this discomfort. Fear of public speaking comes from the anticipation of being embarrassed. It is unnerving to imagine being judged in an unfavorable way.

However, most people set unrealistic standards for themselves. They have erroneous beliefs that in addition to providing valuable information, they must be witty, charismatic, and perfectly polished. Though these are worthwhile qualities to develop, the truth about giving a good-quality speech is that you only need meet the needs of your audience.

If possible, talk in advance with people who will be attending your speech. Or, talk with people who know your audience. Learn what they know about your subject and what they need to know. Then, as you prepare your speech, keep in mind that all audiences want answers to the following eight questions:

(1) *How long will you be talking?* Time is valuable and people want to know when they can move on to other things. Never talk longer than necessary to make your point. And, always finish on time.
(2) *How many parts does your speech have?* People feel better if they can track the status of your talk. Make sure you identify when you transition from one part of your speech to the next. As people see you are on track, they will be relaxed and stay focused upon your message.
(3) *What is your main message?* Audiences want a quick understanding of what you are trying to say. Make your message clear and easy to remember.
(4) *Why should they believe you?* Fill your presentation with logical and sensible facts, examples, and personal experiences that support your main points.
(5) *Why is your message important to them?* People what to know how your message will realistically help them succeed in their work or personal lives.
(6) *What risks will they face if they fail to respond to your message?* Responsibly presented, valid risks hold the interest of your audience.
(7) *What steps should they take?* Provide small, achievable tips.
(8) *What resources do they need?* Audiences want to know what support they need to succeed.

By answering these eight questions, you will be giving the audience what it needs—useful information. Then, it will not matter if you mispronounce a few words, or rely upon your notes. It will not matter if you aren't funny or charismatic. The only thing that will matter is that you will be informative. As a result, you will feel confident about being appreciated, and your fear will disappear.

Arranging Speaking Engagements

If the purpose of your speech is lead generation, and not just practice, then make sure your audience is well targeted. There are many ways of reaching audiences with good-quality prospects. Consider the trade organizations that serve your existing clients. Many of these organizations regularly seek speakers. Consider obtaining speaking opportunities through people you already know. For example, a lawyer serving the banking industry could, through an existing contact at a bank, arrange to speak to all the loan officers of that bank. And finally, consider implementing joint-venture seminars with non-competing professionals who share the same client demographic; this gives you an opportunity to reach your joint-venture partners' contacts.

Conclusion

Lawyers have a high level of verbal skills. But, because of prejudices about selling, they typically do not invest their energies and talents in this important area. With confidence in the propriety of selling, any lawyer can learn how to market through the spoken word and improve the ability to communicate his or her worth. In addition to helping build a practice, this ability enhances self-esteem, self-confidence, and the quality of relationships with clients, prospects, and referral sources.

Proposals and Responding to Requests for Proposals

8

Suzanne Donnels

Competition for new and existing business is an increasing occurrence for law firms in times of conservative economic growth, regardless of firm size or practice. Recent press reports offer clues about the cause of this trend. Dennis Powell, Cisco System's vice president and corporate controller, said to CNET News about the company's fourth-quarter earnings that "Cisco's cost-cutting measures have resulted in a potential savings of $2 billion over the course of the next year—double the company's expectations." Powell may be addressing Cisco's overall expenditures, but it is safe to say that legal services will be subject to cost-cutting measures as well.

As in the 1990s, clients are seeking creative fee and service structures. Some are moving toward convergence—establishing better relationships with far fewer firms. Some clients seek specific new expertise and others use the proposal process to reduce outside legal fees. In a buyer's market, clients look for opportunities to reduce those fees by as much as 20 percent. In-house counsel believe that reducing the number of outside firms improves professional efficiency and intimacy. Whatever the reason, more law firms are being asked to respond to formal or informal requests for proposals (RFPs) or to compete in high-stakes competitions. Winning these contests is a major coup financially and strategically, and competition is fierce. Firms win when they commit to doing everything they can to be victorious.

This chapter highlights the distinctions of a winning proposal, the process that governs its production, and the rules of the game.

Are Proposals Worth the Investment?

For in-house counsel, the RFP process is costly in both time and money. So, why do they continue to host such competitions? Proposals provide good written expressions of how firms will work with in-house legal departments. They put all competitors on the same playing field, allowing for clear comparisons. Law firms use the same process to evaluate technology vendors, Web developers, and designers. The proposal process can be very lucrative for a firm, particularly when it comes away from the competition with new work or an increase in its share of the client's work.

The mere fact that in-counsel engages in this effort can indicate receptiveness to a new type of relationship or change with an existing firm, provided the competition is real and not rigged. The firm should seek expanded opportunities to add value to its work for the prospect.

> *Example 1*
> *Expanding the Opportunity*
>
> *We received an RFP to bid on some commodity real estate work for a reputable company. It had a new general counsel and our intelligence indicated that this person was investigating the concept of a partnering relationship with its law firm. We decided to approach the general counsel with the idea of submitting two proposals—one that directly responded to the RFP and another that proposed to handle all outside legal work as a preferred provider. The prospect loved the idea—we were awarded all outside work, and unseated the incumbent firm.*

How to Get on That RFP List?

An RFP, a request for quote (RFQ), or a request for information (RFI) can be unsolicited or advanced by the firm through targeted marketing efforts. An RFP is very different from an RFQ or an RFI. The RFP asks for a description of how the firm will work with the prospect, including an approach and strategy. RFQs and RFIs are less intensive and typically do not include approach sections.

> *Example 2*
> *Spending Time Wisely*
>
> *Having been in-house in three different large law firms over the last thirteen years, I must ask: Is the time taken to prepare untargeted PowerPoint pre-*

sentations and packets of materials without any due diligence time wasted? Lawyers and marketers should be spending their time enticing competitions. I see it every day: In-house marketers struggle to improve their positions and be viewed as more strategic, yet are kept in the trenches under the fire of the daily material-assembly game. Wouldn't we be better utilized developing strategy and engaging in proven activities that work, rather than pitching anything that moves?

In-house counsel use proposals as a means to select qualified counsel to help them achieve corporate objectives. Because legal bills can run in the millions of dollars, in-house counsel need the tools to make the best choice. This cost may result in a larger decision-making team, possibly including the board of directors, human resources director, and chief financial officer.

Having brand or name recognition in a particular practice area will usually get you a copy of an RFP. Having a close relationship with general counsel or a position on the prospect's board of directors can also grant you such an honor. But what if you do not have a strong relationship, or brand or name recognition? How can you get a copy of the RFP? One way is simply to call the general counsel and ask for a copy, or tap your contacts inside the company to get you on the list.

A still greater challenge is learning when an RFP exists. You must take a strategic approach to identifying opportunities. Select those companies with whom you would like to work or expand your existing book of business. Determine the key decision makers responsible for your areas of interest. Call those persons directly and make appointments to visit and talk about company needs, while remembering to combat the temptation to talk about you, your practice, or your firm. The WJF Institute's Bill Flannery created *20 Questions You Should Ask Your Clients and Prospective Clients*, which can guide you through this conversation.[1] You could also send letters to the targets, informing them of your interest in being included on their RFP distribution lists. Though not nearly as effective as in-person meetings, this approach can work once in a while.

To Propose or Not to Propose

In a recession, clients are in the driver's seat and can use the proposal/competition process to improve service, reduce costs, or send a message to existing counsel that they seek a new type of relationship. To avoid scattershot marketing, you should assess whether each opportunity is viable before you decide to compete.[2] To do this effectively, create and follow a firmwide "opportunity evaluation" process. Marketing personnel should grant firmwide access to information about competition procedures.

Be selective about the competitions you enter. Make sure your firm is qualified, has staffing available to do the work, and has no business or legal conflict. The work should be strategic, enjoyable, and, most important, profitable.

Finally, do not waste time competing if the process is "fixed"—asking simple questions can often uncover this. Also avoid competitions that require repetitive rounds of open bidding—this usually means the competition is based solely upon price.

Example 3
To Propose or Not to Propose: A Checklist of Considerations[3]

- Are there any legal, industry, internal, or marketing reasons not to represent this prospect or client in this particular matter?
- Are there any issue conflicts, or present firm clients for whom accepting this prospective new client would pose serious problems? (For example, hospitals and health maintenance organizations often proscribe their law firms from representing tobacco interests, and Big-Three auto manufacturers may prefer their firms never represent their competitors.)
- Would winning the engagement be profitable for the firm?
- What level of commitment is required to sustain a mutually beneficial relationship with this client? Is the firm prepared to commit such resources?
- Is the size and scope of the matter compatible with the firm's capabilities?
- Is alternative pricing absolutely necessary to obtain the work? Is the firm's management willing to consider such pricing arrangements?
- Is the competition "fixed" (that is, merely a pro forma exercise for the issuer) to produce a predetermined winner? (Even public/government agency bids—often required every several years under public purchasing regulations—can be "tilted" or merely "for show" exercises necessary to reassign the work to the incumbent firms.)
- What other firms are likely to compete, and how do your firm's capabilities measure up to the competition? If you are presenting a comparatively weak specialty of your firm against that practice area's national niche leader, it may be better to pass.

If the chances of winning the competition are slim, are there other valid reasons to compete nevertheless? Even losing can lead to fractional business opportunities later, if the winners should encounter conflicts or disappoint the buyers down the road. Debriefing after a loss can be the platform from which you can "win" the next time. But it is most important that you make a great impression in your response.

Prevent last-minute fire drills by adopting a policy mandating that, *within twenty-four hours of receipt*, every lawyer send a copy of the RFP to the firm's marketing department and the managing partner.

Losing builds character, but wastes time. If you want to improve your firm's win rate, make it a policy to respond only to those RFPs that offer you a reasonable chance of winning. Without such a policy, the well-intentioned efforts of lone rangers in your firm will result in wasted time and effort, as well as lost business and opportunity cost.

So what about that RFP you *really* want to win (perhaps because it is from the number-one client in your practice area), yet you are unsure of your chances? There are no hard-and-fast rules about when *not* to compete; but you should always ask as many questions of and about the prospect as needed to get a good understanding of the competitive landscape. (See Example 4.) If you decide to go for it and you lose, then apply this experience to future competitions. Also, manage your team's expectations so that if you lose, the marketing department does not receive a "black eye" for proceeding with the proposal.

Example 4
Marketing Department Intake Questions

The Prospect:
- *What is the prospect's name? Is this an existing client?*
- *What is the prospect's primary area of business and industry?*
- *For which area of practice does the prospect seek our representation?*
- *What are the prospect's pressures—both legal and nonlegal?*
- *Who are our internal or external coaches? (These are people who can offer great insight into the culture and decision-making processes inside the target's organization.)*
- *What is the typical process the prospect uses to select outside counsel?*
- *Which firm(s) has the prospect used in the past? Are any of those firms bidding on this work? What is the prospect's relationship with those firms? What can our coaches tell us about those firms?*

The Prospect's People:
- *How is the prospect organized?*
- *How does the prospect make its key decisions, and who are the key decision makers? What is our relationship with each?*
- *What or who influences the prospect's business decisions?*
- *Who does the firm know at the prospect's business?*
- *Does the firm have any internal or external friends or enemies of the prospect?*
- *Who is our competition (law firms, others)?*
- *What are the firm's current billings with the prospect?*
- *What have been the firm's billing trends over the last five years?*

The Project and Themes:
- *What is the deadline for this project?*
- *Has there been a conflicts check run on the prospect?*

- Who will serve on the team? Who will lead the team?
- What is the estimated value of the engagement? What are the possibilities that it will lead to future work?
- What are the themes of our "pitch"? What is the strategy/approach?
- What differentiates our firm from the other firms in the mix? In what ways are we equal?
- What are our chances/odds of winning this work?

Relationships Change

Over the years, relationships with clients change—after all, they are human beings and their feelings about their lawyers evolve. An example follows.

> *Example 5*
> *Changing Circumstances Can Mean Changing Relationships*
>
> *A firm's longtime client moved to a new city. This transition was an obvious barrier between the client and firm, and the work the firm did for this client decreased as less expensive local counsel was selected. Several years after the move, the client sent the firm an RFP. It stated that the ideal counsel for this work would be located in the client's hometown. This was a concern for the firm's marketing department, as the firm did not have a presence in that location, and there were many competent local firms that often charged lower rates. The firm's relationship partner asked the client targeted questions. The RFP was challenging and detailed, asking for a great deal of minority and lawyer population statistics. It took a week for the marketing department to generate a response and at least five days of lawyer time to complete it. Though the firm was short-listed for the presentation, it ultimately did not get the business, for the very reasons that raised red flags initially: (1) the firm did not have a presence in the client's hometown, and (2) the firm's work for the client had decreased since the move.*

Early questions to the relationship partner and prospective client can help determine the viability of an opportunity. Develop a bank of questions you can use to assess which competitions are worth the effort. Asking questions that offer significant insight is an art, but you need the right information to make a sound decision. While Example 4 includes a list of questions for accepting assignments, Example 6 contains questions to ask prospects before proposing.[4]

> *Example 6*
> *Preproposal Questions for the Prospective Client*
>
> - *How many firms received a copy of this RFP? Do any of those firms currently work for you? If so, in what capacity?*

- Which firm(s) do you currently use for this area of practice? Will that/those firm(s) be considered for this representation?
- Why have you decided to use a competition to select outside counsel for this work or matter?
- How did you come to select our firm for this competition?
- What one, two, or three things can we offer or provide that will win this work?
- What characteristics do you like to see in outside counsel?
- What characteristics do you NOT like to see in outside counsel?
- What are the important issues in resolution of this matter?
- Who within the company (individual, committee, board) will make the final hiring decision?
- How would you like this matter staffed?
- What are your expectations and preferences regarding budgeting, billing rates, alternative pricing arrangements, and the like?
- Is there any other relevant information about this competition that you can share?

You Have Decided to Propose

Refine Your Strategy

All lights are green, because your research told you there is a strong chance your firm will be selected to represent this prospect. Before you hit the gas pedal, develop your strategy by extending your research to deeper sources and identifying key differentiators. Review the RFP carefully, explore its story, and read between the lines. What does it tell you about the prospective client's goals, selection criteria, terms, language, and culture? What questions does it raise but not answer? Neglecting to answer these questions or guessing about what the prospect wants or needs is risky.

Example 7
A Success Story

Firm XYZ worked on a proposal for a telecommunications company. The firm's contacts inside the prospect offered valuable information about how the decision makers perceived the firm and the lawyers proposed for the team. Plus, they offered key insights into the immediate pressures facing the in-house department and the political landscape. The marketing staff searched all databases relevant to the area of practice they were pitching and located interviews in the press with several of the in-house counsel about how each liked to work with outside counsel. Finally, they asked tar-

geted questions about what the in-house lawyers were seeking and their relationships with competitors. These findings helped Firm XYZ prepare what was ultimately the winning proposal.

Your proposal should contain the most accurate information about the prospect's goals, culture, challenges, and legal needs.

Conduct Preproposal Research and Gather Competitive Intelligence

Research can help shape the proposal's themes and messages. Canvas the lawyers and staff members in your firm to see if they have any knowledge to share about the prospect and its culture, customs, and decision-making processes. Distribute to all members of your firm a list of individuals who have hiring authority inside the prospect's organization. You might find a match that can offer insight about the prospect's operation, decision-making process, and pet peeves. If the prospect is an existing client, interview the relationship partner and the lawyers who serve the client to learn about their impressions and any known service issues to consider. If your firm is proactive about your client relationships and has a client interview program in place, review old interviews to make sure you are aware of the client's preferences, service values, and any problems. If there are any deficiencies in the relationship that have not been addressed, make sure they come to closure before you propose.

Deepen your client research. Many corporate sites feature interviews with corporate executives, including the chief legal officer or vice president and general counsel. Mine the digital and printed interviews of well-known general counsel to gauge what they like to see in their outside counsel relationships. Some sites contain videos of the key executives, which can provide insight about the executives' organizational values, pressures, and goals. Canvas your firm to identify any client coaches (anyone inside the prospect's organization who can offer guidance on corporate culture and decision-making processes). Of course, do standard company research on databases such as OneSource™ and Hoovers™.

For litigation issues, search WestLaw™, LexisNexis™, and Courtlink™. These sites will illuminate the litigation history of the prospect and the degree of success your competitors have achieved over the years. Note that the data and data entry procedures vary from court to court; you must understand each database's limitations.

For information about transactions and deals, try databases such as the Thomson Financial databases, the Asset-Backed Securities database, and *The Deal*'s M&A database.

Know your "enemy." First, ask the prospect which firms received copies of the RFP. Learn about each firm's history with the prospect, how that relationship began, and its status. Most prospects who are serious about finding the best law firm will agree to meet with a firm that requests it before submitting a proposal.[5] A prospect that will not do so is probably signaling that the competition is "fixed."[6] Next, conduct research on competitor firms. Go to their Web sites and conduct keyword searches for the prospect's name—this can often lead to the practice and industry areas the prospect uses and the lawyers who devote considerable time to them. If the competitors' sites do not offer this type of search, use other search engines to locate the information.

Do not forget to tap into favorite strategic vendors and consultants. They are often in your position and are willing to offer assistance in the sales process. This can be an effective way of gathering intelligence in competitions.

Develop Themes, Strategies, and Key Points of Differentiation

How can you develop themes and strategies for your response? How can you differentiate your firm in this competition? As you develop your response, you must continue to ask, "What makes us *truly* different from the other firms involved in the competition?"

One simple technique is to review your research of the prospect and make a list of words and phrases the prospect uses in its written materials when it describes itself and its industry. Adopt those words and phrases when writing your response. For example, if the prospect writes "website" in lowercase letters and as one word, then you should do so in your response (even if you believe "Web site" is correct). The goal is to match and mirror the information so the reader of the response is most comfortable with the content. Remember, you are trying to build a relationship, and typically in-house counsel hire those people who are most like them.

The intelligence you gather can also dictate the tone of your response. If the prospect communicates informally, then your response should be informal. You can obtain additional information about the appropriate tone by asking your contacts inside the prospect's organization.

Identify major themes to echo throughout your response. These themes should be introduced in your executive summary and repeated in every section thereafter. The themes should be a combination of legal and service strategies related to the prospect's needs (which you can discern from the RFP, your research, and interviews). Think about ways you can illustrate the themes by using hypothetical and actual work product.

Explain how you can solve the prospect's problems. Clients want to learn much more from your proposal than your qualifications—they want you to propose solutions, and, oftentimes, very specific and creative ones. Always remember to tailor strategies that speak to the needs of the prospect.

The Process

Draft the Outline

Once you have conducted your research, asked your preproposal questions, and determined strategies, themes, and points of differentiation, you are ready to draft the outline of your response. Following are some suggested steps for that process:

- Read the RFP again—carefully—and highlight important items in one color and items that must be included in the response in another color. This helps you develop a checklist of things you must complete for the proposal to be accepted. And remember this *important* matter—if a proposal is late or does not contain the requested information, it may be rejected. Public agencies are particularly strict on this rule. Obtain *written* dispensation to extend deadlines or change requirements, because if you receive verbal approval from the wrong person, it may not be honored.
- Review the research you conducted. Do you have a sense of the prospect's culture, what it values most, and what it needs? If not, do further research.
- Of all the themes and service strategies you considered, select three. Often people cannot retain more than that in a lengthy proposal. Also, make sure your themes are strong enough to stand on their own.
- Outline your response, and identify when each item on the outline will be drafted and by whom. It is important to distribute this outline periodically to everyone working on the proposal, to ensure the deadline is met.

Select the Team

Based upon the client information you gathered, select the appropriate lawyers (and staff, when applicable) to handle this engagement. This can be a perilous venture, so be cautious. Clients are intolerant of a "bait and switch" with key team members, so propose only those team members who will actively work on the prospect's matters. In other words, do not promise to staff matters with senior partners who are too busy to work on them—even if those partners have the biggest names. Offer only those team members who will work on the matters and who can be present at the "beauty contest."

Select team members with the best mix of experience and expertise for this client. Be sensitive to diversity. Carefully select your team leader. The relationship manager should be someone who has the right expertise and is adept at establishing rapport and trust with clients. Most importantly, the relationship lawyer should understand the client's business and pressures, and be able to craft customized solutions.

Complete All Sections of the Proposal

At a minimum—and unless otherwise dictated by the request—your response should include an executive summary, a legal strategy/approach, a staffing plan, a service plan, and a pricing plan. Make sure you respond to every section and question in the RFP. (In a recent competition, in-house counsel commented that only one firm fully answered all questions asked in the RFP!) The rule to remember is very simple: If the prospect issuing the RFP asked the question, the answer is important to that prospect.

Along the same lines, you should try to adhere to the RFP's structure (as long as it makes sense). The prospect designed the structure, and if the prospect is comfortable with it, you should either be comfortable, or get comfortable. That said, public agencies and financial institutions sometimes share RFPs, so you might see a "disconnect" between a prospect's needs and the request you must answer. In this situation, try to find a structure that supports a balance between the two.

Proposal Ideas

Leverage Your Firm's Technology to Serve the Prospect

Clients interested in cost savings and efficiencies would likely be receptive to using the firm's technology tools, such as extranets, knowledge bases, case management software, document automation software, video conferencing resources, secure e-mail, document transmission, e-billing, chat rooms, and electronic libraries.

Develop Responsive Pricing Plans

If the RFP requests innovative pricing structures, you and your team should strategize about what you are willing to offer the prospect. Ask detailed questions about the prospect's history in this regard, so you avoid offering a strategy that has not worked for them. Concepts to consider include bonuses, phased budgeting, metrics collection, efficiency reviews, fixed fees, and blended or discounted rates.

Consider Bonuses or Risk Sharing

Bonuses or risk sharing can be an enticing proposition for any client. An example: You agree that each transaction will cost no more than X. If the firm comes in at Y, which is less than X, the firm gets paid Y + (X − Y). If the firm goes over X, then the firm is paid its hourly or discounted rate. For the client, this option offers predictability, while for the firm it offers incentives to stay under X for more than 100 percent realization.

Use Phased Budgeting
A phased budget provides a road map of cost and progress; it gives the client a clear picture of the scope of the entire project. Process-oriented clients tend to be comfortable with this approach.

Propose the Collection of Metrics
Many manufacturing and service companies have invested in the Six Sigma approach to the delivery of products and services and the management of vendors, including legal services. These sophisticated clients may look for counsel to employ data collection systems to provide metrics. These measurements can be analyzed to identify efficiencies and predict future costs. The metrics to be monitored are particular to each client, and vary depending upon the area of practice and how the in-house department handles its matters. Because of this, there is no reason to develop and present a detailed and specific plan of what to track; rather, discuss the general value of metrics and the assistance they offer in identifying efficiencies and cost savings. This might be an uncomfortable discussion if you are inexperienced in metrics, but do not fool yourself by avoiding this section. A metrics-savvy prospect would almost surely dismiss a proposal that is unresponsive to its request.

Consider Issues Related to Fixed Fees
Fixed-fee proposals should typically include adjustment mechanisms, so neither the client nor the law firm is unduly penalized or rewarded if legal workloads vary considerably from initial expectations. Keep in mind that one of the worst results would be to win the competition and then discover the work is unprofitable.

Improve Your Proposals through Automation
Most firms spend most of their proposal creation time looking for relevant material and recruiting writers to draft new sections. Automating the proposal process can aid in shifting some of that time to researching and crafting strategic language that truly speaks to the prospect's needs. A myriad of products on the market interact with Mircosoft Word and offer full-text searching. Some of the more sophisticated systems offer proposal management, content-updating assistance, and real-time proposal assembly. The deployment of these systems can be costly in both time and money, but the payoff—in the form of better-tailored proposals—can be great.

Eye Candy—What Should the Proposal Look Like?

Hiring outside counsel for any sizable contract involves many key decision makers, whom you might assume would read all proposals submitted. However, the greater the number of proposals submitted, the less any of them get read. Moreover, for better or worse, the proposals that prospects read first probably are the ones they remember best. And, the thinnest proposal with the most attractive packaging will be the first one read.

Therefore, your package should persuade reviewers to pick up the proposal, often from a stack of twenty to fifty, or more. A proposal with more than ten pages should have a cover and back, a table of contents, and customized tabs that are clearly marked to coincide with the sections of the response—this allows the reader to view the section with the greatest appeal. A good proposal has sidebars or call-outs that add visual interest, as well as wide margins that allow the reader to take notes.

The importance of the visual display of information cannot be overstated. If a graph or illustration can help you make your point, your proposal will be more persuasive. For more information about these techniques, read books by Edward Tufte, an information designer who is an expert on the visual display of data that is targeted and well received by the intended audience.[7]

That said, "high-touch" is just as important as "high-tech." Clients appreciate offers to contact lawyers on their cell phones and at home. Extending invitations to kickoff meetings, "get up to speed" meetings, and face-to-face client satisfaction interviews conducted by the firm's management or marketing staff, at no charge, will underscore the importance of the relationship to the firm.

Good Content

Craft your response with action verbs and simple language. You must keep the reader engaged in what could be a relatively dry subject; good writing can achieve this. When in-house lawyers are debriefed after competitions, many complain that proposals contain "too much legalese." Often, lawyers are not the only ones who read these proposals. Human resource directors, senior executives, and business managers are involved in the decision-making process as well. They sometimes claim that they did not understand what the writers were saying, and neither did the writers.

Also make sure your proposals are proofed and edited before submittal. Poor grammar or spelling will destroy your chances—mistakes show you do not care or cannot be trusted to pay attention to detail.

Winning proposals are written specifically for each prospect. In post-competition debriefings, in-house counsel commonly complain that many proposals contain "off-the-shelf" materials, when they were looking for proposals tailored to their issues, questions, and needs. Your proposal must be focused upon the client, not your firm. Your firm's boilerplate qualifications should be secondary or omitted. This may seem illogical, but the prospect is interested in your solutions, not how many of your lawyers were members of Order of the Coif.

When you do describe client engagements and qualifications, make sure you list them in order of relevance to the prospect—first by area of law and industry. Then include related work in other industries, and, if necessary, unrelated work done in the client's industry.

Keep in mind that prospects care little about how well educated the firm's lawyers are, how cost-effective and collegial the firm's culture is, or how unique, complex, full-service, and leading edge the firm's experience is. Like the saying goes, the proof is in the pudding: *show* the prospect how wonderful you are through evidence. Tell the prospect about your professional relationships and why your work with clients was successful. And never exaggerate your client engagements or outcomes—prospects will see right through it.

The Words to Use

If you were to canvas the marketing materials from your firm and your competitors, you would likely find the same terms in each. This does not differentiate you from anyone. Take, for example, the term, "full-service law firm." By definition, there is no such thing—no one firm represents everything from the personal injury needs of an individual to the high-level finance needs of a Wall Street conglomerate.

Every claim made in your proposal should be supported with proof from a client, evidence in the press, or a filed document. For example, most firms talk about their expertise, experience, quality of work, and responsiveness. The proposal that includes a quote from a firm client attesting to this claim will be better received than one that simply makes the claim.

Follow all the writing principles you learned in school or when you prepared opening and closing jury arguments: frame each paragraph with a beginning and ending sentence, mention your themes throughout your response, and have a strong closing statement reflecting upon all the mentioned themes. Use this as an opportunity to build rapport and lay the foundation for trust with the prospect. Make sure you use consistent terms, spelling, hyphenation, and grammar. For example, if you decide to use serial commas in the beginning of the proposal, use them throughout your response.

The Most Important Sections

Prospects almost always read the executive summary first, followed by either the approach or cost proposal. It is the only section you can be certain the decision makers will read. By far, the executive summary is the most important section in the entire proposal. It is a prospect's first view into how your firm will work with the prospect if it chooses you. Yet, this valuable real estate is too often wasted on how long the firm has been in existence, the number of lawyers by office, or the number and location of offices.

After reading the executive summary, the prospect should be persuaded to hire your firm. Craft an executive summary that is a complete summary of your proposal. It should contain the major attributes covered in your legal strategy/approach, services plan, staffing plan, and pricing plan. Conveying the longevity of your firm and the curriculum vitae of the founding partners will not earn you high marks from in-house counsel looking to see how you will work with the prospect and whether you understand its business and pressures.

The legal strategy/approach is the second most important section, unless the reader is a CFO or controller, in which case the pricing section would be second. The focus of the approach section should be on how you will solve the prospect's problems through the service strategy you tailor.

Proof Is Persuasive

Remember, the most effective "proof" of your good work is that obtained directly from your satisfied clients. If you are fortunate enough to have both a client service program and positive feedback, seek permission to use client quotes in your proposals. A client quote can be as persuasive as a prospect's one-to-one conversation with a client. Also, when you describe client engagements, talk about issues in those examples that are most relevant to the prospect. Be specific with amounts, verdicts, and jurisdictions. Rather than merely listing names, deals, clients, and dates, tell stories about engagements, conveying how you and clients worked collaboratively to achieve success and how you added value to the matters.

Continuous Improvement

Once the proposal is out the door and the adrenaline rush is over, the last thing you will feel like doing is reviewing the process. Nevertheless, as painful as it may be, this is the way to learn how to improve. At some point in your evaluation, you must ask the prospect these questions: How did we do? What did you like and dislike about our response? What did you like best about the winning proposal and presentation? How did we compare?

Conclusion

It is interesting to reflect upon law firm marketing over the last decade. In the early 1990s, during our last recession, many marketers and their firms had the right idea and were creating marketing functions that focused upon targeted opportunities, proposals, and high-stakes competitions. They were tracking their results and refining processes. These same firms were conducting in-person client service interviews. "Total quality management" was the management technique du jour. Then the dot.com boom came to pass and many firms forgot what they learned—that the client relationship is what really matters. The basics of marketing—such as client satisfaction and client-focused materials—were replaced with snazzy image campaigns, high-priced public relations, and mounds of dollars invested in trade organizations and sponsorships.

Those techniques and investments have value, but they should happen only when the basics are in place. We innovate during challenging times; let's learn from the last decade and prepare for change through strategies such as scenario planning and competitive intelligence. By keeping abreast of marketing developments, we will not be surprised when the market fluctuates and we will be able to tap into alternative plans. Staying grounded with targeted research, competitive intelligence, and a systemic approach to responding to RFPs will produce proposals that answer prospects' needs—and that win their business.

Endnotes

1. William J. Flannery, Jr., *20 Questions You Should Ask Current and Prospective Clients*, available at **www.wjfinstitute.com**.

2. William J. Flannery, Jr., *Just Say No: When Law Firms Should NOT Participate in Beauty Contests*, available at **www.wjfinstitute.com**.

3. ANN LEE GIBSON, 50 TIPS TO HELP YOU WIN CLIENT COMPETITIONS: RFP COMPETITIONS, BEAUTY CONTESTS, CONVERGENCE COMPETITIONS. LEARN THE RULES OF THE GAME IF YOU WANT TO WIN (2001).

4. For more insight into the art of questioning and the sales cycle, read *Spin Selling*, by Neil Rackham (1988).

5. Flannery, *supra* note 1.

6. GIBSON, *supra* note 3.

7. Edward Tufte has written several books, including *Visual Explanations, Envisioning Information, The Visual Display of Quantitative Information,* and *Data Analysis for Politics and Policy.* He writes, designs, and publishes his books on information design, which have received more than forty awards for content and design. He is professor emeritus at Yale University, where he taught courses in statistical evidence, information design, and interface design. His current work includes digital video, sculpture, printmaking, and a new book entitled *Beautiful Evidence.*

Using Win-Win Pricing As a Marketing Advantage

9

Felice C. Wagner
Peter D. Zeughauser

Because so much of successful law firm marketing is based upon extraordinary client service, client relationships, and partnering concepts, it is important to look at ways in which firms can compete for business by moving away from the traditional hourly rate fee structure and toward aligned incentives. Simply stated, by presenting creative, alternative pricing and fee structures, lawyers can attract and win new clients.

About Fee Arrangements

All fee arrangements should achieve two goals—generation of profit and increased client satisfaction. While achieving these goals, fee arrangements should strengthen and build the relationships between the law firm and its clients. As simple as this seems, law firms and clients have endured the fidelity of a twenty-five-year marriage to the hourly rate, a fee arrangement that serves neither goal spectacularly well. The hourly rate is far from the most profitable fee arrangement available to firms. Indeed, with the increased importance of technology and depth of expertise in the profession, its profitability is diminishing rapidly. (The best that can be said about the hourly rate is that its "cost-plus" underpinnings ensure some profit, although the margins are often small and realization rates unacceptably low in an increasingly competitive environment for law firms.)

And, although many clients are resistant to—even fearful of—experimentation with alternatives to the hourly rate, they harbor deep suspicion and distrust of the system due to the wrong incentives it provides. The system survives, though, because the readily apparent alternatives appear fraught with problems that are the same as, if not worse than, those associated with the hourly rate. The alternatives do not ensure profit and they pose risks to relationships.

In recent years, the billable hour has come under increasing scrutiny. It has been blamed for a myriad of problems, including lawyer dissatisfaction, associate retention problems, and a decrease in pro bono and public-service activities among lawyers.[1] Nonetheless, the hourly rate remains the most frequently used pricing model.[2] Lagging far behind are discounted hourly rates and fixed fees, capturing only 40 percent and 10 percent of outside counsel fees, respectively.[3]

Dissatisfaction with the billable-hour model exists on both sides of the client/lawyer relationship. For the client, there are numerous reasons to decry the straight hourly rate. For example:

- It does not tie cost to value. Regardless of the value of the work to the client, the same hourly rate is charged.
- It creates incentives to be inefficient. The longer it takes to complete a project, the more the law firm makes.
- It does not account for results. Regardless of whether the outcome of the hours billed is satisfactory in the client's eyes, the cost is the same.

The view from the law firm's perspective is equally negative. In the *ABA Commission on Billable Hours Report*, which was released in August 2002, Robert Hirshon, then President of the ABA, stated in his preface to the report that:

> the unintended consequences of the billable hours model have permeated the profession. A recent study by the ABA shows that many young attorneys are leaving the profession due to a lack of balance in their lives. The unending drive for billable hours has had a negative effect not only on family and personal relationships, but also on the public service role that lawyers traditionally have played in society. The elimination of discretionary time has taken a toll on pro bono work and our profession's ability to be involved in our communities. At the same time, professional development, workplace stimulation, mentoring and lawyer/client relationships have all suffered as a result of billable hour pressures.[4]

Corporate clients are also growing frustrated as they watch their companies' profits decline, but see their law firms continue to operate at 20 to 40 percent profit margins.[5] To address this disparity, corporate clients are using on-line bidding, issuing requests for proposals, and demanding deep discounts from their outside counsel. In addition, many corporate legal departments have either implemented or plan to implement a "preferred provider" arrangement. In a recent survey conducted by the American Corporate Counsel Association, more than 30 percent of the participating corporations reported that they were engaging in "convergence" to reduce the number of outside counsel they use and the total amount of legal fees they pay.[6]

Technology is also challenging the traditional billing model. Through the use of new technology, corporate clients are becoming increasingly sophisticated in the ways they manage budgets and structure fee arrangements. Leading-edge technology allows law departments to process data gleaned from law firm invoices on both the amounts spent and the tasks performed. More importantly, these systems provide a means for legal departments to analyze aggregate financial and performance-based data to evaluate costs, monitor budgets, manage risk, and assess performance. This same technology allows in-house counsel to evaluate alternative fees by using historical data to project costs in new litigation having similar characteristics. Armed with this data, in-house counsel are better prepared than ever to assess the efficacy of any alternative fee arrangement.

A few savvy law firms are also using technology to break the billable-hour model and compete with firms still entrenched in the billable hour. By automating significant portions of their practices and moving to a fixed-fee model for those services, some midsize firms have been able to transform themselves from being only local players into having national reach and national clients.[7]

Impediments to Change

Given the negative consequences of the billable-hour pricing model and these new advances in technology, it is not surprising that many have studied and advocated the use of alternative fee strategies.[8] In fact, the literature on the subject spans almost twenty years, and both inside and outside counsel agree upon the wisdom of implementing structures that are not based upon the hourly rate. Still, the billable hour remains entrenched.

One reason for this dichotomy may be the lack of emphasis placed upon pricing during the process of hiring outside counsel. Although in-house counsel face increasing pressure to reduce outside counsel fees, most in-house lawyers report that they do not view billable rates as one of the top five factors they consider in selecting outside counsel. In the *2001 ACCA Partnering* with *Outside Counsel Survey*, for example, the top five criteria cited for selecting outside counsel, in order of importance, were past relationship, individual lawyer reputation, lawyer expertise in a specific area, firm expertise in a specific area, and geographic location.[9] Other studies have reached similar conclusions.[10]

Another reason for the longevity of the billable hour is the risk aversion and the resistance to change that is endemic to the legal profession. Many lawyers resist experimenting with unfamiliar pricing models—especially when they have used the billable hour during most, if not all, their careers. They understand it, it is simple, and, although the total bill may be unpredictable, the hourly charge is clear.

Lack of trust between lawyers and their clients is also to blame for the staying power of the billable hour. Both clients and outside counsel report a great reluctance on both sides to experiment with an alternative billing strategy. Understandably, neither party wants to be on the short end of a bad deal.

Perhaps most importantly, the billable hour endures because it serves as the fuel for most law firm engines. Annual compensation, bonuses, and performance evaluations depend primarily upon the number of hours billed. Software and related systems are designed around the billable hour. This inertia makes successful implementation of non-hourly models even more challenging.

Thus, to succeed with alternative fee strategies, firms must not only explore fee arrangements that align the interests of law firms and clients, build relationships, and ensure profitability, but also align their infrastructures to encourage and reward the use of non-hourly billing.

Risk/Reward Allocation

Most lawyers would agree that the earnings hierarchy in the profession places contingent-fee lawyers at the top. They make the most money. Taking a look at the Am Law 100 list, one would conclude that lawyers at the big Wall Street firms come in a tidy second. Interestingly, third place seems to fall to the many other lawyers who populate the bottom 80 percent or so of the Am Law 100 firms. These are the big hourly rate firms.

This is significant because of the striking manner in which profit potential parallels risk taking and relationship building in the fee arrangement. From the point of view of a client and its law firm, there are three principal risks one faces in every engagement: the risk of a cost overrun, the risk of a bad outcome, and the risk that quality might be compromised because of the fee arrangement. Reward-based incentives may be used to allocate or shift these risks.

The Alternatives

Following is a summary of most of the alternatives currently in use, including their advantages and disadvantages, when they are used, and how they are combined with other pricing models.

Fixed or Flat Fees

- *Advantages*: Fee is not based upon time, and both client and firm know at the outset what the fee will be. Allows client to budget and avoid billing surprises. Allows firm to leverage its expertise and efficiency. Requires both firm and client to document with specificity the services that will be performed for the fixed fee. Creates an incentive for firm to improve work flow, and make better use of technology and staffing.
- *Disadvantages*: Law firm assumes risk of cost overruns. As a result, lawyers must foresee all contingencies and fully understand costs of providing services, or risk losing money on the engagement. Client assumes risk of a bad outcome. Thus, unforeseen circumstances could lead to tensions around the need for higher-quality work product and/or additional effort from the firm.
- *When Used*: For high-volume, routine, commodity work where costs are easy to predict and surprises are rare.
- *Often Combined With*: Safety valves or "re-openers" that allow both client and firm to revise the agreement should unforeseen circumstances occur; performance bonuses or rewards based upon achieving shared objectives (such as reducing overall costs, improving cycle time, or early disposition).

Contingency/Result-Based Fees

- *Advantages*: Clients pay only when law firms achieve successful results. They do not pay for time. Allows economically challenged clients to obtain legal representation. Allows law firms to leverage their efficiency and expertise fully. Both client and lawyer know at the outset how the fee will be determined.
- *Disadvantages*: Law firms assume all risk. Firms with little experience, inefficient operations, poor screening processes, or weak financial skills risk losing money. In addition, some jurisdictions place caps on contingencies in certain circumstances. If firm achieves successful results for client with very little effort, client may feel firm was overpaid.
- *When Used*: When law firms are highly confident in their abilities to achieve successful results through detailed screening, efficient operations, strong financial skills, and, of course, legal expertise. When

clients with valid claims are unable to pay for legal representation any other way.
- *Often Combined With*: Fixed or flat fees or straight hourly billing. For example, client and firm might agree to segment litigation in such a way that firm bills for the initial investigation phase on a fixed-fee or straight hourly fee basis. Once details of the matter become clearer, client and firm could agree to contingency-fee arrangement.

Retrospective Based upon Value
- *Advantages*: Shifts focus from time spent to value of results. Amount of fee is based upon value to client, as defined by client.
- *Disadvantages*: Requires great deal of trust between lawyer and client. Client and lawyer may not agree upon value.
- *When Used*: When client and law firm know and trust each other—and when value to client of results achieved can be fairly and accurately calculated.
- *Often Combined With*: Straight or discounted hourly billing up to agreed-upon minimum fee, with performance bonuses or rewards based upon achieving shared objectives (such as reducing overall costs, improving cycle time, early resolution, or high-damages award).

Retainers
- *Advantages*: Clients more likely to seek legal help when they know clock is not ticking. Law firms get paid up front and thus can avoid collection and profitability problems, provided retainer kept current and accurately reflects costs of providing legal services.
- *Disadvantages*: Clients must pay up front. Disagreements about what is included in retainer can occur if details not clearly specified in representation agreement.
- *When Used*: When positive cash flow is important for firm. When clients want legal help without a ticking clock or when clients want to ensure law firm does not represent an adverse party.
- *Often Combined With*: Because retainer is a deposit against future charges, it can be used with virtually any billing alternative.

Capped Fees
- *Advantages*: Rewards law firms that know how to leverage their efficiencies and expertise. Client able to predict maximum cost and shift some of the financial risk to law firm.
- *Disadvantages*: Law firm assumes risk of cost overruns. Client assumes risk of a bad outcome. Can hurt law firms if they misjudge costs, but

only client gets benefit of efficiency. If cap set too low, it can discourage law firm from conducting thorough assessment during early stages of matter.
- *When Used*: For high-volume, routine, commodity work where costs are easy to predict and surprises are rare. When client and firm have a strong relationship.
- *Often Combined With*: Safety valves or "re-openers" that allow both client and firm to revise agreement should unforeseen circumstances occur; straight or discounted hourly billing with performance bonuses or rewards based upon achieving shared objectives (such as reducing overall costs, improving cycle time, or early resolution).

Blended Hourly Rates
- *Advantages*: Easy to negotiate and administer. Clients pay low hourly rates and law firm's senior lawyers are encouraged to delegate work to lowest-cost provider.
- *Disadvantages*: Creates incentive for lawyers to bill more hours, not become more efficient or seek early resolution. Often results in use of less experienced and efficient lawyers, which can lead to lower-quality work product and increased hours. Can also threaten firm profitability if lawyers do not fully understand costs of providing services.
- *When Used*: For routine matters that do not require a wide range of expertise and that allow easy prediction of required tasks and personnel mix needed to perform them.
- *Often Combined With*: Performance bonuses or rewards based upon achieving shared objectives (such as reducing overall costs, improving cycle time, or early disposition).

Volume Discounts and Discounted Fees
- *Advantages*: Guaranteed work for law firm, which saves business development costs. Reduced rates give client incentive to send more work to the firm.
- *Disadvantages*: Creates incentive for lawyers to bill more hours, not become more efficient or seek early resolution. Risky for firms that do not fully understand costs of providing services that are subject to discount. Firms risk offending other clients who hear about the discounts.
- *When Used*: For high-volume, routine matters, when cost is client's primary concern.
- *Often Combined With*: Performance bonuses or rewards based upon achieving shared objectives (such as reducing overall costs, improving cycle time, or early disposition).

Relationship-Building Fee Arrangements

Combining fee arrangements and creating hybrids, like flat fees with bonuses, is likely the key for structuring a fee that increases both profitability and client satisfaction. A core element of a successful relationship-building fee arrangement is the "blow-out" or "re-opener" trigger. This contingency kicks in when the fee arrangement, however carefully structured, is not working for one side or the other because of events that were not reasonably foreseeable at the time the arrangement was agreed upon.

Another option is to create "risk corridors," which allow the law firm and client to share the benefit of cost savings and the risk of cost overruns. In this scenario, a law firm and client agree to a fixed fee, with the understanding that if the actual cost of providing legal services is 10 percent above expectations, the law firm assumes the costs over the agreed-upon fixed amount. If actual costs exceed 10 percent of the fixed fee, the law firm and client share the cost overrun at a predetermined level. The benefits of cost savings would also be allocated. If actual costs fall below the fixed fee, the firm might be able to keep the "windfall" profit. However, if cost savings exceed what was anticipated by 10 percent, the firm rebates the client a predetermined share of those savings.

As implied by the creation of risk corridors, there is more than one source of funds from which the reward for a great result can be paid. Most lawyers think of bonuses and premiums as coming from the result achieved by the law firm. Indeed, in recent years, contingent fees have increased dramatically in popularity with the corporate bar. Defense contingencies are the fastest-growing type of alternative fee structures. But another important source of bonus funds is cost savings. In the end, as much as business clients want quality and results, they also want efficiency and predictability. Thus, a fee arrangement that provides incentives for saving the client legal fees is one that builds a stronger relationship. And, bonuses and premiums paid out of money saved can be equally or more satisfying than money paid out of results, if one of the client's top priorities is to save money.

Another tool needed to allocate risk and reward properly in a creative fee arrangement is work segmentation. The risk of windfalls is greatest from the unknown; thus, if a fee arrangement is based upon discrete pieces of work, you can revisit the budget when the work is required. (For instance, you could negotiate a "mini" fee structure for a motion when the decision to file the motion is being made, a time when more is known about the likelihood of success than at an earlier time.) This reduces the likelihood of a windfall for either the lawyer or the client. The key is to build a budget plan that anticipates discussion of different fee arrangements at important junctures. Though some clients will find it too cumbersome to keep revisiting the fee issue, others will welcome the chance to control costs more carefully.

These basic principles illustrate how fee structures can be used to increase profitability and strengthen client relationships at the same time. The keys to success are to (1) allocate and share risk rather than shift it, (2) identify a source for payment of the premium or bonus that is aligned with the client's interests, and (3) segment the work so the fee structure is agreed upon at a time when the unforeseeable can be best avoided.

The Impact of Fee Structures Upon Quality

One unintended consequence of a movement away from hourly billing may be a decline in quality. With all its shortcomings, the hourly rate does create an incentive for good-quality work more than it creates an incentive for anything else. After all, if you take a lot of smart people, which lawyers tend to be, and tell them you will pay them by the hour to solve difficult problems correctly, they will get it right. The incentive for producing high-quality work under some of the other arrangements described above is as indirect or nonexistent as the incentive for efficiency under the hourly rate.

Many clients and big-firm lawyers share the belief that good-quality work has become the standard commodity of big-firm work product—an integral component of what they all offer. However, when you squeeze profits in a free marketplace, you might also squeeze quality. Good quality is rampant only because clients pay handsomely for it under the hourly rate.

In a capped-fee scenario, for example, when the fee is exhausted, morale and enthusiasm for winning may wane as economic pressures require the firm to reevaluate strategy and resources. The same problem can arise under a contingent-fee scenario. As the promise of a high recovery fades along with the corresponding ability of the lawyers to earn a profit on the case, a firm's willingness to invest time may wane. In both cases, lawyers might be forced to look for shortcuts to remain profitable. Thus, the thoroughness and exhaustive preparation that is the hallmark of high-quality work may be at risk as firms move away from hourly billing models. Strange things happen on the frontier of change.

Often, things do not happen as one would expect. The profession is clearly at the frontier of change when it comes to alternative billing. It needs to take a very hard look at how it will avoid quality failures as risk and reward shift. When confronted with the basic question of whether to make money or die, most law firms will choose to make money. They will find ways to remain competitive, by cutting costs and providing predictability. Fee structures must reward the behavior the client desires for the matter at hand. If clients want predictability, cost cuts, good quality, *and* improved results, then firms better build in rewards for all three, because flat fees by themselves do not reward results.

Ultimately, no single fee structure is appropriate for all legal work. Every fee structure has incentives for behavior that may be adverse to the client's interests. As a result, the appropriate fee structure for any matter must be tailored to the client's interests and priorities. It requires thought and knowledge to develop. And, it must reward desired behavior.

The Proper Role of Discounting

Generally, discounting is ill-advised, especially if done *indiscriminately*. Clients who hire firms based upon price are likely to leave for better prices. More importantly, firms spend umpteen years developing brand-name equity. Why diminish it by selling top-line service and quality on the cheap? One cannot dispute, however, the effectiveness of discounting as a tool for improving client relationships and law firm profitability. There are, in appropriate situations, a few good reasons to discount.

Effective, win-win pricing should be the glue for a strong relationship between a client and law firm. After all, the right price is the sine qua non of value in any client's mind. Defining and producing value is often difficult when the seller is selling something that is invisible, like legal services. Ensuring that value is perceived in the client's mind is likewise difficult. And, when it comes to value, like many other things in life, perception is reality.

When a law firm charges by the hour, its interest in selling hours is often inconsistent with what a buyer wants to buy. The problem with *indiscriminate* discounting is that it does not address the fundamental flaw of the hourly rate. Before one can align interests, one must discover interests. Clients and law firms actually share several interests: They both want to manage legal work in a way that makes each of them more profitable. They both want a fee arrangement that encourages great results and high levels of expertise brought to bear on the work at hand. They both want cost-effective fees. And, they both want robust and trusting relationships. Discounting is an effective tool for aligning all these interests.

Discounting can also be used to encourage good results. The simplest example of this is supplementing a discounted hourly rate or a flat fee with a contingency, so the discount is recaptured if an agreed-upon result is achieved. This fee structure can be used for an entire matter or a discrete piece of work. When a client seeks to obtain a result and the lawyer has confidence in his or her ability to achieve the result, this fee structure aligns interests and influences the perception of value by conditioning payment of the full fee upon achieving what the client wants and what the lawyer thinks is possible.

Clients also want to create incentives for cost savings. A discounted hourly rate fee structure can be employed to encourage cost savings just as it can be employed to drive a certain result. For example, a client and law firm may agree that the reasonable cost of documenting, negotiating, and closing a transaction is $50,000. Posit that the client closes five of these transactions a year, and has paid its law firm $250,000 a year for the past five years to do this work. The client wants to reduce its fees by 5 percent, or $12,500. It is "shopping" the work to other firms. In this instance, the law firm offers a 5 percent discount, but has the ability to recapture the discount if it can reduce the fees beyond $12,500.

Thus, if the law firm can close the five transactions for $200,000 at full rates by pushing the work to a lower level or through technology, knowledge management, or other techniques, the law firm and the client split the difference between $237,500 and $200,000. The law firm would recapture its $12,500 discount first from the savings, and the client and firm would split the balance of the savings, with the firm being paid a total of $225,000 for the $200,000 in work, or a 112.5 percent realization rate (which, for most firms, would improve profitability by 20 percent or more). And the client has achieved a 10 percent discount as opposed to the 5 percent it sought. Will clients pay extra for these kinds of savings? Well, they frequently do when they hire contractors to construct buildings. Perhaps the most commonly used construction contract is one with a guaranteed maximum cost and a clause that provides for a sharing of any savings.

Even when a relationship is already strong and the client develops a need for services in a practice area outside the law firm's areas of expertise, the client usually has reservations about "paying for the education" of a lawyer in the firm. This is especially true if the client can buy the expertise "off the shelf" at another law firm. In this instance, the firm can offer a deep discount equivalent to its profit margin while a lawyer develops expertise. The firm not only prevents incursion into the relationship by another firm, but also expands the relationship.

Building market share might be a legitimate reason to discount. Market share can be measured not only by the amount of the geographic market a law firm dominates, but also by the amount of a specific client's budget for legal services the firm wins each year. Offering a discount as part of a cross-selling strategy, thus allowing the client to consolidate its legal work and achieve efficiencies and perhaps other benefits (like better opportunities to practice preventive law), may prove worthwhile. Similarly, a discount can be an effective way to develop a dominant market position or win a new marquis client, both of which can be the prelude to raising rates.

It does not follow, however, that discounting always makes sense. In a free market, buyers and sellers perform best where and when the greatest rewards can be earned. Indiscriminate discounting can cause a law firm to lose interest in good-quality work and clients, and might even provide greater incentives for excessive hourly billing than the straight hourly rate. But, when deployed as a strategy for achieving specific (often shared) goals and allocating risks and rewards, discounting is an effective tool.

Best Practices in Pricing

So, if "win-win pricing" can be used by firms to make more money and build stronger client relationships, why is there not greater use of creative, alternative pricing structures? The answer to this question is not mysterious. Although there are great incentives in corporations for in-house counsel to budget predictably and achieve good results, there are few, if any, incentives for lawyers in law firms to do so, even if a fee structure results in great benefits for the firm. Given the lack of incentives, it is not surprising that few law firms and clients have strayed far from the billable-hour model. Many that have, however, have had great success. Though they are still few and far between, most of these successful alternative strategies share three key components:

(1) *Relationships Based upon Trust*: The law firms and clients share an unwavering faith in the desire of both parties to ensure mutual fairness and mutual benefits. Review and renegotiations are anticipated and provided in the fee agreements.
(2) *Knowledge of Alternative Billing Methods*: The lawyers and clients have an intimate understanding of the various pricing alternatives and the advantages and disadvantages of each.
(3) *Authority and Incentives to Explore Creative Alternatives*: The lawyers and clients are empowered with the authority to explore creative alternatives and be rewarded for their efforts.

Without these key components, any alternative fee strategy runs a high risk of failure. If your goal is to win (and maybe keep) more clients and business by using creative, alternative pricing and fee structures, then you must be diligent about working in a way that allows both your firm and the clients to achieve their goals.

Endnotes

1. AM. BAR ASS'N, ABA COMMISSION ON BILLABLE HOURS REPORT vii–viii (2002) [hereinafter ABA Report].
2. AM. CORPORATE COUNSEL ASS'N, 2001 ACCA PARTNERING WITH OUTSIDE COUNSEL SURVEY 158 (2001) [hereinafter ACCA Survey] (more than 75 percent of in-house legal departments reported that 80 percent of their fee arrangements were based upon straight hourly rates).
3. *Id.*

4. ABA Report, *supra* note 1, at ix.

5. Robert Lennon, *The Bottom Line Flattens*, The American Lawyer, July 2002, at 114.

6. ACCA Survey, *supra* note 2, at 59.

7. Hildebrandt Int'l, White Paper: Relationship Management in a Competitive Market 3 (2002).

8. For an extensive list of articles and resources, go to the ABA's online toolkit at **http://www.abanet.org/careercounsel/billable/toolkit/bib.html**.

9. ACCA Survey, *supra* note 2, at 120.

10. *See, e.g.,* Corporate Legal Times Second Annual Survey of Chief Litigators (2001); PriceWaterhouseCoopers 2001 Law Department Spending Report (2001); Greenfield/Belser Ltd. & FGI Mkt. Research, Branding Your Law Firm § 11 (2000).

Let Strategy Drive Your Internet Marketing

10

Deborah McMurray

Spending money on designing and building a Web site without first developing a written marketing strategy that defines target markets and clients, buyers of your services, and firm and practice goals is like starting construction on a house without any architectural blueprints. And, at the high end, it can cost about the same amount of money.

Too many law firms are approaching their third- and fourth-generation Web sites as they would a print brochure. While there should be a consistent message and design from medium to medium, the Web requires a dynamic—not static—approach. The concept of "shelf life" is irrelevant to the Web, because content should *always* be changing. The point of a Web site is to offer your target audiences relevant material that they can easily find, so they will visit not only once, but again and again.

Firm leaders can control visitors' perceptions of your firm and the Web experience you offer. But it requires diligent planning and maniacal attention to "information design."

The First Step: Strategy

Strategy comes first. Answer these questions before you spend a dollar on a new or improved site:

(1) Your Practice
- Analyze your practices—and be specific. Who are your clients? Are they business owners and executives, corporate counsel, or consumers? If you have a commercial practice, what are your clients' industries and who are their customers?
- How will your practice change over the next five years? Will legislation affect how you deliver services?
- How will your clients' companies and industries change over the next five years? (Will they experience increased or decreased regulation? Deregulation? Consolidation? Globalization?)
- What are the important problems your clients face? What keeps them awake at night?
- How does your firm help them solve these problems?

(2) Marketing Your Practice (answered by key practice leaders in the firm)
- How do you market your practice?
- How often do you participate in beauty contests? How do you prepare? Do you ever use PowerPoint presentations?
- What *sells* new clients on your firm?
- Who are your competitors?
- Why is your firm different and better?
- What are your goals for a Web site?

(3) Perception of the Firm
- How is the firm perceived by clients? By prospects? By other lawyers? By law students?
- How should these perceptions be changed?
- How would you *like* to have the firm perceived?

(4) The Firm
- How would you characterize the firm's culture and atmosphere? What is your style of doing business?
- What is unique about this firm?
- If your firm were a car, what car would it be today? What car do you want it to be five years from now?

The answers to these questions will help you formulate your market position, and identify differentiating features and key messages. This information will help you choose one course of action over another and will prevent you from launching a "one size fits all" Web site. This information will also drive all design ("look and feel") decisions.

The next questions relate more specifically to your approach to the business of law. Corporate clients want to know three things: what you have done, for whom you have done it, and what you can do for them. If your Web site does not provide the answers quickly, you are not successfully communicating with these visitors.

(1) Are you comfortable listing business client names under representative matters and on lawyer résumés? Does your state bar permit this? (*Note: Always get client permission before doing this.*)
(2) Are you comfortable giving special content (such as white papers or research studies) to visitors at no charge?
(3) Or, are you comfortable charging clients and prospects for white papers and other substantive industry information?
(4) Are you committed to keeping your site current and relevant? Whose responsibility is it?
(5) Do you want to have password-protected extranet areas for clients so they can see and retrieve proprietary and confidential information?

Interview or Survey Your Clients

Many lawyers are shy about asking for their clients' opinions on matters involving the firm's offerings, marketing activities, or delivery of services. Yet experience continues to prove that clients not only can provide a wealth of information on these topics, they are delighted to be asked.

In addition to information you can obtain from your own clients, research studies can tell you what corporate counsel and visitors want from law firm Web sites. For example, *Finding and Working with Lawyers on the Web*, published by Greenfield/Belser Ltd. and fgi Research in 2001, summarizes telephone interviews with corporate counsel and executives about how they connect law firms and the Web. The survey answers the following questions:

(1) Do buyers of legal services search online? How often? For what?
(2) Where do they start? What are they thinking?
(3) Do Web sites replace familiar methods of law firm marketing, such as ads, newsletters, or brochures?
(4) Once a buyer finds a site, which features are preferred? Which are disdained?
(5) Once a buyer chooses a firm, how does the buyer want to use the site to work with the firm?

The study confirms that different buyers search the Web differently. For example, business executives frequently seek industry expertise first, and corporate counsel often search by practice area first. Organize your information to accommodate the wishes and habits of each kind of visitor. Three examples of firms that have done this well are Godwin Gruber LLP (**www.godwin**

gruber.com), Andrews Kurth LLP (**www.andrewskurth.com**), and Manning Fulton & Skinner PA (**www.manningfulton.com**).

Your Site

Domain Names

In the early days of law firm Web sites, firms typically abbreviated their names; for example, Carrington Coleman Sloman & Blumenthal LLP became **www.ccsb.com**, and Thompson & Knight LLP became **www.tklaw.com**. Many firms still use these abbreviations. Today, visitors (including law students) search intuitively—they type "Carrington" and "Thompson Knight" and hope the firms' Web sites will appear. Sometimes they do, and sometimes they do not. Your domain name is an important part of your firm's positioning and branding strategy—it should advance your firm's name in the marketplace. Initials can't do that because they aren't intuitive. Don't force the marketplace to remember two things about you, when one will do.

Cybersquatting is less problematic than it was even a couple years ago. However, if you are still using initials for your domain name, reregister with your "street" name—people should not need to remember more than that. For example, Gardere Wynne Sewell LLP's domain name is **www.gardere.com**. However, someone unfamiliar with that name might search for **www.garderewynne.com**. Previously this led to the site of a cybersquatter who had registered hundreds of derivations of law firm names. As of our date of publication, it led to a "Can't find **www.garderewynne.com**" screen.

Also register all ".net" and ".org" versions—the price of name and reputation protection is worth the few hundred dollars this will cost. Get clever with your domain name. The Texas state bar and other state bar associations say you cannot use names like "www.thebestlawyerintx.com" or "www.winyourlawsuitinflorida.com." However, most—if not all—state bar associations enable you to create vertical sites and call them names such as "antitrustlitigation.com," for example. We borrow from the real estate industry when we call these vertical sites "category killers" or "big box" sites. Put an intellectual stake in the ground with one of these sites and you can measurably advance your firm's reputation in a niche area. It is a great strategy. But be careful—it is imperative that you keep these sites up-to-the-minute with current and relevant content.

Remember: Your domain names are not merely locating devices—they have the capacity to convey a very important message about who you are and what you do.

Trademark and register all derivations of your domain name and firm name, including misspellings. Bieser Greer & Landis, a Dayton, Ohio, law firm (**www.biesergreer.com**), has also registered a frequent misspelling—"beiser-greer.com." Think of your domain name as intellectual property that should be protected.

Traditional Marketing Tools That Drive Traffic to Your Site

A Web marketing plan should include tactics to keep your Web site top-of-mind in your target audiences. According to *Finding and Working with Lawyers on the Web*, traditional marketing materials draw buyers of legal services online. Survey respondents stated that "law firm Web sites depend on tried-and-true print media to drive site traffic." Nearly half the buyers surveyed visited a law firm Web site because of a promotional mailing. Almost as significant, just under half went to a site after seeing a law firm's print ad. Internet banner ads in 2001 were not moving much of anyone, however. Though more recent and reliable statistics are not available, anecdotal evidence suggests that banner ads still are not driving traffic to law firm sites.

Consider implementing the following ideas:

- Write a clever e-mail message announcing the new site and noting its unique features. All lawyers and staff should send the e-mail to friends and clients of the firm. Invite them to visit and give you feedback. This costs nothing and you will receive valuable information about what these visitors value.
- Print a catchy postcard mailer announcing your new site. Think ahead, however. Do not be content to drive traffic just this once. When you design your postcard, think of ways to get visitors to return.
- Mail a signature toy with the firm's URL on it.
- Create a simple brochure that gives readers a tour of site highlights. What can your new site do for visitors? What is unique about it? Why should visitors care?
- Create a CD-ROM mailer that takes your audience on a tour of the site and that links to various sections.

Online Marketing Tools

The best online tool is having all lawyers and staff e-mail the site link to firm clients, referral sources, and friends. Be prepared to accept both praise and criticism. Share responses with your Web development team.

According to research, other online promotions fall flat. Only a miniscule number of buyers of legal services want to download lawyer announcements, other new developments, or press releases.

If your firm pays to be listed in *Martindale-Hubbell*, check your online listing at **www.martindale.com**. Add your firm's URL to your listing, as well as e-mail links to your lawyers' listings. Pay a little extra each year to be able to link to your Web site—it costs about $200, and is well worth it.

More Online Marketing—Making Your Firm "The Expert"

Take a lateral step left and think of nontraditional sites that can market your firm's capability in a particular area. The Outsourcing and Technology Solutions section at Hughes & Luce LLP created **www.commercebynet.com**. This is a site that digs deep into e-commerce trends, companies, laws, and news. It pulls content from major news sources, plus includes articles from firm lawyers on relevant topics, such as Internet technology, the ABCs of bankruptcy, and international e-commerce. There is a small reference and a link to Hughes & Luce at the top, but it has the appearance of being an independent, third-party site.

Search Engines—An Important Part of Your Strategy

When you launch your new site, it should be search engine "optimized." Search engines are moving targets—what is effective today will not necessarily be the standard a few months from now. Keep current with search engine registries, and register key words from your practice areas. This process is highly specialized, and requires the expertise of someone who lives in this space twenty-four hours a day. To get maximum benefit, it will cost a few hundred dollars. If your Web developers do not have this specialization, make sure they recommend someone who can provide it.

Google™ has leapt forward as the leading search engine. You can "pay to play" at Google™ and other search engines—you pay to appear in the favored first, second, or third position in the search results. However, if you keep refreshing the content on your home page, Google™ will continue to search your site. It sees current content and rates your site higher in the search results than sites that do not have new content on the home pages. For more information about how Google™ works, visit Chapter 11.

Grow Your Site

Building a Web site is a process, not an event. You cannot simply forget about your site and assume it will continue to work for you. Your marketing plan should outline how you might expand the scope and reach of your Web site over the next twelve to fourteen months. For example, consider taking the following actions:

(1) Translate the site into a foreign language (see **www.pillsburywinthrop.com** or **www.goulstonstorrs.com**).
(2) Add an intranet or extranet.
(3) Add a "quick guide" that gives visitors one-click access to their favorite information (such as practice and industry areas, lawyers, or offices).

(4) Add personalization so visitors can choose their areas of interest. Each time they log in, your site greets them ("Hello, Tom") and displays only those areas of interest they selected.
(5) Introduce new vertical, single-issue sites (**www.deregulation.com**, **www.securitizationlaw.com**, or **www.mbpprojectfinance.com**).
(6) Add a virtual tour of your firm that will bring your offices to life (see **www.goulstonstorrs.com/virtual_frame.htm**).

What Do Clients and Prospects Want from Your Site?

According to *Finding and Working with Lawyers on the Web*, on-point experience matters—71 percent of the respondents ranked experience with specific matters as one of the most important pieces of information on a site, with industry expertise a close second at 69 percent.

Equally important is what did *not* matter to respondents. News releases, diversity statistics, and recruiting activities were all low on the list of features they cared about. Pro bono activities ranked next to last. Does this mean you should not include these items? Certainly not—just don't lead with them. Pro bono work and community involvement often define the heart and soul of a firm. But as important as they are internally, they do not always translate as well externally.

Because recruiting is an important aspect of a law firm's Web site (though your clients and future clients may not care about it), why not create a separate recruiting page? It can look and feel similar to your main site, and can be linked to your home page, but you can go to market with a more contemporary and fresh personality on the recruiting page (your URL might be "www.firmnamerecruiting.com"). To view some unique approaches to recruiting, visit **www.sonnenschein.com**, **www.hellerehrman.com**, **www.foley.com**, or **www.womblecarlyle.com**.

Practice Descriptions and Industry Strength

A Web marketing plan will ensure that your site is client focused and that you are offering current and relevant information. *Finding and Working with Lawyers on the Web* states that "along with legal skills and experience, sophisticated buyers expect outside counsel to offer in-depth industry knowledge." About 57 percent of the survey respondents consider industry knowledge to be a critical feature of online practice descriptions.

Industry overviews, white papers, and other industry briefings establish your mastery of a particular business sector. As a large firm, Mayer Brown Rowe & Maw has created numerous industry- and topic-specific sites that all link to the firm's home page (**www.mayerbrownrowe.com**). The goal is to know your audiences and know how they search for information.

Lawyer Résumés—Still a Critical Part of Your Strategy

Your Web marketing plan should include a template for your online lawyer biographies. Keep them short, current, and focused. As mentioned earlier, buyers of legal services want to know what you can do for them—and specifically, what you have done lately. List industry experience, specific matters, and outcomes (but watch the various state bar association rules and restrictions regarding these matters). Do list your alma maters; do not list dated civic involvement or other personal and family information. It is better to include community and pro bono activity in a specific section of the site, rather than having lengthy presentations of this material in your résumés.

The best lawyer bios are one page in length. If lawyers in your firm are noted experts in certain areas and require more space, include links on their bios to additional information. Also use links to list numerous speeches and publications, rather than forcing visitors to scroll through pages and pages.

The bios should link to relevant articles in your publications section (and vice versa), as well as to descriptions of the practices and industries in which each lawyer is involved. Some content management systems are robust enough to allow lawyers to develop multiple bios—such as one for intellectual property, another for agribusiness, and a third for business litigation. The intellectual property bio links to the intellectual property practice description, the agribusiness bio to that industry description, and so on.

Include current photos—even consider the full-body shots like those used at the sites for Goulston Storrs (**www.goulstonstorrs.com/lawyersearch.htm**) or Tonkon Torp LLP (**www.tonkon.com**), or more informal shots like those used at **www.biesergreer.com/lawyers.asp**.

Breathe life into your site. It is your firm's face to the world.

(For additional information on this topic, see The Lawyer's Guide to Marketing on the Internet, *Second Edition (ABA, 2002).)*

Weblogs   11

Richard P. Klau

Overview: What Are Weblogs?

In the early days of the Web, to admit to a personal Web site was to invite any number of groans. Personal Web pages were the antithesis of the Shoeless Joe mantra, "If you build it, they will come." People built them, and if everyone else knew what was good for them, they stayed away. In droves.

That has all changed, thanks to a relatively new concept called a Weblog. In truth, Weblogs (also known as blogs) have been around in one form or another since the late 1990s. But thanks to a veritable explosion of easy-to-use, inexpensive applications, Weblogs have gone mainstream. Personal Web sites, no longer groan-inducing vanity presses, are now legitimate. Rather remarkably, blogs are proving to be excellent marketing vehicles for lawyers at large and small firms alike.

What distinguishes blogs from traditional Web sites? A few characteristics are common to most:

- frequently updated content
- chronologically organized posts
- posts containing links to news items, other blogs, or Web sites of interest, along with comments about the linked item

Successful blogs focus upon particular topics or subjects and are updated frequently (at least several times a week, if not daily). Most blogs are run by individuals and often espouse the opinions of the authors. The advantage is that readers get a feel for the blog owner's point of view—and often form stronger bonds with that individual than they would with a more "corporate" site where the company message trumps that of particular individuals.

A challenge in maintaining any Web site is adding content with as little effort as possible. Though tools like Microsoft FrontPage made the design of Web sites easier, they did not make the addition of new content simple. The result? Sites looked good, but nevertheless required effort and facility with HTML programming on the part of the site owner to keep the site current, which, in turn, resulted in stale sites that did not get updated nearly often enough.

Blogs simplify this. Blogs are designed to publish content to the Web effortlessly, so the only thing you need to worry about is what to say. Everything else—formatting, uploading of the content, linking of all the items—is taken care of by the particular application.

Third-Party Endorsements

Weblogs received considerable attention in 2002, with write-ups appearing in *Newsweek*, the *New York Times,* and the *L.A. Times*, and countless articles in the computer trade press. All focused upon the ease with which individuals could establish their own blogs. (If it takes more than five minutes, something is wrong.) By 2003, Weblogs became part of mainstream Web strategies used by all types of lawyers—from those in large firms (Denver's Holland & Hart's Health Care Group) to sole practitioners (lawyer and Internet pioneer Erik Heels, who tabled his firm Web site in favor of a Weblog-only approach). Legal Weblogs (also known as blawgs, thanks to a term coined by Reed Smith's Denise Howell, an early lawyer/blogger) had arrived.

Largely as a result of their Weblogs, lawyers who previously enjoyed limited, if any, national visibility are now well known and often quoted in the press. Many point to the Weblog as a critical element—if not the only element—of personal marketing strategy.

Weblogs as Marketing Vehicles

There is nothing about the Weblog that makes it an inherently effective marketing tool. Much of the early press about Web strategies centered around the philosophy that "content is king"—but only now does that mantra hold true. Whereas countless hours can be spent over-designing firm Web sites (with predictable results: sizzle and no substance, which fails to encourage repeat visitors), Weblogs emphasize substance almost to the exclusion of style. Many Weblogs are text-only endeavors, and even those that do incorporate graphics do so sparingly and retain a heavy emphasis upon text.

The effectiveness of Weblogs as marketing vehicles stems from (1) the popularity Weblogs enjoy with the leading search engine, Google, (2) the cross-linking nature of many Weblogs, which drives traffic from one to another, and (3) the inherently personal nature of many Weblogs, which encourages unique personalities to shine through in text, something that visitors like.

Google

Although Google keeps its search algorithm proprietary, several things are known about how it ranks pages for search results:

(1) *Inbound Links*: The more links to a particular page, the more "votes" that page has.
(2) *Link Titles*: The words others use to link to a page tells Google about the words that might be most important on that page, thereby helping it establish the relative importance of those terms in a search result.
(3) *Updates*: The more frequently a site is updated, the higher the rank.
(4) *Text on the Page*: Google searches text for keywords.

There are other factors, but the best way to get Google to give your pages high rank in search results is to have many other sites link to your pages using the same term. If one hundred sites link to your mesothelioma Weblog with the words "mesothelioma news," then you will almost certainly be the number-one search result for "mesothelioma news."

Weblogs encourage linkable content. Each post becomes a separate Web page, and others who maintain other Weblogs and see something they want to pass along to their readers can link to that individual page. Google interprets that link as a "vote" in favor of that page—the more votes, the more important Google decides the linked page is.

No matter how compelling your law firm Web site may be, there are probably not many inbound links to your content from other sites. That is not a criticism of your site, but a reflection of the fact that even the most dynamically updated site is geared more for casual visitors than for people who maintain their own Web sites. As a result, Google will index content at your Web site but will view the content as being of relatively low importance, given the number of inbound links.

Jerry Lawson, author of the ABA publication, *The Lawyer's Guide to the Internet, Second Edition*, recently addressed this issue in an article, available at **http://www.llrx.com/features/lawyerWeblogs.htm**. He compared the inbound links at several large-firm Web sites with those of a single lawyer, Ernest Svenson (publisher of the popular Weblog, "Ernie the Attorney," at

http://radio.Weblogs.com/0104634/). Inbound links to Svenson's site were as much as ten times higher than those of many other sites. In particular, Svenson's site is ranked higher on search terms than Skadden Arp's site.

If you view your Weblog as a public-relations campaign, one way you would measure the effectiveness of the campaign is to evaluate the reach of the Weblog. While any given Weblog might have just a handful of regular readers (most individual lawyer Weblogs have several dozen to several hundred regular readers), its reach expands geometrically as a result of Google's distribution—if the Weblog covers popular, current topics, its author can expect hundreds of additional visitors *per day* simply by writing about issues in his or her area of expertise. Multiplied across numerous individuals in a law firm, the effect could be dramatic.

For an individual seeking to establish expertise in a particular area, there is no better way to do so than by using a blog. Within weeks, Google will update its index of your site each day: type something in your blog today, and anyone searching for that topic at Google tomorrow will see your blog. In many cases, it will be one of the top ten search results.

The more focused your area of interest, the more likely Google will steer more visitors your way. (Incidentally, these tips are equally applicable if you choose to maintain your Web site manually instead of using a Weblog application. The advantages to using a Weblog application are ease of use and speed of publication.)

THE APPLICATIONS

Blogger	Credited by many for bringing blogging to the masses, blogger.com is a Web site that makes creating, hosting, and maintaining your blog simple. Once at the site, pick a username and password, click on "create a blog," and you are ready. If you have an existing Web site, or have space on a Web server, you can simply add your server's settings to your Blogger blog: Blogger will take care of uploading your blog to www.yoursite.com. Alternatively, you can create a free account on blogger.com's partner BlogSpot (**http://www.blogspot.com/**), and your blog will be ready for visitors at yoursitename.blogspot.com. (But see below for a discussion about why this is probably not a good idea.) You have complete control over the appearance of the site, using templates that apply to all pages in your blog.	Free for basic use

	Creating a new entry is simple—go to **http://www.blogger.com/**, type your post into the edit field, click on "post & publish," and your new content is now online. Blogger.com is free. The advantages to blogger.com are that it is purely Web based, the interface is exceedingly simple, and it is free. The disadvantage is that there is no software installed on your machine, so if you are a mobile user, you are limited to posting when you are online. **http://www.blogger.com/**	
Movable Type	Based upon a similar model as blogger.com, Movable Type is Web-based software that allows you to publish your Weblog. Whereas Blogger is maintained on a central server, Movable Type is software that you install on your own server. It consists of "scripts" that install on your Web server, so you must be relatively comfortable with installing and configuring Web server software. If you are not, the good folks at Movable Type will do it for you for a small fee. Though the software itself is free, a donation is requested, and future versions with increased functionality will likely require fees. Conceptually, Movable Type is similar to blogger.com. It offers more for those who are capable of doing some of their own programming, and offers more control over presentation of content. It is not for novices who are uncomfortable with doing some programming. **http://www.movabletype.com/**	Free if you can install your own software on your Web server; otherwise you must pay to have it installed. Future versions are likely to require fees. In addition to the software-based Movble Type, Six Apart (the company behind Movable Type) also offers TypePad, a hosted service that starts at $5/month and goes to $15/month depending on the feature set you want.
Userland Radio 8	Userland makes Radio. Radio gives a user complete control over page layout, text formatting, and post archiving. Radio allows a user to establish a blog in a matter of minutes. Many enhancements exist as "tools" for Radio, which expand its functionality (including categorization of posts and rendering of outlined content).	Cost is $39.95/year; includes 40 megabytes of storage.

	Unlike the other applications, Radio is software that installs on your desktop. The advantage is that you can always contribute content to your site. However, if you use multiple computers, this can be a hindrance. **http://radio.userland.com/**	

What to Say on Your Blog

Knowing that you want to *start* a Weblog does not answer questions about what to *say* on the Weblog. There is no magic or single method for maintaining a Weblog; posts can be brief, include long commentary, or simply point to an interesting link somewhere else. Focus upon your area of interest and write about that. Spend some time following other Weblogs to get a sense of their style; after a while you will find a format that feels comfortable for you. Following are some examples of Weblogs that cover a range of styles:

- *Ernie the Attorney*: Author Ernest Svenson is a technology partner at Gordon Arata McCollam Duplantis & Eagan, a midsize New Orleans law firm. He writes primarily about law practice, law technology, and a variety of technology-related issues (**http://www.ernietheattorney.net/**).
- *Bag & Baggage*: Maintained by Reed Smith appellate lawyer Denise Howell, this Weblog focuses upon a wide range of legal and technology issues, with occasional forays into many other topics (**http://www.bagandbaggage.com/**).
- *SCOTUS Blog*: A blog maintained by the D.C. law firm of Goldstein & Howe, this focuses exclusively upon each Supreme Court term and the cases heard, and has some of the most current and detailed information about the Court (**http://www.goldsteinhowe.com/blog/**).
- *Overlawyered*: Walter Olson (who frequently appears on NPR, Crossfire, MacNeil-Lehrer, and other media outlets) chronicles the litigiousness of American society on this Weblog, often with witty comments about unnecessary litigation. This is a good example of an expert's commentary coupled with a very personal point of view (**http://www.overlawyered.com/**).
- *Holland & Hart's Health Care Blog*: A good example of a group blog maintained by lawyers in the healthcare group at Denver-based Holland & Hart, this focuses upon news from within the healthcare industry (**http://www.hollandhart.com/healthcare/blogindex.htm**).
- *How Appealing*: One of the most popular legal Weblogs, How Appealing is maintained by Buchanan Ingersoll appellate partner Howard Bashman. Focusing entirely upon appellate case law, Bashman pro-

vides in-depth commentary as only an expert could (**http://www.appellateblog.com/**).
- *The Volokh Conspiracy*: This is one of the best group blogs, maintained by UCLA law professor (and former U.S. Supreme Court clerk) Eugene Volokh. Coconspirators include practitioners and other law professors, many of whom, like Volokh, are considered to be foremost experts in their fields. The content covers a wide variety of legal topics, with insightful commentary that often later appears in journal articles (written by the bloggers themselves) or in news interviews (Volokh is a regular on NPR and is frequently interviewed by many of the cable news channels) (**http://www.volokh.com/**).
- *The Lawyer's Guide to Marketing on the Internet, Second Edition—The Blog*: This is the book blog for the ABA's October 2002 release. Maintained by the authors—Rick Klau, Deborah McMurray, and Greg Siskind—the purpose of the blog is to share current and sometimes controversial opinions about Web site design and development. Postings about law marketing in general are also included (**http://www.bookblogs.com/lawmarketing**).

Where Should the Blog Reside?

Several of the popular Weblog applications give you the option of hosting your blog at their domain (for example, Blogger users can host at yourblogname.blogspot.com; Radio users can host at radio.weblogs.com/usernumber). Although this is convenient (the application can be preconfigured to work with the default server settings), it is strongly recommended that you opt out of this choice, for several reasons:

- *Portability*: If you were to choose to switch Weblog applications, your blog's URL would have to change (only Blogger-created Weblogs can publish to blogspot.com; only Radio users can publish to radio.Weblogs.com). This creates confusion for your readers, makes your content harder to find (because links from Google and other sites will point to the old site), and creates additional work due to the need to maintain multiple versions of the site.
- *Brand Awareness*: If you are blogging as a member of a law firm, you want to reinforce your firm's brand at all times. You should therefore publish your blog to your firm's Web server, rather than to a generic site, which does nothing for your firm's name recognition.
- *Control*: All the major Weblog companies are small, and you want to be protected if something were to happen to them. If Blogspot shut down its servers for some reason, you would be left without a backup (leading to the portability issues noted above). If you publish at a domain

under your control, or at least under your firm's control, then you have far more certainty about the blog's longevity.

Publicizing Your Weblog

Once you start your Weblog, you must let people know about it. Start by telling other bloggers about your site—if you read some blogs today, send the site owners an e-mail and let them know about your site. If they are interested, they will tell their readers and include a link to your site. Several people—most notably Denise Howell (**http://www.bagandbaggage.com/**) and Ernest Svenson (**http://www.ernietheattorney.net/**)—maintain large directories of fellow lawyers who keep Weblogs. Getting included in their directories is a good way to announce to the broader community that you have a site.

Another good tactic for attracting readers is, oddly enough, to link to other sites whose focus mirrors your own. Because most bloggers monitor traffic to *their* sites, they will see the incoming links from your site. And they will often return the favor by sending readers your way.

Enhancing Your Weblog

Besides posting good content to your Weblog, there are other ways to enhance it.

Comments

Depending upon the content of your Weblog, it may make sense to let visitors leave comments to continue the discussion. Though there is some risk—people can write whatever they want—it is always possible as an administrator of the site to delete offensive or inappropriate remarks. The real advantage in allowing comments is that readers feel more connected to the content and they may well contribute additional information that you and other readers find useful.

If you use Movable Type or TypePad, you have the ability to include comments on your site without adding any software. Other weblog applications require you to enable third party systems, several of which exist which are free to use. The two most popular comment sites are YACCS (**http://rateyourmusic.com/yaccs/**) and Haloscan (**http://www.haloscan.com/**). Both offer detailed instructions about adding their services to your Weblog, and have extensive help forums to assist with any troubleshooting.

Subscriptions

There are two separate ways to let readers subscribe. The most popular option is to let people subscribe by e-mail; whenever you post to the Weblog, your readers can receive an e-mail message with some or all of the post attached. This becomes a convenient way to ensure that frequent readers are informed immediately about new content, and permits readers to follow your writing without needing to remember to visit your Web site every day. Bloglet is one subscription service on the Web, and is free (**http://www.bloglet.com/**).

A more powerful subscription feature is likely to be leveraged only by your more technically oriented readers (which may include other bloggers). Every Weblog application endorses a standard known as RSS (Really Simple Syndication); it is an Extensible Markup Language (XML—a markup language for documents that contain structured language) version of your Weblog that allows other applications to "monitor" your posts. The premise is simple: Every time you post to your blog, the Weblog application generates an XML version of the post. Applications known as "aggregators" (also called "news readers") are configured to check those XML files frequently (usually once per hour). Whenever you post, your readers' aggregators will download the new content and display it for the readers.

Either mechanism is a wonderful way of extending the reach of your Weblog and ensuring that your message will be heard consistently by your readers.

Linking to Other Sites—Keep a "Blogroll"

You will notice that many Weblogs link to other sites, both in the content of the posts to the blog and in the margins of the site itself. The links in the margins—popularly referred to as blogrolls—offer your visitors a chance to see which other sites you find interesting or informative. It is also a way to reward other bloggers for keeping good sites by sending traffic their way.

If you know a little HTML, you can always maintain the list of links yourself; if you do not, you can use a third-party system like BlogRolling (**http://www.blogrolling.com/**) to keep track of sites you think are worth mentioning. BlogRolling includes nice features like noting when sites on your list update, so visitors to your site can get a visual indication that there is new content at the sites you think are worth visiting.

To find sites worth linking to, consider visiting a few of the largest directories of blawgs:

- Denise and Ernie's directories, already mentioned above (**http://www.ernietheattorney.net/; http://www.bagandbaggage.com/**)
- Detod—a company with a terrific directory of blawgs (**http://blawgs.detod.com/**)
- Daily Whirl—a collection of posts from more than 100 blawgs, updated throughout the day (**http://www.dailywhirl.com/**)
- The Blawg Ring—a list of blawgs that link to each other and allow visitors to navigate from one to the next (**http://www.geocities.com/blawgring/**)

Tips and Tricks

- *Do Not Make the Site "Corporate"*: Readers of Weblogs expect to see the personality behind the blog. Blogs, by their very nature, are personal publications. If you make the blog too "official," you risk diluting the message and you may fail to capitalize upon whatever traffic is generated to the site. Do what Reed Smith does: link to the individual's blog from the firm Web site. (And if you are a lawyer working for a law firm, link back to your firm's site so people can find out more about what the firm does.)

- *Make It Interactive*: Fans of the book *The Cluetrain Manifesto* by Rick Levine, Christopher Locke, Doc Searls, and David Weinberger, published by Perseus Books in December 1999, will remember that marketing is a conversation. (Incidentally, all four coauthors maintain their own Weblogs.) To take advantage of a Weblog as a marketing tool, you should encourage conversation on the site. Let readers leave comments, and engage your readers in dialogue.

- *Change the Content Regularly*: If you fail to update the site, readers will notice and Google will ultimately ignore you. The value of a blog is directly related to the currency of its posts.

- *Track Readership*: It is standard practice among bloggers to reciprocate when someone links to them. Not only does this acknowledge a favor of someone steering traffic to you, it can genuinely aid readers of your site. If someone linked to you, presumably it is because you said something the reader found interesting. Chances are good that the reader focuses upon similar issues and may have content that is interesting to your other readers. Though your Web hosting provider might keep track of statistics, they may be either too difficult to read or too cumbersome to access; consider using a free service like SiteMeter at **http://www.sitemaster.com/** to let you track visitors in real time.

(For additional information on this topic, see The Lawyer's Guide to Marketing on the Internet, *Second Edition (ABA, 2002).)*

Section IV

Maintaining Your Program

Business Development, Sales, and Marketing Training

12

James A. Durham*

Introduction: Setting the Stage

Most lawyers are ill-equipped to meet the challenge of developing new business. They have not been taught the requisite skills, and many harbor deep-seated resistance to the very notion of business development. Historically, ethical restrictions precluded aggressive marketing, and a form of "pride" in the legal profession caused some lawyers to think, "I'm a licensed lawyer and I didn't go to law school to be a salesperson." The fact that most firms—in the past—were sufficiently profitable with just a few major rainmakers has also contributed to the lack of marketing by most lawyers.

Further, the resistance most lawyers have to "management" (or, more accurately, "being managed") limits their interest and involvement in business development initiatives. The reason many lawyers join larger law firms, rather than becoming sole practitioners, is to leave administrative headaches to someone else; they also want the steady flow of work that comes from the so-called "rainmakers." They do not, however, like being told what to do.

---

*Special thanks to William J. Flannery, of the WJF Institute in Austin, Texas, for his contributions to the background portions of this chapter.

To be sure, there have always been lawyers who can get new business just by sharing a cab to the airport with somebody. The reality is that great lawyers *can* be great salespeople. The unsettling point, however, is that many rainmakers are tired—tired of bearing such significant responsibility, and tired of the increasing effort required to face the incredible competition that has emerged. Simply stated, lawyers who work in law firms founded or grown by such titans had better find ways to replenish the supply of clients before the "Great Ones" fade off into the sunset. (Marketing is, in many respects, a matter of succession planning!) It is in this new competitive environment that firms have begun offering a variety of marketing training programs.

The Advent of Training

It is certainly a watershed that training exists on a fairly widespread basis, often involving significant investments of time and money. Sometimes lawyers must be dragged into training programs kicking and screaming—usually after some enlightened managing partner or management committee insists upon their participation. In recent years, however, it is clear that the resistance has ebbed dramatically. What makes the very existence of marketing training so remarkable is that it suggests the transformation of professional attitudes and the professional culture of most law firms.

Lawyers are learning that they cannot simply "market" in the traditional sense, by writing and speaking to their peers ("reputation building"); they are learning that "selling" involves changing the way they approach and manage entire practices. The good news is that they are coming to realize that marketing is best done by delivering extraordinary service to existing clients and by building meaningful relationships within their networks, not by pushy sales pitches and discounting. As lawyers learn this, they become even more receptive to training. Training must, at a minimum, help them improve service and relationship-building skills.

Implicit in lawyers' willingness to be trained is their realization that they do not need to have a certain type of personality to succeed at building a practice. In every endeavor, there are "naturals," and there are those who must learn the skills of the trade painstakingly. In music, the person with perfect pitch is not necessarily as successful as the journeyman with modest natural gifts who practices constantly. Sports offer other obvious examples. In golf, there are those, like Tiger Woods or Bobby Jones, who are innately gifted, and others, like Ben Hogan or Nancy Lopez, who have worked notoriously hard to compete. In the fullness of time, all these athletes commanded equal respect from historians of the game.

This same pattern can be seen in the legal profession. Countless numbers of lawyers who believed they could never bring in business because they were not natural rainmakers now have solid six- and seven-figure "books of business" as a result of learning and practicing the fundamentals of service, communication, sales, and relationship-building skills. Once marketing is understood in these terms, the transformation in lawyer attitudes is palpable.

Today, it is actually possible at some law firms to use a word like "selling" in a skills training program, partly because of competition fears and partly because lawyers now understand it to mean "relational sales." An increasing number of firms have even hired full-time sales professionals.

Making the Case: Why Do Training?

Often lawyers ask for specific training programs. The marketing director or partner should be responsive to these requests. But what should happen when there is *no expressed demand* for training in your firm? (Or worse, what about when the firm is openly hostile to bringing in consultants?) It is up to the person in charge of marketing to identify the firm's training needs and "make the case" for training to management. If successful at selling the training concept, then he or she must manage the entire process. In essence, the law firm marketer must do the homework, identify the options, and make something happen.

The person who proposes a training program should anticipate a lot of questions and objections, such as these: "Do we really need this?" "What is the measurable benefit?" "Can this stuff really be learned?" (Many lawyers think one either knows or does not know how to sell from birth.) "Consultants don't understand our business." "It costs too much."

In reality, a firm cannot afford *not* to offer good training programs. The very reputation of the firm, and each lawyer in it, turns on the service delivered to clients. Lawyers must learn extraordinary client service skills—beyond "be responsive and do good work." Staff persons also must know how to impress clients with service. Lawyers must know how to prepare for and deliver presentations to clients and prospects, and they must know how to network more effectively.

Studies show that the most common complaint about lawyers is that they are not good listeners. (This helps perpetuate the image of arrogance that haunts lawyers.) So maybe it makes sense to start by proposing a training program for "active listening." Regardless of how rational it may be, however, this type of "soft skills" training is particularly hard to sell to lawyers.

It also might make sense to start by offering training on a "pilot" basis. Training has a better chance of getting off the ground if people are assured that those responsible for training will elicit feedback from the participants, and assess the "value" of the training before committing to a major program.

The Nature and Extent of Training

Regardless of who does marketing training, it will not be effective if it is an isolated event. It should be a component part of an integrated business development and firm strategic plan. Training should blend with, support, or modify the strategic plan. And there should be an ongoing coaching component to the training. Having said that, it is never a bad idea to give lawyers the opportunity to improve individual service, sales, or other skills, even when a firm has not yet developed a strategy.

Many law firms have gone as far as they can go in developing conventional marketing tools (such as brochures, newsletters, seminars, published articles, and media relations). These are essential to successful marketing programs, but the benefits of these tools cannot always be easily quantified. On the other hand, training lawyers to expand relationships with current clients and to win work from new clients *can* result in specific, measurable increases in revenue. Moreover, *a firm can improve client satisfaction and client retention dramatically by offering business development and client service training to all associates, as well as nonlawyer staff persons.* By showing these individuals what critical roles they play in the firm's success, they get energized to deliver incredible service to everyone who deals with the firm.

If you ask lawyers what they want to learn during training, their answers typically include these: how to develop a strategic business development plan, how to leverage present work to gain new work, how to find the time to market, how to target appropriate clients for additional work, how to discover client needs, how to turn contacts into clients, how to talk to strangers, and how to network more effectively.

When lawyers are asked what they see as the greatest obstacles to business development, they typically mention these: fear of looking like a pushy salesperson, not enough time, not enough reward for marketing *efforts* (only for results), lack of information about the firm's existing clients and contacts, insufficient understanding of other practice areas, and a general lack of teamwork in the firm. These answers illustrate that training cannot be done in a vacuum, and that firms must address serious management and cultural issues if they want newly trained lawyers to be successful business producers.

The Training Process

Training can be broken into a number of distinct stages. It makes good sense to start with individual training that addresses the expressed desires and concerns of the lawyers. This can be followed by—or supplemented with—relational sales training and programs designed to improve communication skills, particularly "active" listening and presentation skills. Next, lawyers can be taught how to form client-focused teams, and how to tailor targeted strategies to capture new business. All of this can be supplemented with individual coaching. Coaching can be done in person or by phone.

Training, like any successful marketing effort, must have the strong ongoing support of firm leadership. The level of management support is *directly proportional* to the level of measurable success and the depth of cultural change that flows from the training.

Selecting a Trainer

Because the marketing director or marketing partner is typically responsible for developing or arranging training programs, he or she can have a real impact on the firm by managing the process effectively. This important role is not without risk, however, as the internal promoter will typically be held responsible for the results of the training. Accordingly, it is important to get as many members of the firm as possible involved in the selection of the trainers. Although most trainers have a good understanding of the substantive material covered in training programs, they must offer a lot more than basic knowledge and checklists for training programs to succeed. Trainers must have the ability to connect with the lawyers and staff they are training.

Some firms have the partners teach programs on business development for other lawyers. This has limited impact, usually because the lawyers attribute too much of the partners' success to their personalities. Moreover, most lawyers do not have training skills or programs, so they just talk. A better way to introduce service training concepts initially is to invite clients to the firm for informal presentations on what they seek in working with outside counsel.

Assuming the firm cannot do the training itself, it will be best served by finding trainers who have considerable experience working with lawyers and law firms. Law firm experience should not, however, be the sole criterion; it is helpful but not dispositive. Getting trainers with personalities that "fit" the firm can be even more critical.

Whether offering programs on presentation skills, "working a room," developing case budgets, or sales training, the person in charge of training should use his or her network of contacts and as many resources as possible to find the trainer best suited for *each* undertaking. Seldom will "one size fit all." The effort should include asking for referrals, reviewing information on the Web, conducting personal interviews, and checking multiple references. The person responsible for training should also present the firm with options for trainers and programs, and make recommendations based upon his or her sense of which programs will fit the firm's culture.

A so-called "name brand" training organization can have credibility with lawyers, but "canned" or "cookie-cutter" programs should be avoided. There should be no hesitation in asking a trainer about specific changes he or she plans to make in a "typical" program to address issues unique to your firm. Friendships and personal loyalties should not be relied upon in selecting a trainer, either. Choosing the wrong trainer can be a serious setback to the firm's efforts.

Ultimately, the best trainers have excellent knowledge of the legal industry, *practical* understandings of lawyers' specific challenges, flexible approaches, the ability to withstand the most intense lawyer scrutiny, and proven track records. Marketplace feedback on the value of any proposed program—from a variety of prior clients, and not just those the consultant/trainer chooses—should be solicited.

Management's Role

Keep in mind that there is no perfect program or ideal person for the challenging job of training lawyers. What has worked famously at one firm may not have any measurable impact somewhere else. Much of the success of a training program depends upon the firm's willingness to support, reward, and even enforce application of the skills and processes taught in the training sessions.

In other words, if the lawyers do what they are taught (such as rehearsing before beauty contests, spending time "off the clock" advancing client relationships, organizing client teams, supervising junior lawyers, and managing matters better), their efforts must be recognized and appreciated, even if the payoff is not immediate. Instead, many firm structures create roadblocks and penalize lawyers for these activities because they result in less billable time, too much independent authority, increased infrastructure requirements, and other expenses. The mixed messages that management can send will frustrate even the most enthusiastic trainees. Also, if no systems of accountability or measurement are put in place, results will be minimal.

The success of the training also depends upon the attitudes of the participants. Were they willing volunteers or were they forced by management to attend training sessions? Were they the "best and brightest," or were they part of the remedial group? The best results tend to occur when those in attendance are volunteers, but a few "stars" and skeptics should also be mixed into the program. Obviously, if the skeptics see value in the program, more volunteers will appear for future programs. Other variables include the willingness of the trainers to be flexible, and management's ability to manage expectations.

Flexibility and Costs

Because the impact of law firm training can vary considerably depending upon the firm's culture and the makeup of the attendees, it is essential that the trainer have the capability (and willingness) to adapt the program to the specific needs and constraints of the firm and the group members. The trainer must create a program to achieve the firm's specific goals, not the trainer's.

Training programs can be packaged in a series of sixty- to ninety-minute workshops, or a single program can extend over several full days off-site; training can even be technology based, using interactive multimedia or Web-based approaches. The best programs will have the participants role play, strategize, and do exercises to practice new skills.

The costs for training programs can range from several hundred dollars for a one-hour awareness program to $40,000 for a three-month or five-day training program, depending upon how it is structured and who conducts it. Most consultants who do so-called "high-end" training charge a daily fee ranging from $5,000 to $10,000, which typically includes all preparation, customization, testing, handouts, and travel time (but not expenses).

Managing Expectations

Even the best training programs can have only limited impact in the first instance. If the program goals are not clearly defined and limited, the attendees will be disappointed. And even when realistic expectations have been established, it is important to have a well-defined plan to follow up, monitor, and support the initial training program, because it is from the ongoing reinforcement, encouragement, and accountability that positive results will occur. Accordingly, for maximum effectiveness, a training program should have an ongoing *coaching* component. The case study set forth below illustrates how a combined training/coaching program can lead to measurable business development results.

Business Development Training: A Case Study

Dr. Harry Keshet, Ph.D., and I created a three-month training program for a high-powered law firm that wanted to see fairly immediate results—new revenue.

We started by having each of the dozen attendees complete a pretraining questionnaire asking about things such as type of practice, knowledge of other practice areas, network/contacts, internal networks, known business development opportunities, and perceived obstacles, strengths, and weaknesses. We also asked each participant to take the Myers-Briggs Type Indicator, a widely used measure of the different personality styles found among all individuals.

This data was reviewed in advance so we could use it to customize elements of a full-day group training program in which we had two goals: to help the lawyers understand how to sell legal services, and to start developing the skills they need to do it. We distinguished marketing and sales, showed the lawyers where business comes from, demonstrated the value of internal and external networks, grappled with the obstacles to business development (such as compensation, time, habits, and fear), and set the stage for the bi-weekly coaching sessions that would follow for the next two to three months.

Harry met with each lawyer for one hour during the next two days, as the first in a series of coaching sessions. The subsequent individual coaching sessions took place on the phone every ten days or so. These calls ranged from thirty to sixty minutes in length.

After two months of coaching, we reassembled the group for an additional half-day group session to continue training in key skill areas, such as listening, asking for the business, preparing for new business presentations, and assembling teams.

This half-day program was followed by another series of phone coaching sessions, with most of the calls aimed at helping the lawyers craft their messages for scheduled "new business" meetings they had arranged during the earlier coaching phase. Some of the planned marketing meetings were with referral sources, and some were with other lawyers to talk about joint business development opportunities.

At the end of the first program, the new business and new leads that had been generated were so significant that the firm immediately launched a second program with another group of partners. It is hoped that all the partners eventually will participate in the program, and that a version of the program (with the marketing director doing the coaching) will be offered to associates.

This type of comprehensive training/coaching program is becoming more commonplace in law firms, and will likely be the approach all firms will take once they accept that it is not sufficient to rely upon a few rainmakers to bring in business, and not wise to expect other lawyers to do it without meaningful training and assistance.

Conclusion

We certainly have come a long way from the days when marketing was seen as a diminution of professional practice, and the idea of marketing training was nearly insulting to most lawyers. In fact, for all that remains to be done, marketing training has accomplished more than many might have expected.

Law firm marketing is no longer just about helping law firms generate more revenue. Good training actually contributes to the profession by reaffirming the primacy of the client. This moves the profession closer to its roots, and can help enhance the perceived value of legal work. Marketing, rightly understood, plays a key role in this reaffirmation because it is ultimately about getting lawyers to be helpful and to communicate more effectively.

Following is a list of training programs. Although not exhaustive, the list offers plenty of options from which to choose a training program that is right for your firm. All are probably necessary if you want to have a truly successful and enlightened "sales" force.

Types of Marketing-Related Training Programs You Might Offer

- Active Listening Training
- Client Service Training (for lawyers and staff)
- Client Satisfaction Interview Training
- Presentation Skills Training (for lawyers who run meetings, give speeches, and participate in beauty contests)
- Cross-Selling Training
- Networking Skills Training and "How to Work a Room"
- Relational Sales Training
- Case Management and Budgeting Training
- Responding to Specific Requests for Proposal (how to win beauty contests)
- Time Management
- Media Training
- Key Client Team Management (for client retention and growth)
- Leadership, Management, and Delegation Training
- Understanding Communication Styles
- Personal Business Planning
- Alternative Fees Options
- How to Talk to Clients about Fees
- Effective Billing Strategies

Ethical Aspects of Client Development

13

William Hornsby, Jr.

As lawyers market through client seminars, trade-show booths, and the distribution of coffee mugs and key rings; advertise on billboards, Web sites, television, and the Yellow Pages; or solicit through direct mail or personal contact, they must always consider the application of their state ethics rules. Regardless of the type of media or the content of the message, these rules of professional conduct shape—and often limit—client development endeavors. The failure to abide by the rules can lead to adverse consequences for lawyers and their firms.

This chapter provides an overview of the ethics applicable to client development, looks at the limitations the rules impose upon the content of marketing materials, examines some of the advertising housekeeping rules, explains limits on solicitations, and considers a variety of other ethics issues important to those involved in law firm client development.

An Overview of the Ethics of Lawyer Advertising, Solicitation, and Marketing

Lawyers frequently think that the ethics rules apply only to advertising, and not to marketing. Therefore, if they "market," but do not "advertise," they are not subject to the limitations imposed by the rules. This view is too narrow, however. The state ethics rules apply to *commercial speech*. The U.S. Supreme Court gives different levels of protection to different types of speech. Speech known as political discourse, where people express their opinions about issues, is highly protected and the government has very limited rights to impose restrictions. On the other hand, commercial speech, used to advance the flow of commerce, has the potential to mislead consumers and is subject to substantial state regulation.

The courts think of commercial speech as communications that beckon business. Anytime a lawyer or firm communicates in a way that "beckons business," that communication is subject to the ethics rules. The type of media used makes no difference. If a lawyer beckons business on an Internet listserv or on a highway billboard, the content of the message must comply with the ethics rules.

What rules do lawyers need to follow? The ABA promulgates the Model Rules of Professional Conduct, which address all ethical conduct by lawyers, including rules of confidentiality and conflicts of interest, as well as communications of legal services. However, the ABA has no authority to discipline lawyers and drafts the Model Rules to encourage the states to adopt them. The ABA Model Rules have no force and effect unless and until the states adopt them. Lawyers must abide by the rules of the states where they are admitted to avoid the possibility of disciplinary proceedings.

Unfortunately, most states have adopted only portions of the ABA Model Rules governing communications of legal services. The rules vary substantially from one state to another. The burden this places upon multijurisdictional marketing practices is discussed below. Note that the rules of the states may be accessed through the ABA Web site at **www.abanet.org/adrules**.

Limitations on the Content of Marketing Material

Although the state ethics rules governing communications of legal services vary, they all include the common element of prohibiting communications that are *false or misleading*. The rule in place in most states reflects ABA Model Rule 7.1, as it was before amendments adopted by the ABA in 2002. This rule defines "false and misleading" in four ways:

(1) communications that include a *material misrepresentation* of fact or law,
(2) communications that *omit something* that makes the representation misleading,
(3) communications that are likely to *create unjustified expectations* about the results the lawyer can achieve, and

(4) communications that *compare the lawyer's services* with those of other lawyers unless the comparison can be factually substantiated.

The first of these four limitations is relatively straightforward and should not be difficult for lawyers to follow. Lawyers disciplined under this rule usually exaggerated their capacity, experience, or circumstances. For example, lawyers were disciplined when they ran a television commercial for their personal injury practice showing a lawyer arguing before a jury when, in fact, no lawyer in the firm had ever tried a personal injury case to its conclusion. A lawyer referred to himself in a Yellow Pages ad as prosecutor of a county when he was, in fact, deputy prosecutor. This was considered a material misrepresentation. Similarly, a practitioner who practiced under his name "and Affiliates" but who had no affiliates, and a sole practitioner who used the title "Senior Attorney and Director of Services," violated this rule. A lawyer who listed a series of "offices near you" but merely had meeting space available also crossed this line.[1]

Occasionally lawyers communicate in ways that do not include material misrepresentations, but that make implications that confuse or mislead potential clients. In these situations, lawyers omit information that makes the communication, as a whole, misleading. For example, a lawyer was disciplined when he sent letters to potential medical malpractice clients stating that his background gave him a strong basis of knowledge to protect the potential client's interest, but failing to mention that he had never handled a medical malpractice matter. Lawyers who advertise contingency-fee matters and state "no recovery, no fee" violate this rule when they charge clients with the costs of the case. Clients may not be able to differentiate fees and costs and may believe they have no financial obligation when they see "no recovery, no fee."

This rule also requires that on firm letterhead, announcements, and Web sites, law firms clearly identify those who are lawyers and those who are not. If firm personnel have titles that may not clearly indicate they are not lawyers, then leaving out the fact that they are not lawyers could be an omission that violates this rule.

The prohibition of statements that "create unjustified expectations" provides a greater challenge to those involved in client development. The rule is predicated upon the belief that every legal matter is unique and therefore prospective clients cannot rely upon the results of the lawyer's past performance to assess the potential outcome of their cases. However, this provision has been interpreted broadly to preclude client testimonials or endorsements when the content of those testimonials goes to the outcome of the cases. Note that a few states prohibit testimonials outright, deeming them to be misleading. But, most states follow the former ABA provision that separates testimonials that go to the outcome of cases from those that have been characterized as "soft testimonials." A Philadelphia ethics opinion concluded that these soft endorsements "describe characteristics of the lawyer's concern for the client, and do not relate to the actual success or failure by the attorney in his representation of the client."[2] Again, it is important to note that the content of the communication is generally what determines its ethical propriety.

Lawyers may also violate this rule when they communicate specific jury verdicts, other case results, or "box scores" giving win/loss records of their cases. Some states have concluded that the use of honorific titles in marketing materials violates this rule, when, for example, a former judge or officeholder such as governor is referred to as "Judge" or "Governor" before the individual's name. Such reference could not only create unjustified expectations, but also imply that the lawyer has connections that could result in a resolution of a matter in violation of the ethics rules.

The final prong of Model Rule 7.1 also presents challenges to those involved in client development. Though a primary function of marketing is to differentiate a firm from its competitors, this rule prohibits comparisons that are not factually substantiated. In other words, you can say you are the biggest, if you are, but you cannot say you are better. The following are examples of statements that breach this rule:

- "quickly become recognized as a premier firm"
- "We Do It Well"
- "low-cost alternative"
- "Big-city experience, small-town service"

These representations were deemed as making unsubstantiated comparisons to the services provided by other lawyers. One court went as far as permitting the state to prohibit use of the words, "experienced," "expert," "highly qualified," and "competent."[3]

The great majority of states share these limitations on false and misleading communications, and many states have additional limitations. As noted, some states have concluded that testimonials are inherently false or misleading. A few states prohibit self-laudatory statements. South Dakota lists seventeen areas that are prohibited as false or misleading.

In 2002, the ABA substantially amended Model Rule 7.1. It retained the first two parts, prohibiting material misrepresentations and omissions, but it deleted the second two parts. Under the amended rule, communications that create unjustified expectations or make unsubstantiated comparisons are misleading only if they rise to the level of material misrepresentations. Note, however, that this version of the ABA Model Rule will become effective only when and if states adopt it. Until then, lawyers must comply with the more restrictive provisions found in their state rules.

Housekeeping Rules

Even when commercial speech is not false or misleading (and therefore is truthful and nondeceptive), it is subject to state restrictions. These rules do not govern the content of the communication so much as the process. Therefore, they may be viewed as housekeeping rules. They involve the obligation of a lawyer to submit or retain copies of communications, the obligation to include disclaimers, and the circumstances under which a lawyer may pay for a recommendation of his or her services. ABA Model Rule 7.2 and its state counterparts address these issues.

Because the states are concerned about lawyers complying with the rules governing communications of legal services, one of the provisions in this section of the state rules involves the obligation of lawyers to submit or retain their communications, be they advertisements or mailed pieces. The states impose some combination of the three requirements. A few states—including Florida, Kentucky, New Mexico, and Texas—require lawyers to submit their materials for screening, either before or when they are distributed or published. A few other states, including Tennessee and Alabama, require lawyers to submit their copies, which are not screened, but merely accessible by the state if disciplinary action is initiated. The most common method is to require lawyers to retain their materials for a set time, which varies from one to six years depending upon the state, and is most commonly two years. ABA Model Rule 7.2(b) had required lawyers to retain their materials, along with records of their dissemination, for two years after the last dissemination. However, when the ABA amended its rules in 2002, it deleted this requirement. The ABA concluded that disciplinary counsel did not ask lawyers for their copies with any regularity, and the burden placed upon lawyers to retain their communications was an unnecessary one, particularly for those firms with active Web sites that change frequently.

State housekeeping rules also frequently impose certain types of disclaimers, disclosures, and labeling requirements. ABA Model Rule 7.2 requires only that the name and office address of at least one lawyer or the firm be included in a communication. However, several states require more extensive disclaimers; some provide the exact language to be used and, in a few jurisdictions, specify the type size and print color. The problem is compounded because these disclaimers address different state concerns, and lawyers or firms with multistate marketing must include an array of statements in their communications.

Sometimes required disclosures are general and must be applied in all communications except those that fall under safe-harbor provisions. For example, Florida requires lawyers to state, "The hiring of a lawyer is an important decision that should not be based solely upon advertisements. Before you decide, ask us to send you free information about our qualifications and experience."[4] This statement must appear in print that is no smaller than one-fourth the size of the largest print in the communication. However, if the content of the ad is limited to a list of matters protected as a safe harbor, the ad need not include the disclaimer.

Alabama requires lawyers to state, "No representation is made that the quality of legal services to be performed is greater than the quality of legal services performed by other lawyers."[5] Comparing this disclaimer with that required by Florida illustrates that there is no common denominator. The statements are simply different, and lawyers or firms marketing to clients in both Florida and Alabama would be required to include both statements. Of course, firms marketing to clients in other states would have to comply with their disclaimer requirements as well.

Some states mandate disclaimers that apply because of the circumstances of the firm or the content of the communication. For example, Texas requires firms that advertise fields of practice where the state certifies lawyers as specialists to include the phrase, "not certified by the Texas Board of Legal Specialization" when any of the lawyers in the firm is not so certified.[6] Disclaimers are also required by various states when lawyers advertise information about their fees or use models to portray lawyers or clients in marketing materials.

One other very important housekeeping rule involves the flow of money to obtain clients. ABA Model Rule 7.2(b), formerly Model Rule 7.2(c), prohibits lawyers from giving anything of value to anyone for recommending the lawyer's services, except as provided in the remainder of the rule. Of course, this provision is designed to prevent "ambulance chasing," which undermines the public's respect for lawyers and the law. Note that lawyers who are not in the same firm are permitted to divide fees under the provisions of the state counterparts to Model Rule 1.5. Similarly, lawyers may pay for the services of employees, under the provisions of Model Rule 5.4. Otherwise, referral fees are substantially restricted under the terms of Model Rule 7.2(b).

Lawyers may pay the reasonable costs of advertisements and may pay the usual charges of legal service plans and nonprofit or state-qualified lawyer referral services. This rule prevents lawyers from participating in for-profit lawyer referral services that are not qualified by the state, if the service requires any division of the fees generated from referrals. On the other hand, lawyers may participate in directories and other advertising mechanisms that charge a reasonable and predetermined cost for the listing or publicity. Note, however, that if the marketing vehicle operates outside the ethics rules in any way—such as by creating unjustified expectations or failing to include required disclaimers—it is the lawyer who is subject to discipline for these ethical breaches.

Solicitation Rules

States address the propriety of solicitation in ways that differ from their treatment of lawyer advertising. Several states have criminal statutes prohibiting the solicitation of legal services, some of which go back more than one hundred years. New Mexico's law is typical of these barratry statutes. It states that barratry consists of "any attorney-at-law seeking or obtaining employment in any suit or case to prosecute or defend the same by means of personal solicitation of such employment, or procuring another to solicit employment for him."[7] These statutes are rarely enforced and when so, only for the most egregious matters. Nevertheless, they reflect both a societal and professional disdain for the abuses that are possible as a result of solicitation.

Though only some states have antisolicitation statutes, all states have specific ethics rules governing solicitation. ABA Model Rule 7.3 and its state counterparts address this issue. Unlike their regulation of lawyer advertising, states have a constitutional right to ban some forms of solicitation. The U.S. Supreme Court has determined that people in need of legal services are often emotionally vulnerable, and that lawyers are trained in the art of persuasion. As a result, most states ban in-person and live telephone (as opposed to recorded) solicitations to someone with whom there is no family or prior professional relationship, when the solicitation is for pecuniary gain.

However, state rules vary on the scope of permissible in-person solicitation. For example, Iowa prohibits in-person and telephone solicitation without exception. Other states, such as Connecticut and Massachusetts, allow lawyers to solicit business organizations, nonprofit organizations, and governmental bodies. This is consistent with the Court's protections, as such an institution is not likely to be emotionally vulnerable and therefore in need of the same level of protection against the overreaching of lawyers as an individual who may never have had the need for a lawyer before facing a crisis.

In 2002, the ABA amended Model Rule 7.3 in three significant ways. First, it decided not to permit in-person solicitation to businesses across the board. Instead, it reasoned that small businesses were more like individuals and needed the protection provided by the ban on in-person solicitation, but large businesses were more likely to be sophisticated purchasers of legal services and did not need these protections. Consequently, Model Rule 7.3 was changed to allow lawyers to solicit other lawyers in person, thus enabling lawyers to solicit those businesses large enough to have a lawyer in-house. Second, the ABA reverted to the rule it had in place twenty years earlier that permits in-person solicitation of close personal friends. Third, the rule was changed to prohibit solicitations through real-time electronic contact, such as chat rooms. The rule recognizes that electronic communications can be as powerful as telephone conversations. Again, note that these changes have not yet been adopted by the states, but are likely to be considered and adopted in some jurisdictions soon.

When considering the limitations on solicitation, it is important to keep in mind that a lawyer may not use agents to do what the lawyer cannot do. Some states explicitly address this issue in their rules governing communications, while others have issued ethics opinions on it.

Although the status may ban in-person solicitations, they may not ban written or direct-mail solicitations. However, as with advertising, states may impose regulations designed to protect consumers when lawyers seek their business through the mail. Under both ABA Model Rule 7.3 and the rules of virtually every state, some forms of direct mail must be labeled as advertising material. The required wording changes from state to state, with most jurisdictions mandating that lawyers label envelopes with the phrase "Advertisement" or "Advertising Material." Some states require an elaborate disclaimer, such as Missouri, which mandates this notice: "ADVERTISING MATERIAL: COMMERCIAL SOLICITATIONS ARE PERMITTED BY THE MISSOURI RULES OF PROFESSIONAL CONDUCT BUT ARE NEITHER SUBMITTED TO NOR APPROVED BY THE MISSOURI BAR OR THE SUPREME COURT OF MISSOURI."[8] Some states require labels to have print of a certain size or color.

Model Rule 7.3, and the rules of many states, require the labeling to accompany only those solicitations sent to prospective clients "known to be in need of legal services in a particular matter." Thus, the rule addresses targeted mail, but not general, widespread solicitations in these jurisdictions. Those who market legal services should look for this language in the applicable state rules. Otherwise, they may have to include the label for all mailed solicitations. The label is designed to avoid alarming people who receive mail from lawyers, and to alert them immediately that the contents involve only solicitation for services.

A few states impose a waiting period on direct mail for certain types of legal needs. For example, Florida requires lawyers to wait thirty days from the time the need for legal services occurs for those in need of personal injury or wrongful death representation. About ten other states have adopted similar provisions, but the ABA considered and rejected the requirement when it reviewed the Model Rules.

However, Model Rule 7.3 and the rules of most states require lawyers to refrain from any type of solicitation when the potential client has made it known that he or she does not want to receive the solicitation, or when the solicitation involves coercion, duress, or harassment.

Special Issues

Specialization

Lawyers must use caution when they identify their practice areas and designate themselves as specialists. Before a 1990 U.S. Supreme Court decision, most states permitted lawyers to identify their practice areas, but not to state that they specialized in particular fields, even if they were certified as specialists by non-state-sponsored organizations that used objective standards to verify expertise. Currently, ABA Model Rule 7.4 provides that a lawyer may identify his or her certification of specialty if the applicable state or the ABA approves of the certifying entity and the lawyer's communication identifies that entity. In addition, lawyers may state that their practices are limited to certain fields of law or that they specialize in their fields, assuming the representations are true, of course. Under Model Rule 7.4, lawyers may also state that they are specialists if they can do so in compliance with Model Rule 7.1. This may be difficult for lawyers who are not certified as specialists in those states that prohibit the creation of unjustified expectations or unsubstantiated comparisons, however. The rules of some states expressly prohibit lawyers from stating they are specialists unless they are certified by organizations that provide objective criteria for certification. A few other states require lawyers to attach disclaimers when they communicate their certifications.

Firm Names and Trade Names

States vary in their regulation of firm names. ABA Model Rule 7.5 and the rules of most states allow firms to practice under trade names. However, a trade name may not state or imply that the firm is connected to a government agency or a public or charitable legal organization, or otherwise be false or misleading. The "People's Law Firm" and "University Legal Center" are examples of trade names that have been found to violate this provision because they suggest the firm is either a public-service law firm or a university-affiliated entity.

Some states prohibit trade names, having concluded they are inherently false or misleading. These states require firms to practice under the names of lawyers who are current partners or shareholders or who are retired or deceased firm members. However, it may be misleading for a firm to include the name of a member who left the firm and began practicing elsewhere.

Domain Names

A law firm's domain name is not considered a trade name and does not have to be the name of the law firm, according to the ethics opinions that have addressed this issue. However, because a domain name has the capacity to communicate a message, in addition to serving as the location device to find the firm's Web site, that message cannot be one that violates the ethics rules. Therefore, "www.thebestlittlelawfirmintexas.com" or "www.ialwayswin.com" would be as much a violation of Rules 7.1(b) and 7.1(c) as if the firm included those boasts in the Yellow Pages, on billboards, or in brochures.

Lawyers should think about using a domain name that will not become misleading with a change of circumstances. For example, if a lawyer used the name "www.janedoe-and-assoc.com" and had associates at the time, but then went solo, the domain name would imply a capacity that the lawyer did not have and would violate the rules. Similarly, if a firm used "www.largestfirminillinois.com" and it no longer was, the domain name would be inappropriate.

Multijurisdictional Compliance

As we have seen, the rules of the different states vary widely. This, obviously, creates substantial difficulties for those who market legal services through multistate or national media. Which rules apply in these situations? First, a lawyer must comply with the rules of the states in which the firm has offices. Second, a firm should comply with the rules of the states in which its partners or shareholders are admitted to practice. Each lawyer is ethically responsible for the acts of the firm. A lawyer is subject to disciplinary proceedings in the states where he or she is admitted to practice. Consequently, a firm that undertakes client development in ways that violate the rules of its partners' states is exposing the partners to the risk of discipline.

What about the states in which the firm seeks clients, but no partner is admitted? As the purpose of the state rules is to protect those in the state, it seems incongruous for a state to protect its residents only from the unethical behavior of *its* lawyers, but not from the unethical behavior of *other* lawyers. In an Indiana disciplinary matter, California lawyers were enjoined after they sent direct-mail solicitations to Indiana residents without complying with Indiana's rules. This served to nullify the marketing effort and suggests that firms must comply with the rules of those states in which they seek clients.

What about communications that spill over into states where the firm does not seek clients and does not wish to comply with the rules? Marketing through the Internet, cable television, and regional or national magazines has the capacity to deliver the firm's message beyond its intended boundaries. Some firms include disclaimers modeled after sweepstakes law, providing the notice that the endeavor is "void where prohibited by law." Although untested, a disclaimer that notifies viewers that the firm is not in a position to accept clients, based upon the communication, in those states where the communication fails to comply with the state's rules of professional conduct has a logical appeal. To make the disclaimer effective, the firm may need an enforcement mechanism to screen out potential clients from the states where the communication fails to comply with the rules.

Disciplinary Actions

Reports from state disciplinary agencies indicate that actions taken against lawyers who breach the rules governing communication of legal services are uncommon. Anecdotal information suggests that prosecuting breaches of advertising rules is a low priority for disciplinary counsel, and the resources of their offices are limited. Generally, therefore, discipline is not pursued proactively, but reactively, when a complaint is made against a lawyer or firm. Frequently, these complaints come not from the public, but from other lawyers who are competing for business with offending firms. Under these circumstances, disciplinary counsel often focus upon bringing communications into compliance, rather than seeking punishment such as suspension or revocation of law licenses. Nevertheless, this orientation should not lead lawyers to conclude they have "a green light" to communicate in violation of the rules. Formal disciplinary proceedings are always possible when a rule is breached, and even an informal notification is an embarrassment that could lead clients to conclude the firm conducts business unethically.

Resources

To access the Model Rules of Professional Conduct governing the communications of legal services, go to **www.abanet.org/adrules**.

A more thorough discussion of the issues presented in this chapter is found in *Marketing and Legal Ethics, Third Edition*, published by the ABA Law Practice Management Section (**www.lawpractice.org/catalog/511-0432**).

The most comprehensive resource on the ethics of lawyers in general, and on client development in particular, is the *ABA/BNA Lawyers' Manual on Professional Conduct* (**www.bna.com/products/lit/mopc.htm**).

Several state disciplinary agencies operate hotlines to answer specific questions about ethics. Members may contact these resources for quick advice on the ethical propriety of their marketing materials. For more formal assessment, lawyers can ask state or local bar associations or court committees to issue ethics opinions on specific questions. Because these opinions are typically drafted and approved by committees, they can take some time. Although the opinions are not binding authority, the lawyers generally need to comply with the findings.

For more thorough analysis and multistate review, particularly for matters integral to client development endeavors such as selecting a slogan, firms should consider engaging independent counsel.

Endnotes

1. *See* WILLIAM HORNSBY, JR., MARKETING AND LEGAL ETHICS, THIRD EDITION 20–24 (2000).
2. Phila. Bar Ass'n Ethics Op. 91-17 (1992).
3. *Spencer v. Honorable Justices of Super. Ct.,* 579 F. Supp. 880 (E.D. Pa. 1984).
4. FLA. RULES OF PROF'L CONDUCT R. 4-7.3(b).
5. ALA. RULES OF PROF'L CONDUCT R. 7.2(e).
6. TEX. RULES OF PROF'L CONDUCT R. 7.04(b)(2)(i).
7. N.M. STAT. ANN. § 30-27-3.
8. MO. RULES OF PROF'L CONDUCT R. 7.3(a).

Appendix

Research: The Foundation of Intelligent Marketing

Mark Greene, Ph.D.
Ann Lee Gibson, Ph.D.

We live and work in a time when we can find as much information as we care to consume. But as many have learned to their chagrin, unvetted information may be neither reliable nor helpful. In the Winter 2000 issue of *Corporate Board Member*, William S. Rukeyser, longtime financial commentator and editor at CNN, ABC, CBS, and *Fortune* and *Money* magazines, said the following:

> These ought to be the best of times for decision makers. After all, there's so much information around on which to base decisions. Yet judging from the prevalence of failed mergers, election chaos and index-lagging stock portfolios, the avalanche of data seems to be doing at least as much harm as good. *It turns out that so many of the things we know aren't true.* (Emphasis added.)

The inclination to find out the truth by conducting research is indeed an admirable one. Looking inside the horse's mouth to count its teeth, rather than engaging in endless debate about how many teeth might be in there, has long been considered intellectually correct. In the legal marketing arena, lawyers and marketers responsible for marketing and selling their firms' legal services readily appreciate the need to understand buyers' needs and preferences and to predict and adapt to buyers' behaviors by conducting, commissioning, and consuming market research.

But what constitutes conclusive market research? What makes a poll reliable or misleading? In what situations can a focus group be useful or dangerous? How large must your respondent sample size be if you wish to generalize the responses to larger populations? What kinds of survey questions elicit useful information and what kinds generate nonsense? In short, how can we distinguish market research that allows us to make informed decisions from, to use Bill Rukeyser's term, statistical sewage?

This appendix attempts to answer these questions. It has been designed as a primer about research that supports the marketing of legal services—primarily by business and corporate law firms. Admittedly, it approaches its topics—the types of research, research methodologies, and the application of those methodologies—rather pedagogically. Readers seeking to understand the basic concepts and assumptions that underlie reliable research will find this appendix to be a useful reference when designing or commissioning research to inform their firms' marketing and business development decisions.

Although the appendix includes many research descriptions and critiques, it is not a cookbook offering research recipes for every imaginable situation in which research might be done. We encourage readers to absorb the concepts presented here and then to consider carefully how they can design, execute, and commission research that will produce reliable intelligence that will inform and improve the tough marketing decisions they and their firms must make.

Setting the Stage

Today's legal industry is not a continuation of the historical "it's business as usual." Firms seem to be merging every day, the industry is rapidly becoming truly global, and, unfortunately, some of our oldest firms are dissolving.

Like it or not, this is a time of rapid business change for the legal industry. As a result, some of the most successful firms are rapidly embracing many of the practices of mainstream corporate business. Among these are the tools of risk management.

Successful executives who hire law firms see any important decision as an exposure to risk of one sort or another. The strategies and tactics employed to manage risk range from hedge insurance to the "safe choice" law firm that can handle an important merger. Smart decisions are based not only upon intuition and sound judgment, but also upon data of many sorts. Very successful management tools—such as the Six Sigma paradigm adopted by many of our most successful corporations—are strongly data-driven.

Many of the sources of this data come from market research in its many forms. Over these first twenty years of legal marketing, law firms have moved from very little understanding of the relevance of market research to today's embracing of research by many of our most successful firms.

Law firm marketing and market research are here to stay. Law firms will require sophisticated marketing plans based upon solid understandings of their markets to flourish in the increasingly competitive legal marketplace. This appendix presents the fundamentals of formal market research and demonstrates its application in the marketing of legal services.

First, a few words about what market research is, and what it is not. A great many definitions of market research exist. Some differ so much that it is hard to believe they are defining the same term. Here, market research is defined as follows:

Market research is the systematic gathering, recording, and analyzing of data relating to the marketing of goods or services.

This is a broad definition, one that does not limit market research to traditional surveys but includes the many forms of data collection that will be discussed in this appendix.

Market research reduces the level of uncertainty in marketing decision making. It does not replace good management judgment based upon intelligence and experience. It is a tool that reduces—but does not eliminate—uncertainty. Market research facilitates decision making based more upon information and less upon intuition. Still, there is a danger of overreliance on research. Care must be taken not to rely too much upon research or to follow it blindly, letting it make decisions for you regardless of its apparent correctness. Market research is one of many tools to be considered in the planning of marketing.

A situation may be divided into that which is known, that which is presumed, and that which is unknown. The proper province of market research is the investigation of the presumed and the unknown. Market research should not be expected to part the clouds and allow some sort of mysterious light of truth to shine down.

Most research findings confirm beliefs already presumed. Few organizations would be in business for long if they lacked at least some understanding of their markets. Thus, the utility of research often lies in moving ideas from the realm of that which is believed (or presumed) to that which is known.

Practically, the function of market research is the answering of marketing questions. This function is technically known as hypothesis testing. Because of the inherent nature of statistical laws, research sometimes fails to provide conclusive results. In response to such a failure, a researcher may require a second effort to collect more data, to modify the research methodology, or to consider the question in a new way.

Reality also dictates that research occasionally results in unpopular answers. For instance, a survey was conducted for a large law firm considering the possibility of a branch office in a nearby city. The study was intended to ascertain the need for various services, the degree to which the need was being met, and the marketing strategy most likely to be effective in selling those services.

The research determined that while a moderate demand for several services existed, it was being more than adequately met by several local firms, and that most buyers were reluctant to use a firm that was not well connected to the local community. The research report recommended that the law firm not pursue opening a branch office in that community. Though many members of the firm did not "like" the findings, or consider this the "right" answer, it probably saved the firm a great deal of time and money that would have been spent in an unsuccessful attempt to establish the branch office.

So, in addition to confirming the presumed and answering questions, research findings occasionally contradict expectations. In a very small percent of the cases, even well-designed research will provide erroneous results as a result of sampling error. This phenomenon can be precisely controlled through use of large sample sizes and care to ensure sample representativeness (more about this later). More often, expectations are contradicted either because the expectations themselves were incorrect (for example, though it seemed like a good idea, it would be a mistake for the firm discussed above to open a branch office), or because the perspective of the respondents differed from that of the people commissioning the study.

For instance, a firm conducted a survey of its clients to determine why estate planning services were not being more effectively cross-sold. The expectation was that clients were not aware that estate planning services were offered, or that boutique firms had a better reputation in estate planning, or that the clients did not perceive the need for estate planning. The purpose of the survey was to determine which of these situations needed to be addressed.

The survey determined that none of these problems existed on a widespread basis. As it turned out, the clients knew or assumed estate planning was offered by the firm, few were using boutique firms to provide estate planning, and they appreciated the need for such services. The expectation that the cause of the problem would be one of the three possible causes tested was contradicted.

A more exploratory follow-up survey revealed that the main reason clients had not bought estate planning services was that, although they perceived the need, it was not an urgent priority, and they just had not gotten around to it. In many cases, the need had been perceived for many years, but it was easy to put off.

As a result of this survey, lawyers in the probate practice successfully implemented a program of initiating calls to the clients and following up by sending them an easy-to-answer list of questions to start the planning process. Once this relatively painless start to estate planning had been initiated, it was easy to build momentum to reach the right conclusion.

In this example, the firm quickly and effectively moved from the analytic phase of the research project into the implementation of marketing programs based upon the findings. Unfortunately, this is not always the case. Failure to implement marketing programs on the basis of research is a problem especially common in law firms. They frequently undertake market research, briefly examine the results, but then fail to act upon them. Such studies are a waste of time and money.

During the entire research process—from design meeting through the presentation—implementation should be the key focus. Studies should be designed to develop information that will result in concrete steps to accomplish well-defined goals. The population to be studied should be chosen because of specific marketing goals. Questionnaires should be designed to provide actionable information. Data analysis and report writing should always be pointed toward the development of plans for action.

The primary result of any market research study should be the development of an action plan, the assignment of actions to individuals or groups, and the monitoring of progress toward the assigned steps. Many firms use marketing teams, often supported or directed by marketing professionals, to implement plans based upon market research. Marketing teams usually consist of the group of lawyers most involved with a particular client or market segment. These teams develop client- or market-specific marketing plans and implement those plans. Such teams can be focused upon a particular practice area, industry, or even a specific company.

Before proceeding to a discussion of the research methodologies employed by law firms, it is necessary to define the various types of market research and their applications.

Types of Research

Market research is generally bifurcated along four lines: primary versus secondary, qualitative versus quantitative, exploratory versus conclusive, and tactical versus strategic. See Table 1 below for an overview of how these types

Table 1: Examples of the Many Types of Research

	Primary				Secondary			
	Qualitative		Quantitative		Qualitative		Quantitative	
	Exploratory	Conclusive	Exploratory	Conclusive	Exploratory	Conclusive	Exploratory	Conclusive
Tactical	Accumulate the firm's collective wisdom regarding a prospective client			Client-specific reports from client satisfaction/ loyalty survey program	Review of the history of a corporation targeted for business development			Financial analysis of a prospective client based upon D&B or S&P data
Strategic	Focus groups to support the development of positioning strategy	Ad testing to discover flaws in advertising concepts	Heuristic use of syndicated market surveys	New-practice feasibility research employing various methods				Economic analysis of a marketplace considered for firm expansion

of research relate to each other, as well as some examples of different types of research.

Primary Research

Primary research is the collection of data to provide original information. Any time original data are collected, the activity is considered primary research.

Data collected through primary research may describe any attributes about the subjects or topics being studied. In primary research about the legal marketplace, the types of data typically collected describe behavioral or attitudinal attributes of individuals (such as buyers, sellers, competitors, opinion leaders, and influencers), organizations (such as clients, prospects, law firms, and media), and environments (such as industries, companies, and marketplaces). For example, calling a city's ten largest corporations and asking the names of their general counsel would be primary research.

Secondary Research

Secondary research is the collection of data originally gathered by previous studies. For example, going to a library and using a directory to find the names of the general counsel of a city's ten largest companies would be secondary research.

Any research study should begin with the question, "What information is already available that may help answer the research question?" As Wimmer & Dominick put it, "Never begin a research project without first consulting available literature. [The] literature review not only allows [us] to learn from previous research data, but also saves time, effort, and money."

Libraries (legal and public), publications, and on-line sources are also valuable sources of data and information regarding the demand for legal services and the economic climate influencing the demand for legal services.

EXAMPLES OF PRIMARY AND SECONDARY RESEARCH

Primary Research:

- Interview prospects to learn about their legal needs
- Survey clients to measure their satisfaction with a firm's services
- Ask lawyers and staff for their opinions about possible directions the firm may take to help the firm determine support for several possible firm strategies
- Conduct focus groups of clients to assess their reactions to marketing materials.

Secondary Research:

- Review news stories to identify legal issues common to a specific client industry
- Examine court records to determine the demand for certain types of legal work within a particular geographic area and during a specific time period
- Analyze Am Law 200 data reported over a multiyear period to understand how the legal market is changing
- Review a database of companies to develop a list of prospective clients that meet certain standards of revenue, number of employees, participation in specific industries, and locations in specific geographic areas.

Qualitative Research

The term "qualitative research" describes the collection of data whose value exists not in quantification, but in depth of anecdotal evidence. Qualitative research is usually exploratory in nature, intended to provide a rich understanding of the factors at work in a situation, rather than to provide a precise numerical account of the relative importance or prevalence of those factors. Most historical research is qualitative in nature.

Empirical measurement tools such as rating scales and multiple-choice questions generally are not used in qualitative research, nor are large sample sizes needed to generalize findings to a population. The strength of qualitative research lies in its depth, not in its precision.

An example of qualitative research would be calling the general counsel of a city's ten largest companies and conducting an informal twenty-minute telephone conversation with each, discussing the law firms they use and how happy they have been with them. The purpose of the call would be to get a "feel" for the qualities that distinguish firms that clients "like."

Marketing plans based entirely upon qualitative information are likely to fail. Qualitative research is very useful in the development of quantitative research strategies, but it should not be considered conclusive.

Quantitative Research

Technically, all information can be counted or otherwise quantified and thus can be considered "quantitative." However, this viewpoint is not very useful. Quantitative research is more appropriately defined as:

> research conducted for the purpose of obtaining empirical evaluations of attitudes, behavior, or performance. Most quantitative research is implemented to provide the user of the data with information developed from a relatively small group that is representative of a larger universe.

For most law firms, the ultimate goal in conducting market research is to develop a better understanding of a population of clients or potential clients. Such conclusive research requires a quantitative component. Quantitative research is usually conclusive and always empirical. It is quantitative information that is most often used in the development of marketing plans.

An example of quantitative research would be a formal telephone survey of the general counsel of a hundred randomly selected companies, asking them what awareness and image they have of local law firms. Such a survey might include a series of questions asking counsel to rate the firms on attributes that previous qualitative research deemed important.

Exploratory Research

Exploratory research is the collection of data for the purpose of discovering hypotheses and insights, rather than testing hypotheses.

Exploratory studies have three purposes: to discover significant variables in the held situation, to discover relationships among variables, and to lay the groundwork for later, more systematic and rigorous testing of hypotheses.

It is obvious from this definition that most exploratory research is qualitative in nature. But not all exploratory research is qualitative. For instance, one might call ten colleagues and ask each to rate the quality of services provided by a competing firm. The results of such an informal poll would be quantitative (for example, a mean rating of 3.4 on a 5-point scale) but certainly not conclusive, because of the small, nonrandom sample.

Another example of exploratory research would be a roundtable discussion with general counsel from ten companies to determine the criteria they consider when selecting law firms. Such "focus groups" are probably the most popular form of exploratory and qualitative market research (and are discussed later in this appendix).

Conclusive Research

The purpose of conclusive research is to test research hypotheses. Conclusive research is always quantitative and may be generalized to the sampled population.

As an example of conclusive research, a law firm might conduct interviews with general counsel from a hundred randomly selected companies to determine whether small and large companies consider the same factors in selecting law firms. Conclusive research most often consists of formal surveys or experiments.

Discerning Differences between Exploratory and Conclusive Research

The utility of any research finding must be evaluated in terms of the study's design and methodology. Just because a study reports findings to the third decimal point and includes sophisticated-looking charts and graphs does not mean that the study's findings may be extrapolated with impunity beyond those individuals who participated in the study.

A common error made in many research studies disseminated and sold to law firms and legal departments is that of presenting findings from qualitative exploratory research as though the research were quantitative and conclusive in nature. Confusion about the conclusiveness of these studies is often created when the results of qualitative research—in which interviewers posed open-ended questions to respondents or in which sample sizes were small or in which the respondents varied in significant ways from nonrespondents—are reported using distribution statistics extended to the third decimal point and sophisticated-looking charts and graphs.

For example, we have seen numerous instances of exploratory studies that report findings like this one: "38.5% of U.S. marketing directors think their firms' Web sites are critical to their firm's success." This finding sounds very scientific. It has the added charm of being succinct and quotable.

Looking behind the methodology curtain of the research that produced this "finding," one might discover that 39 marketing directors volunteered to participate in a telephone survey. Of them, 17 opined that their firm's Web site was "critical" (whatever that means) to their firm's "success" (whatever that means). However, 39 marketing directors do not represent a large enough sample to warrant the extrapolation of even this vaguely worded opinion to the greater population of U.S. marketing directors, who currently number between 500 and 1,000.

Strategic Research

Strategic research is conducted for the purpose of developing plans or strategies to be used in marketing goods or services to a general population (for instance, all large corporations in Chicago or all healthcare institutions in Connecticut). Almost all market research has—or should have—strategic intent. For instance, a firm considering the development of marketing materials such as newsletters should precede the design of the materials with a market survey to determine the firm's current image and the image that would be most attractive to the market. Such a survey would have strategic intent.

Tactical Research

Tactical research is conducted for the purpose of developing plans or tactics to be used in marketing goods or services to specific potential clients or customers. While strategic market research is intended to support marketing efforts that address a wide audience, tactical market research supports marketing that targets individual potential buyers.

A common example of tactical market research conducted by law firms is the secondary research conducted to develop an in-depth profile of a company to be approached in a sales effort. Such research may collect a wide variety of data, including the following:

- financial performance data
- biographic information about corporate executives
- records of legal proceedings

Armed with this information, a marketing team can develop more effective tactics for selling services to the target corporations than would be possible without the information.

> **To conduct an individual analysis of any questionnaire ethically, it is essential that the respondent know that information from the interview will be studied individually.**

Tactical information is often a secondary benefit, not the primary purpose of market research conducted for law firms. For instance, in client satisfaction research (discussed later), the primary purpose is usually the development of strategic plans to better serve the firm's client base. However, in addition to the aggregate statistical analysis, it is possible (and very useful) to study each individual questionnaire or response to identify and learn how to correct problems that may exist in that specific client relationship, as well as to identify cross-selling opportunities.

To conduct an individual analysis of any questionnaire ethically, it is essential that the respondent know that information from the interview will be studied individually. In client satisfaction research, this does not substantially reduce the survey response rate. In other survey situations, the value of tactical analysis must be traded off against the potential effect on survey response rates of alerting the respondent to the absence of confidentiality. One way around this dilemma is to provide the respondent the option of confidentiality.

Surveys of nonclients conducted for the purpose of determining the market potential of practice areas, geographic areas, or industry groups are generally conducted for strategic purposes. However, the interviews conducted for such studies are also of tactical value. Each completed questionnaire may be considered a qualified sales lead. (Again, ethics prohibit such individual analysis if the respondent has been told or led to believe the interview will be treated confidentially.)

The tactical benefits of research are also important for firm politics. As mentioned earlier, many law firms are not yet completely comfortable with market research, nor are all lawyers convinced of the value of investing in market research. Such skeptics can be convinced of the worth of market research when they see relationships with valuable clients improved—or even saved—as a result of tactical application of the findings of client satisfaction surveys. An investment of perhaps $80,000 in a client satisfaction survey can result in saved or improved client relationships worth millions of dollars to a firm.

Why Clients Leave

A law firm, like any organization, is best motivated to action by some sort of crisis. Unfortunately, the loss of a large institutional client often occurs without such a call to action. In many cases, the scenario is more like this:

(1) In Year One, a large corporation is one of a firm's top ten clients, receiving services from several practice areas. Life is good.

(2) In Year Two, the client drops to number 53, but those noticing the drop attribute the decline in billing to the end of a major litigation or the settlement of a large transaction. It is believed that nothing is wrong and that work will return when the company has need. (Actually, the firm's share of the client's business has dropped because of aggressive marketing by one competitor and substantial relationship-building efforts by another.)

(3) In Year Three, the client drops to number 206, but the decline does not receive immediate attention because the firm is focused on cross-selling services to its top twenty clients. (Actually, the firm is receiving little business from this large corporation because those responsible for initially building the relationship with the firm have moved on, and those now engaging outside counsel do not believe the firm is very interested in their work.)

And that is the way much work is lost, "not with a bang, but a whimper" (apologies to T.S. Elliot). A client satisfaction survey, conducted when this institutional client was still one of the firm's top ten clients, would have revealed the competitive threats to the firm's position and, one would hope, spurred the firm to action to prevent the decline.

Research Methodologies

There are many research methodologies. The following section presents those methodologies found to be of greatest utility to law firms, in the order in which they are usually employed. Most studies conducted for law firms fall into one of these classifications. (The table below identifies the type of research each methodology represents.)

Table 2: Research Tools

Methodology used	Typical type of research represented
Web / Library research	Secondary
	Qualitative or quantitative
Focus groups	Primary
	Qualitative
Mail surveys	Primary
	Quantitative
Web surveys	Primary
	Qualitative or quantitative
Telephone surveys	Primary
	Quantitative
In-person surveys	Primary
	Quantitative or quantitative
Experiments	Primary
	Quantitative
Competitive intelligence	Secondary
	Qualitative or quantitative

Web/Library Research

As stated the section entitled, "Secondary Research," time and money can often be saved by beginning data collection efforts with a search in existing sources of the needed data.

For example, a law firm conducting a survey regarding the demand for environmental law began by searching records of applications for waste disposal permits. This search resulted in a list of potential survey participants in the geographic area of interest.

Common sources of information for Web/library research include court records, census records, league charts, transactional databases, regional economic reports, industry analyses, analyst reports, directories, government records, news stories, and the Internet sites of clients, prospects, and competitors.

Focus Groups

Focus groups are interviews conducted with six to twelve subjects simultaneously, with a moderator who leads a relatively free discussion about a specific topic. The identifying characteristic of the focus group is *controlled group discussion,* which is employed to gather preliminary information for a research project and to help develop questionnaire items for survey research. All focus group research contains four common elements:

(1) multiple respondents performing together,
(2) interaction of participants,
(3) the presence of a moderator, and
(4) a discussion outline.

Focus groups are appropriate for preliminary exploration of a topic or problem about which there is little prior understanding. The strength of focus groups lies in the rich, qualitative nature of their results. Focus groups are used to explore issues and define questions that can be definitely addressed by quantitative research methodologies, such as surveys and field experiments.

> **Focus groups are one of the most commonly used *and* misused research methodologies.**

Focus groups are one of the most commonly used *and* misused research methodologies. Although focus groups are powerful exploratory research tools, they generally employ too few participants for testing hypotheses or providing conclusive answers to marketing problems. Because of the peer and societal pressures at work during focus group discussions, as well as the probing nature of the discussions themselves, the results of focus group sessions must be interpreted with extreme care.

FOCUS GROUP STUDIES ARE NEITHER QUANTITATIVE NOR CONCLUSIVE

Dr. Mark Greene, one of the authors of this appendix, recalls an incident that demonstrates a misuse of focus groups:

> Regarding the danger of focus group "observer epiphany," I recall a focus group I conducted several years ago for a national video rental chain. Several sessions were conducted with wide geographic spread. The intent was to provide guidance in the develop-

ment of an important survey questionnaire and develop hypotheses concerning new store layouts.

One afternoon in Alexandria, Virginia, the vice president of marketing was viewing a session through the one-way mirror when a participant made a particularly compelling case for a way to redesign stores. This concept rang true for the marketing executive—so much so that he scrapped plans to test various store layouts and ordered national implementation of the new concept posed by the focus group participant. But because of the new, untested layout's negative impact on business, it was scrapped, and the original layout reinstated within six months.

Focus groups are powerful types of qualitative, exploratory research. They should not be treated as quantitative or conclusive.

Participants often leave the sessions holding opinions or beliefs not held at the beginning of the discussions. (Focus groups are an exception to one of the most important principles considered in the design of research studies—that the act of conducting research should influence the population under study as little as possible.) For example, in focus groups used to evaluate advertising concepts, opinions of the concepts tested are often changed by the participants' discussion of the ads. Thus, the participants' initial reactions (based upon the beliefs they came in with) are not the same as their final reactions (influenced by the other participants). The former provide the more valuable picture of participants' true opinions.

The small sample sizes and lack of random sampling involved in participant recruitment also preclude the generalization of focus group findings to any population beyond the participants themselves.

Firms are often tempted to employ focus groups as a conclusive methodology, due to their short time frame and low cost. Though a powerful tool for generating ideas or hypotheses, focus groups are not an end unto themselves. An inappropriate substitute for quantitative research, focus groups should be followed by surveys, experiments, or other empirical research. They are not a conclusive research methodology.

Still, focus groups have an important place in the development of answers to marketing questions. When properly used, they are a powerful method for generating hypotheses and exploring topics.

A focus group research project typically consists of the following steps:

(1) *Project Design Meeting*: At this meeting, the project objectives are defined and the methodology is spelled out in detail.
(2) *Sample Development*: A list of potential participants is prepared. This list should be as representative as possible of the population of

interest. For instance, assume the intent of the research is to discover which law firm attributes midsize suburban companies consider when selecting providers of general corporate work. The potential participants should be representative of all potential buyers in midsize suburban companies. The companies should not be limited to those that are high-tech or those with which the firm already has contacts. The participants should not include individuals from large companies, those not involved in the decision-making process, or those who work downtown.

(3) *Development of a Discussion Guide*: A focus group discussion guide lists the topics to be covered during the session. It is not a formal questionnaire that must be rigorously followed. As the discussion proceeds, the moderator may decide that certain topics should be covered in greater depth than planned, or that others should be touched upon only briefly. The guide provides some degree of structure to the session, but does not prevent the moderator from rearranging the order of discussion as the flow of the session may suggest.

(4) *Participant Recruitment*: The potential participants are contacted by telephone to request their participation in a focus group session. They are told the topic of the discussion and the length of the session (typically two hours). The potential participants are told that taking part will allow them to influence the development of the service or its marketing, whichever is appropriate. As an added incentive, they are usually told they will be paid for their time (typically $250 to $350 for senior counsel), depending upon the location and the level of the participants, and will be given a light meal or refreshments. Limousine service is sometimes provided for senior executives. Participants coming from distant locations are usually given hotel accommodations and compensation for their travel.

Because usually fewer than the full number of participants recruited actually come to the session, some overrecruiting is almost always done. To ensure eight to ten participants, twelve to fourteen are usually recruited. If a larger number of participants come than can be comfortably accommodated in the session, the extras are given their incentives and sent on their way.

(5) *Preparation*: Focus groups are usually conducted at facilities specially designed for that purpose. Participants enter a waiting room to check in, and are given any required presession questionnaires. At the appointed time, the participants are directed to the session room, where they find a large table and chairs. They sit at the table, leaving the head chair open for the moderator. Behind the chair at

the head of the table is a wall-size mirror. The mirror is one-way glass, behind which observers from the client firm are usually found. Almost all focus groups are recorded on audio or videotape using microphones in the session room ceiling and a video camera behind the one-way mirror.

(6) *The Session*: When the participants are seated, the moderator enters the room, takes the head chair, and introduces himself or herself. The observation and taping are explained, as are the purposes and logistics of the session. The discussion then begins, usually with the participants briefly introducing themselves. During the session, participants may be asked to complete questionnaires, watch videotapes, or examine exhibits of advertising or marketing concepts.

(7) *Post-session*: When the discussion is complete, the participants leave the session room, and receive their participation incentives as well as thanks for attending. Meanwhile, if observers from the client firm are present, the moderator goes behind the one-way mirror to debrief the observers on their reactions to the session.

(8) *Analysis*: The moderator's notes taken during the session and the debriefing of observers are combined with a study of the audio tapes to form the basis of the focus group report. To facilitate this process, the audio tapes of the session are usually transcribed before report writing.

(9) *Implementation*: Focus groups can provide valuable input to quantitative research design. The focus group process is complete when the report is used for that purpose.

To protect against the influence of a few particularly persuasive individuals and to preclude geographic bias, a focus group study usually includes several sessions, often geographically distributed. For instance, a focus group project conducted to discuss potential branding strategies might include two sessions with purchasers of legal services from large corporations and two sessions with buyers from smaller companies. When a law firm engages a research firm to conduct focus groups, the research firm should be expected to do the following:

- work with the law firm to define the population of interest and develop the discussion guide
- recruit participants for each group, possibly employing monetary or other forms of recruitment incentives
- provide an experienced moderator to conduct the focus group sessions, ensuring that each topic area of the discussion guide is covered, and exploring any relevant questions that arise during the discussions
- prepare a written report of the session results.

Focus group projects usually require three to four weeks, from proposal acceptance to presentation of final report. Focus groups typically cost approximately $7,500, plus variable recruitment and travel expenses. The total per group is usually about $12,000.

If properly handled, focus group research will achieve the following:

- provide general guidance in the design of quantitative research, increasing the likelihood that the correct questions will be asked using the appropriate methodology (including elimination of unnecessary questions and addition of questions not previously considered)
- generate hypotheses to be tested by quantitative research methodologies, such as telephone surveys
- lower the cost of conclusive research by "closing up" open-ended questions

The Difference between Open-Ended and Closed-Ended Questions

Open-ended questions have answers that are not restricted to a predefined set. Examples include the following: "What do you like most about working with Jones, Jones & Jones?" "What could Jones, Jones & Jones do to improve your relationship with the firm?"

Closed-ended questions have predefined response sets. Examples include these: "Which Jones & Jones lawyers have you worked with?" "Using a 5-point scale where 1 means 'not at all satisfied,' and 5 means 'completely satisfied,' how would you rate your satisfaction with the fees charged by Jones, Jones & Jones?"

As a final example, a large Midwest firm decided to hold a series of seminars. To identify the topics of greatest interest to their key clients and to explore other administrative matters regarding the seminars (such as when and where to hold the seminars, their length, and whom to invite), ten clients were invited to the firm's offices to discuss law firm seminars over dinner. Two such dinners were held. These informal discussions could be considered a form of focus group research.

Using Focus Groups to Test Marketing Materials

One exception to the rule that focus groups not be treated as conclusive involves their application by law firms to test marketing materials. Though focus groups should not be treated as quantitative, and thus able to be generalized to a larger population, they can be used to discover "fatal flaws."

For instance, a few years ago, Dr. Greene was employed by Womble Carlyle (a law firm in the Southeast) and Greenfield/Belser (its design firm) to test some new ads featuring "Winston," a bulldog representing the firm in an advertising campaign. In one ad titled, "Be Virtually Anywhere," the intent was to show Winston being "beamed" somewhere, à la *Star Trek*.

Participants in two sessions reported that they thought the dog was being rained upon rather than transported. There was no need to know what percentage of the audience would misperceive the ad's intent. The design firm tweaked the artwork, and the problem was eliminated. This was conclusive, qualitative research.

A similar result occurred when a major Washington-based firm discovered during a focus group that a historic figure slated for inclusion in a campaign would be perceived by some as anti-Semitic. Again, quantitative research was not required to decide to remove that person from the ad series, but without the focus groups, the problem with the historical figure would not have been recognized.

Mail Surveys

Mail surveys are an inexpensive way to gather a large amount of quantitative data. They are especially effective for collecting data from populations with a vested interest in participating in the research (for example, those with strong interest in the survey's topic or the belief that their responses will substantially influence the services they receive). They are often used in panel designs or other situations in which the participants have been given substantial inducements (usually financial) to participate in the project.

Panel research consists of a series of data collection efforts, separated by time, in which the same respondents participate more than once. The primary strength of panel research is the ability to track changes in the attitudes or behaviors of specific individuals. The primary weakness of panel research is the sensitization that may be caused by the survey process. The act of participation changes respondents, causing them to behave differently in subsequent waves of data collection than they would otherwise behave. For instance, answering questions about alternative billing methods may cause respondents to think about the issue after the survey, thereby causing them to react differently when next questioned.

The response rate is the percentage of potential respondents who actually participate in the survey. The higher the response rate, the more confident you can be that the findings from the sample apply to the larger population from which the sample was drawn.

The steps involved in conducting mail surveys are the same as those involved in conducting telephone surveys (see section entitled, "Telephone Surveys"), except that questionnaires are mailed to potential respondents instead of being administered by telephone.

Without substantial participation inducements or very interested respondents, mail surveys typically achieve response rates of about 10 percent.

(A recently published syndicated survey of corporate counsel by ACCA/Serengeti yielded a response rate of less than 3 percent!) Because such low response rates preclude confidence that the opinions of the respondents match those of the population of interest, many mail surveys cannot be considered conclusive research. High response rates are necessary if we are to generalize the findings to the larger population of interest. The principles of statistical inference upon which such generalizations are based assume the respondents represent a random sample of the population.

If anyone asked to participate fails to do so, the representativeness of the sample becomes suspect. It is not only possible—but even likely—that those who fail to respond do so because they are in some ways different from those who do respond. For instance, if a survey is intended to measure image and awareness of local firms among general counsel, it is likely that those counsel who do not participate are not as involved in work with outside counsel as those who do respond. Therefore, the survey participants will report higher awareness of firms than is actually present in the population.

In conclusive survey research, nothing can substitute for a high response rate. It is essential that a large proportion of those given the opportunity to participate do so. Any response rate less than 100 percent should result in a degree of skepticism regarding the extrapolation of the research findings. However, some steps can be taken to increase confidence in research with a less-than-perfect response rate. For instance, the characteristics of respondents can be compared with known population parameters. In the survey of general counsel discussed above, information might be available regarding the population of companies in the community (such as number of employees, annual revenue, or location). As a check of sample representativeness, it would be possible to compare the sample with the population on each of these variables. Close agreement between the sample and population parameters on several such variables would increase confidence in the sample. Still, such checks cannot test all possible sources of variance, especially those related to attitudes and behaviors of individuals. Such checks are reassuring, but they are no substitute for a high response rate.

Because mail surveys usually result in unacceptable response rates, it is common practice to send those who have not responded a second mailing within a week or two of the first. Third and fourth waves of mailings, even telephone calls, are commonly used to increase mail survey response rates. These repeated mailings and telephone follow-up calls might increase the cost of mail surveys beyond that of telephone surveys, and greatly increase the time required to collect the data. Targeting respondents who are highly motivated to participate and providing financial incentives offer the best hopes for high response rates in mail surveys.

In general, participants may be expected to spend a maximum of five to ten minutes completing mail survey forms, depending upon the relevance of the topic under study and the inducements offered to participate. Most market research undertaken by law firms requires the collection of more data than could be collected in this short period.

Though mail surveys are effective for collecting responses to rating scale and yes-or-no questions, they generally perform poorly in collecting rich verbatim responses. When asked open-ended questions—such as, "What criteria do you consider in the selection of a firm to provide ERISA services?"—respondents who might respond at length by telephone will generally jot down only a few brief comments on a mail survey questionnaire. Mail surveys do not afford the opportunity available with telephone surveys or in-person interviews to react to responses and elicit elaboration on the answers given.

Mail surveys tend to take longer to accomplish than other survey methodologies. Data collection usually requires between six weeks and three months, and may run even longer. Most surveys must be completed much more quickly.

Some research projects require that something (often ads or advertising concepts) be shown to respondents. Some materials can be mailed with questionnaires, but large, bulky, or expensive materials are not generally practical to send en masse. Still, limited demonstration of materials is possible with mail surveys.

A large sample is necessary for confidence that a population statistic is very similar to a sample statistic. For instance, if we were to interview ten randomly selected clients and find that half intended to give a firm more intellectual property work the following year, it is not possible to conclude that exactly half of all clients intend to do so. If we interviewed one hundred clients and found that half intended to do so, we could be much more confident that half of all clients intend to do so.

More precisely, on the basis of ten interviews, we would be correct 95 percent of the time in concluding that between 10 and 90 percent of all clients intend to increase this work next year (50 percent plus or minus 40 percent). This level of precision renders the data useless. One hundred interviews would decrease this margin of error to plus or minus 10 percent, allowing us to be 95 percent sure that between 40 and 60 percent of all clients intend to give the firm more intellectual property work next year. Interviews with five hundred clients would increase our precision to plus or minus 5 percent. (See the next sidebar for a graph and discussion about the maximum margins of error corresponding to various sample sizes.)

Contrary to intuition, the sample size required to reach a given level of precision is not generally related to the size of the population. Only when the population is very small does that parameter affect the required sample size. For instance, if we were to conduct a survey to determine the level of satisfaction of corporate counsel with law firm billing rates, two hundred respondents would provide a maximum margin of error of plus or minus 7 percent, whether our sample was drawn from corporations in Southern California or the entire United States. Of course, in either case, our findings would be restricted to the population from which the sample was drawn.

95 Percent Confidence Intervals

To calculate the maximum margin of sampling error for a given number of interviews (assuming the respondents represent a random sample of the population), find your number of interviews on the horizontal axis (for example, 100 interviews). Draw a line directly up from that number until your line meets the curve. From that point, draw a horizontal line to the left until the vertical axis is met. That point corresponds to the maximum margin of sampling error (in this case, +/– 9.8 percent).

The maximum margin of error occurs when opinion is evenly split (that is, 50 percent "yes" / 50 percent "no") and decreases as opinion becomes evenly divided. For instance, for 100 interviews with a 90/10 split (or 10/90), the margin of sampling error drops from 9.8 to less than 6 percent.

In many cases, this error figure will be less important than the error introduced by nonresponse bias. When some of those asked to participate choose not to do so, the potential for nonresponse bias exists. This violates the assumption of "random sample of the population," and the difference of opinion between the population and your sample is likely to be substantially greater than the figure suggested by the margin of sampling error.

Standards Error of Proportion
(95 Percent Confidence Intervals)

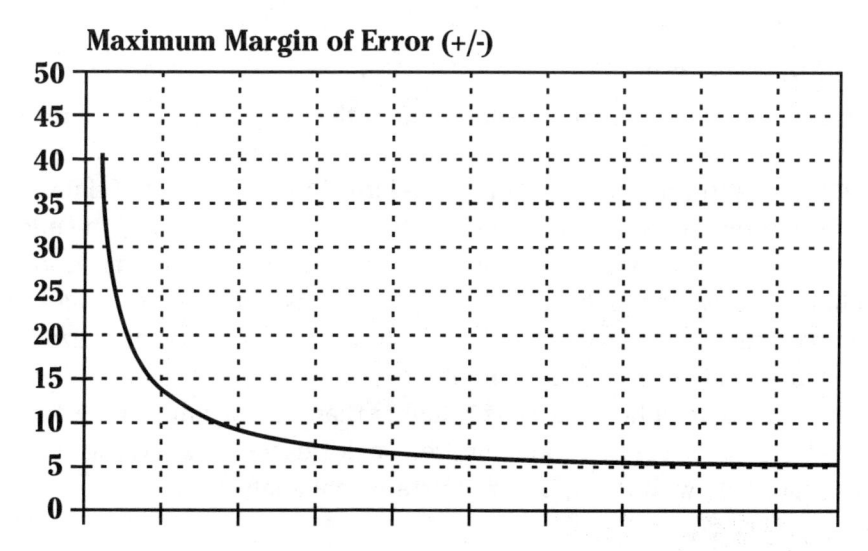

A typical one-page mail survey that targets executives, with sufficient follow-up procedures or incentives to result in one hundred returned questionnaires and a 70 percent response rate, should be expected to cost between $40,000 and $60,000, and to require twelve to sixteen weeks, from design meeting through report presentation.

Web Surveys

A mail survey is a type of self-administered survey. This genre also includes evaluations found in hotels and other establishments, e-mail/Internet-based questionnaires, Web-based surveys, and, for consumers in public places, kiosk surveys. Of these, Web-based surveys are of most interest to law firms.

Web-based surveys usually consist of e-mails sent to members of a population of interest. The e-mail invites potential participants to visit a Web-site where the survey is administered. These sites range from being visually very plain and difficult to navigate to highly designed sites with elegant and inviting navigation. Such factors have substantial impact upon the response rates achieved.

Web surveys improve on mail and e-mail surveys in that they are generally easier to complete and they support complex "skip patterns," in which the questions posed depend upon answers given to other questions or participant characteristics (for example, if question 1 is answered "yes," then skip to question 6). Web surveys also avoid the time and possible errors involved in typing mail survey results into a database, as the data are directly entered into a computer by the respondent. In some cases, Web survey results are available the day after fielding is completed.

Law firms use Web surveys most often for inexpensive client satisfaction surveys and for internal surveys of the firm's lawyers.

Many of the telephone survey principles discussed below apply to Web-based surveys.

Telephone Surveys

Law firms use telephone surveys more often than any other market research methodology. And rightly so—this is an efficient method for gathering a large amount of quantitative information in a relatively short period of time.

Telephone interviews allow researchers to ask effective open-ended or probing questions, as well as yes-or-no and rating scale questions. Moreover, telephone surveys typically achieve response rates that are six to eight times as high as mail surveys, allowing for much more confident generalization of findings to the larger population of interest.

The cost of telephone surveys is higher than that of single-wave mail surveys. A telephone survey of one hundred senior executives, averaging fifteen minutes per call, with the appropriate statistical analysis and a good written report, should be expected to cost between $80,000 and $120,000, depending upon the response rate required, the participants' interest in the topic, and the number of open-ended questions.

Telephone surveys share with mail surveys the weakness of not allowing for sufficient demonstration of materials, such as brochures or Web sites. However, before the survey phone calls, certain materials can be mailed to potential respondents for evaluation during the calls.

A respondent can be expected to participate in a telephone survey for ten to thirty minutes, depending upon the salience of the topic, the respondent's status as either client or nonclient, and the participation inducement offered. Telephone interviews of nonclients commissioned by law firms typically last about twenty minutes. Client interviews may last up to thirty minutes.

Telephone survey studies usually include the following steps, which are addressed in turn below: goal establishment, research design, sample construction, instrument design, pretesting, data collection, coding scheme development, questionnaire coding, data entry, statistical programming, detailed statistical analysis, report preparation, presentation, and implementation.

Goal Establishment

The project objectives are discussed at a meeting with the research firm. Care should be taken to discuss objectives in terms of actionable results, not things that would be "nice to know." For instance, a firm might be curious to know more about its image among lawyers in local law firms, but if it were not seriously considering using that information in referral-based marketing, resources would be better spent in collecting data likely to influence marketing actions.

As many objectives as possible should be listed, making sure that no important goals are omitted. Next, the priority of each research goal should be established and the depth of information required should be discussed. The goals of a telephone survey conducted to guide the development of a firm brochure and other printed materials might be as follows:

- Discover which firm attributes are most attractive to the companies desired as clients.
- Measure the degree to which the firm's primary competitors are now seen as having those attributes. (Items 1 and 2 will reveal how the firm's image needs to change.)
- Determine how receptive the target companies are to aggressive advertising by law firms.
- Learn which publications are most often read by those who make or influence decisions regarding the selection of outside counsel.

Research Design

Substantial effort should be devoted to selecting the best research design for the stated project goals. Considerations include the information needs and constraints involving time and money. Law firms should be wary of research firms that offer only one approach to every marketing problem; such firms usually offer only focus groups or only telephone surveys. (See the section at the end of this appendix for a discussion of vendor selection.) For this example, we will assume that a telephone survey is the appropriate methodology.

Sample Construction

Having decided the questions to be asked and the methodology to be employed, the next step is careful construction of the list of potential respondents. This critical step is the fatal flaw in many studies. The findings of a telephone survey can be extended only to the population of which the respondents are representative. Findings from a survey of firm clients cannot be extrapolated to nonclients. The results of a survey of suburban companies cannot be reliably generalized to the population of companies located downtown.

For the survey to support the development of a marketing effort, a list of the sort of companies to be influenced by the campaign would be developed. Law firms are often interested in the 250 largest corporations in a metropolitan area (in terms of annual revenue).

Having defined the target population, it is necessary to acquire a list of companies. The largest companies in most metropolitan areas are listed annually by local newspapers. Other sources of such lists include list brokers and on-line information services. Most sources will provide each company's annual revenue and its address and telephone number, but not all will provide the name and telephone number of the company's general counsel. Collecting this information usually requires making a telephone call to each company. (The completed list of the area's 250 largest companies with their addresses and general counsel names and telephone numbers can also be used as a database for future marketing activities, such as mailings of brochures and newsletters.)

The result is a comprehensive list of the area's largest companies. A representative sample of that list will be used.

Instrument Design

Professional assistance is most critical in this stage of telephone research. Though questionnaire design may seem simple enough, it is both a subtle art and a well-studied science. Questions that sound fine may have fundamental methodological flaws.

For instance, few professional researchers would ask questions such as the following: "Please rank the importance of the following attributes to your selection of a law firm to provide corporate tax services." "Please rate the importance of the following attributes to your selection of a firm to provide corporate tax services. Use a 1 to 10 scale, where 1 means 'not at all important' and 10 means 'extremely important.'" These are two simple examples of common questionnaire design mistakes. The first question is problematic because of its use of rankings, and the second because of its use of an even-point scale. Despite the fact that questionnaire design has been the subject of an enormous amount of research, the number and variety of such mistakes seem to be limited only by the number of do-it-yourself questionnaires written.

EXAMPLES OF GOOD AND BAD SURVEY QUESTIONS

A provider of services to the legal industry recently included the following question in one of its surveys:

> Which are the two most important uses of XX for your department? *Check only two.*
>
> | | Two Most Important |
> |---|---|
> | Dlkjh asd;h afg;dsoihfa a;odihfas;df | ___ |
> | Vyuig ;ohqfgaa adsf hyt re | ___ |
> | Ilkh iug ig yfgyuf iuyg uigiulg | ___ |
> | Pkjh iug iug ug lglg lglkjgl;ouiy | ___ |
> | Other _____ | |

There are several problems with this question. First, the list of possible uses was not developed on the basis of input from users. It was simply made up by company executives. Second, this is not an effective way to measure the relative importance of concepts. From this question, it is not possible to determine whether the two concepts selected are equal in importance, or one is much more important than another. It is also impossible to determine whether the top two are much more important than the others.

A much better approach to this research question would be to pose the following questions:

1. What is the most important use of X for your department?
   _____

2. Please rate the importance of the following attributes on a scale of 0 to 10, where 0 means "not at all important" and 10 means "extremely important."

Dlkjh asd;h afg;dsoihfa a;odihfas;df	___
Vyuig ;ohqfgaa adsf hyt re	___

Ilkh iug ig yfgyuf iuyg uigiulg   _____
Pkjh iug iug ug lglg lglkjgl;ouiy   _____
Insert attribute from respondent given above _____

With the second approach, we can measure the distance between each concept in terms of its importance, including that spontaneously offered by the respondent. Ideally, the concepts would have been developed through focus groups or other qualitative/exploratory research.

Pretesting

A great deal of regret can be avoided if questionnaires are "pretested" before fielding begins in earnest. Questionnaires should first be tested internally by one researcher interviewing another. This pretest will uncover most problems of logical flaw in "skip patterns" and awkward question wording. The term "skip patterns" refers to instances in which certain portions of a questionnaire may be passed over depending upon responses to prior questions; for instance, "If question 4 is answered no, skip to question 7."

Pretesting should continue with interviews of ten to twenty actual respondents. Based upon the responses they receive, the interviewers who conduct these "real" interviews are debriefed as a final check of questionnaire wording and logic.

This is also the time to make sure that respondents are answering as expected. For instance, if we ask twenty people about the best media for law firm advertising, and ten respond that law firms simply should not advertise, we probably should rework the questionnaire to determine whether the respondents oppose law firm advertising in general. If indeed they do, we should avoid posing the "best media" question, so we do not alienate them.

Rating Scales Should Clarify, Not Confuse

Use of 1-to-10 scales can be almost as troublesome as use of rankings. If a respondent wishes to assign a neutral rating, he or she will usually choose 5. In fact, 5 is below average on a 1-to-10 scale (5.5 is the midpoint). If a respondent realizes that 5.5 is the midpoint and tries to respond with that number, the interviewer, who has been trained to accept only whole numbers, will force the respondent to choose 5 or 6. This flaw of any scale with an even number of choices requires the respondent to decide whether to respond positively or negatively to the question, even though the respondent's opinion before the survey was neutral. It is important that research be as unobtrusive as possible and stick to measuring attitudes, rather than creating them.

RANKINGS CAN BE MISLEADING

Rankings can be very misleading, because the amount of difference between each ranking is not known. For instance, it might be the case that a company considers experience in its industry and experience with a particular type of case to be absolutely critical to its selection of a firm to provide a particular service. The next most important attribute is cost, but it is a very distant third and only slightly more important than accessibility of the firm's partners. In such a case, it would not be very useful to know that industry experience ranks first, experience with the type of case second, and cost third.

Data Collection

Once pretesting is complete and the questionnaire has been fine-tuned, it is time for full fielding. As with most phases of the telephone survey process, the interviewing is best done by full-time professionals, for four primary reasons:

(1) Experienced interviewers can get a high response rate without alienating the respondents or their secretaries. This is vital because low response rates are the most common fatal flaw in telephone surveys. As discussed above, without a high response rate, one cannot be confident that the findings can be extrapolated from respondents to the population of interest.

(2) Full-time professional interviewers (trained, supervised, and monitored) can complete fielding in a reasonable time frame. There have been several cases in which law firms have assigned interviewing duties to paralegals, secretaries, and temporaries, only to turn the job over to professionals when it winds up taking months, rather than weeks, to complete a few hundred interviews.

(3) It is critically important that each question is worded the same way each time it is asked. Otherwise, it is impossible to determine whether variance is due to real differences in the population or to differences in the way interviewers administered the questionnaire. This important skill is more difficult than it may sound; once a "real" respondent is on the phone and the interview is underway, it is difficult not to paraphrase or reword questions to make them more comfortable for the particular interview situation.

(4) It is also important that the interviewers in no way agree or disagree with respondents. This may seem obvious, but it is hard not to offer supportive comments such as "OK" or "Uh-huh." Many times the agreement or disagreement is more subtly expressed as a tone of approval or disappointment in the voice of the interviewer. Profes-

sional interviewers do not have a vested interest in any particular survey outcome, so they can be perfectly neutral in administering the questionnaire.

Coding Scheme Development

Before responses to open-ended questions can be entered into a database for statistical analysis, it is necessary to categorize the responses and assign numbers to the categories. Those numbers can then be entered for analysis. The categorization is called the coding scheme.

As a simple example of a coding scheme, suppose 100 clients were asked, "What do you like most about Jones, Jones & Jones?" Examination of their 250 responses (most would provide more than one answer) might result in the following categorization of responses:

- like a specific lawyer
- quality of service
- responsiveness
- understanding of my industry
- "team" attitude
- other responses

In developing a coding scheme, the most critical facet is ensuring that the responses fit the categories well. Effort must also be made to minimize the number of categories, make the categories as mutually exclusive as possible, and have few responses left over as "other responses."

The process is best accomplished by entering all responses into a database and then repeatedly arranging them in tentative groupings until a satisfactory scheme emerges. It is very much an iterative, trial-and-error process.

Questionnaire Coding

Once the coding schemes have been developed, each response to the open-ended questions is assigned a numeric code.

Data Entry

Next, the numeric codes assigned to all responses to all questions are entered into a data set for statistical analysis. For best results, the data entry step is done twice, and the two resulting data sets are compared to make sure they are identical. This greatly reduces the chances of entry errors in the final data set.

Statistical Programming

The analysis of the data set should be done by a computer program specifically designed for that task (not a spreadsheet)—one that can read the data set and conduct a comprehensive analysis of the data.

Other types of programs, such as Excel or Access, are not suited to this task. A great deal of programming time is required to set them up for even the most rudimentary statistical analysis. The best programs for this task are SPSS and SAS.

Detailed Statistical Analysis

The initial statistical analysis will provide basic information such as the number and percentage of respondents giving each answer to each question (for instance, 18 percent of all clients are aware of the firm's intellectual property practice), the averages for any data appropriate for such calculation (for instance, clients use an average of 1.3 other firms; the average client has been using Jones, Jones & Jones for 5.2 years), and the breakdown of responses by preselected subgroups (for instance, the average rating of satisfaction with litigation services was 3.4 for clients of the suburban office versus 4.2 for clients of the downtown office; 67 percent of the firm's litigation clients consider the firm "aggressive," compared with only 11 percent of the probate clients).

Statistical analysis should not stop with this initial review of the data. In fact, it should be only the beginning. Examination of the initial statistical output will usually suggest as many questions as it answers—questions that often cannot be anticipated before the results are studied. For instance, wide variation in the number of the firm's services used by clients would lead the analyst to investigate the types of clients that use more or fewer services. The number of services used could be broken down by the clients' Standard Industry Classification (S.I.C.) Codes, their size in terms of employees and annual revenue, the number of years they have been using the firm, the specific services they used, the number of other firms they use, and the services received from others.

BE WARY OF S.I.C. CODES

The S.I.C. Code is used to differentiate companies by industry type. Care should be taken in its use, however, because it tends *not* to be terribly accurate. The classification of many companies reflects lines of business they have since left, and the classification of many corporate divisions reflects parent companies' lines of work, but not the divisions' focus.

Such follow-up analysis can lead to much better understanding of the types of clients using more or fewer of the firm's services and, in turn, the development of strategies to maximize the number of services used by each client. It might turn out that those using few services tend to be manufacturing companies, regulatory law clients, and companies new to the firm, and that manufacturing companies tend to use the services of other firms to a substantial extent while new clients do not. These findings suggest the firm should direct a great deal of cross-selling effort toward the manufacturing sector, and perhaps toward clients of the regulatory group, but that aggressive cross-selling will probably not be very effective with new clients. This scenario assumes that the information has been provided by a telephone survey, but most firms need look no further than their billing systems to find all the data necessary to support an analysis such as this.

In short, it is important that the firm decide early in the study that specific analytic steps will be undertaken to answer the questions that motivated the study. It is also important that the data be further studied to extract additional value from the many questions that could not be anticipated during study design.

Report Preparation

Report preparation is often given short shrift. The final report should be an easily read and understood document that answers the research questions that motivated the study. It should also go substantially beyond addressing the fundamental research questions. The report should explore the motivations behind the opinions and behaviors discovered, as well as the relationships between the various research findings. Most important, it should discuss the implications of the findings. The results should present "intelligence"—information pieces that have been filtered, distilled, and analyzed—as opposed to mere "data," or even "information." "Intelligence" can be thought of as information that has been turned into something that can be acted upon.

To add qualitative depth to the quantitative findings, the report should include—in an appendix or separate document—the complete verbatim answers to all open-ended questions. Examination of answers in the respondents' own words can add substantially to understanding the reasons behind attitudes and behaviors. However, it is very important that the reader not consider a handful of particularly pithy remarks representative of all respondents. The answers should be considered as a whole or used to illuminate the meaning of a specific coding classification. There is danger that a particularly memorable quotation will be given more weight than it is due and generalized to the population under study.

An added benefit of using an outside research firm to prepare the report is that an experienced researcher can apply the perspective that comes from having asked similar questions of other groups. Thus, the fact that 13 percent of small businesses near the suburban office are aware of the firm may be reported as an unusually high or low number.

It is also helpful for the report to include graphic representations of the findings, which adds a dynamic view of the data. Many quantitative concepts are much more easily understood if presented graphically.

Presentation

It is important that the research findings be presented in person to members of the firm. All those who might be involved in the implementation of the findings should be invited to the presentation. The presentation should not be limited to a set of slides summarizing the written report. Rather, the presentation should be an interactive session during which the meaning—and especially the implications—of the research are discussed at length.

Those responsible for conducting the research should be available to assist with data interpretation, but members of the firm should be encouraged to challenge the findings, explore their meanings, and work toward the development of action plans based upon the knowledge gained.

It is quite likely that ideas generated during the presentation will result in still more follow-up statistical work to investigate the reasons behind opinions and behaviors in the marketplace.

Implementation

Research is of little worth if it does not result in marketing plans that are implemented. Unfortunately, law firms seem particularly prone to failure when it comes to implementing actions on the basis of their research.

Many firms have found that the best way to ensure effective implementation is to assign *specific* tasks to *specific* individuals with *specific* due dates. Such individual accountability, with appropriate follow-up, has been shown to be effective in preventing marketing activities from being put off or forgotten. Keep in mind that market research has little or no inherent value—its value is realized when it results in decisions and actions.

In-Person Interviews

Personal interviews have all the qualitative and quantitative strengths of telephone interviews, and more. This type of interview enables the researcher to show items to the interviewee (such as brochure samples), it provides for collection of more in-depth information through even more probing than possible with a telephone survey, and the interview may last more than an hour.

However, face-to-face interviews are much more expensive than telephone interviews, and, because of the logistics involved in scheduling and conducting the interviews, projects using this approach generally take much longer than telephone surveys to complete. Also, although the rich qualitative depth of information that can be collected through in-person interviews is extremely valuable, it is also expensive and time-consuming to analyze.

As with telephone interview respondents, in-person survey respondents must be representative of the population to which findings will be generalized, and a sufficient number of interviews must be conducted to provide for the desired level of precision in extrapolating the findings. As is the case with telephone surveys, it is important that the interviewer do nothing to influence the responder. While collecting information, the interviewer must be careful not to give either verbal or nonverbal cues to the respondent. The interviewer should not express interest in a particular topic by leaning forward, for instance, or express agreement or disagreement with an inadvertent smile or frown.

In most cases, the benefits of personal interviews are not needed to accomplish the objectives of research studies. The additional time and expense is rarely warranted. However, law firms occasionally employ in-person interviews to survey their most important clients. Such projects can result in detailed understandings of clients' perceptions, and demonstrate strong interest in the clients. Because of the extreme importance of each such interview and the care necessary in properly conducting each interview, the use of professional interviewers in such cases is strongly recommended.

Experiments

According to research mavens Donald T. Campbell and Julian C. Stanley, experimental research is that portion of research in which variables are manipulated and their effects upon other variables are then observed.

As an example, suppose a firm is planning to hold a seminar on loan workouts, and intends to mail invitations to 500 companies (a mix of clients and nonclients). The firm's marketing department has recommended that design A be used for the invitation, but the managing partner believes that design B would be more effective. The firm decides to conduct an experiment to determine which design approach should be used for future invitations. The variable to be manipulated is invitation design (A versus B), and the variable to be affected is the number of companies attending the seminar. Each of the 500 companies would be randomly assigned to receive one of the two invitation designs. The firm would track which design was mailed to each company and whether the company attended the seminar. Analysis of the results would provide conclusive evidence regarding which design prompted the highest response rate and therefore should be used in future mailings.

Experiments are powerful research tools because:

(1) they do not rely upon the recruitment of a large, representative number of volunteer participants
(2) they usually represent a completely "real" situation in which participants react as they normally would in that situation, rather than as they anticipate they would
(3) participants usually do not know they are participating and thus do not "play games" with the researcher, trying to manipulate the results to achieve the preferred outcome

However, experiments are subject to a number of limitations not relevant to survey research. For instance, suppose a large firm is considering raising the hourly billing rate charged for its mergers and acquisitions work. To test the impact of the increase, the firm selects two very similar branch offices, Cleveland and Detroit, each of which have six partners specializing in mergers and acquisitions and each of which billed about $5 million in such work last year. The experiment will consist of increasing the billing rate in Cleveland from $275 to $300 per hour, while leaving the Detroit rate unchanged. At the end of the year, the profitability of the two offices will be compared and a conclusion reached regarding the superior billing rate.

Experiments like this are frequently conducted in American business. In fact, this experiment is better designed than many. Still, the experimental design has so many possible sources of trouble that it should not be seriously considered. The following discussion presents some of the most glaring problems.

- The six partners in each city are not identical sets of lawyers. It may be that the lawyers in Cleveland are actually worth more than those in Detroit and can reasonably charge more. In an experiment such as this, the lawyers must either be identical (impossible), or they should be randomly assigned to the two cities (certainly not a practical approach).
- Cleveland and Detroit are not identical cities. It may be that companies in Cleveland are used to paying more than companies in Detroit for mergers and acquisitions services, or that they are generally in better financial shape and are therefore less price sensitive. The potential clients must either be identical, or they must be randomly assigned to the different prices (again, not very practical).
- During the course of the experiment, events may have an impact on one city and not the other. Perhaps Detroit's automobile industry will experience a downturn not felt by most companies in Cleveland. This would certainly affect the amount Detroit companies are able to pay for legal services. An experimental design such as this requires that no external events affect one of the groups and not the other. This is rarely the case.
- The normal year-to-year variance in the mergers and acquisitions activity of each office may be so large as to mask the more modest effect of the rate increase. For instance, if the average annual change in profitability of the offices is plus or minus 30 percent, then it will not be possible to detect any small impact of raising the rates in Cleveland.
- Unforeseen problems within the structure of the experiment may occur during its execution. For instance, one of the Cleveland lawyers

might leave the firm during the year. Or, a client from Cleveland might mention to a client in Detroit that his rates have gone up, causing the Detroit client to feel that he is getting a particularly good deal and the Cleveland client to feel cheated.

Law firms sometimes combine experimental and survey methodologies by field testing their marketing tactics. For example, to test the impact of an ad or advertising campaign, a firm first conducts a survey to measure image and awareness of the firm among target companies, then does the advertising, and finally conducts a second survey to measure image and awareness of the firm again. Any change in the target companies' responses is assumed to have been caused by the campaign. But in fact, many other factors could have caused the change. Perhaps the firm received press coverage because of an important case it handled or because of the addition of an important practice area. The ongoing efforts of individual lawyers through seminars, speeches, publishing, and networking could also change outside awareness of the firm and its image. It is even possible that the first survey sensitized the target companies to the firm under study. Mention of the firm in the initial survey might cause the respondents to take more notice of the ads than they would have otherwise.

The field testing approach just described was taken by a large corporate law firm. In that case, the research was contaminated by press coverage of the fact that the firm was advertising. Articles in the primary newspaper in the firm's city and in several national legal publications probably received more attention than the ads themselves, making it impossible to measure their effect.

A better approach to testing the effect of an advertising campaign, or any other marketing effort, uses experimental and survey techniques with a control group. In this case, a group from the population of interest is randomly excluded from the experimental stimulus. The members of this group become the control group. An example of this design would be as follows: Suppose a national firm wishes to measure the impact of an advertising campaign run in a national magazine with many regional editions. The firm makes arrangements with the magazine to run the campaign in only half the editions (assigned randomly). Before the campaign begins, a survey is undertaken in each region to assess awareness of the firm and its image. The campaign is then executed and run in the randomly selected regional editions. Next, the firm conducts a follow-up survey to assess awareness of the firm and its image for a second time, being careful to contact only those companies *not* interviewed in the first survey.

This design overcomes almost all the problems of the previous example. Because different companies are interviewed in each wave, none are sensitized by the first survey. Because this design includes a control group of randomly selected regions where the campaign did not run, the effect of the campaign can be isolated by subtracting the effect of any other influences on awareness and image.

In relatively few instances are experiments an affordable methodology for use in law firm market research. However, because experimental research is so powerful and lacks many of the constraints present in survey research, it should be considered whenever possible.

Hybrid Studies

In many instances, some combination of methodologies is the most appropriate design. For instance, suppose a firm is considering offering a series of seminars concerning several practice areas for small businesses. The firm needs to know whom to invite, where to hold the seminars, and, obviously, which topics the seminars should address. The research design for this project might consist of focus groups and a telephone survey.

Focus groups would be conducted with small-business owners to discuss their needs for such educational seminars. At these sessions, the owners would be encouraged to discuss in depth their business situations and their knowledge of legal services. They might be asked when they believe they should turn to a law firm versus an accounting firm for tax help. They would also be asked to discuss the strengths and weaknesses of other seminars they have attended and their general preferences concerning such events.

The focus group sessions would be followed up by a telephone survey to determine (1) the degree to which the specific educational needs of small businesses are being met by other firms, (2) the number of small businesses interested in each seminar topic that might be included, (3) the preferred style of seminar (for example, case studies, interactive and participatory, or lecture), and (3) the best time and location for the events. The focus group results would serve as the basis for designing the telephone questionnaire.

Competitive Intelligence

Competitive intelligence is frequently defined as a systematic and ethical program for gathering and analyzing information about your competitors' activities and general business trends to further your own company's goals. Competitive intelligence allows companies to anticipate market developments, rather than merely react to them. Competitive intelligence, or CI, is also widely defined as *not including* activities that are illegal or unethical or could be described as espionage. In fact, the Society of Competitive Intelligence Professionals (SCIP) requires members to sign and follow a strict ethical code (see **http://www.scip.org/ci/ethics.asp**).

Although CI is a relatively new term within law firms, CI professionals constitute an older and larger profession than do legal marketers. SCIP claims over 7,000 CI professionals as members, who work in fifty countries, mainly for public and private companies.

Conducting CI requires researchers to look at a collection of different kinds of information and then filter, distill, and analyze that information to produce "intelligence" until it is something that can be acted upon. CI generally involves secondary research, although in some instances, primary research is conducted to collect data that will become part of the suite of information that CI researchers analyze to develop actionable intelligence.

One of CI's guiding principles is that organizations that are the first to spot industry and competitive trends accurately can gain great advantages if they take effective action on the basis of that CI. Conversely, otherwise valuable CI is worthless to organizations whose leaders fail to act.

Another CI guiding principle is that multiple sources of information yield the most reliable three-dimensional intelligence. For example, a CI researcher attempting to understand a competitor's strategies would delve deeply into the competitor's financial performance, employment data, legal troubles, acquisition history, patents, and other intellectual property history. A CI researcher would readily include psychological profiles of its competitors' leaders as part of the suite of information he or she uses to develop actionable intelligence.

Another principle of CI is that a company should track its competitors constantly. Eleventh-hour responses to cries for CI usually fail, because some of the most useful CI is developed through scanning a variety of types of information over time, thereby permitting CI professionals to notice small but meaningful changes and deviations in competitors' behaviors.

CI researchers are making increasing use of research tools that quickly identify and report on new Web site content on competitors' sites and other sites of interest. Better CI tools are being developed to automate much of the "searching for information" aspects of CI, leaving more time and energy for analysis. Common analytic tools used to develop CI include competitor profiles, financial analysis, SWOT analysis, scenario development, win/loss analysis, war-gaming, conjoint analysis, and simulation/modeling.

Summary

Table 3 presents a summary of the most important strengths and weaknesses of the major primary research methodologies used by law firms.

Application of Research Methodologies

In this section, the methodologies discussed above are applied in the types of research studies most often undertaken by law firms. This is not intended to

Table 3: Strengths and Weaknesses of Traditional Research Methodologies

Methodology	Strengths	Weaknesses
Web / Library Research	• Inexpensive • Great depth of information • Quick turnaround	• Limited by researcher's access to information
Focus groups	• Generate ideas • Respondents can be shown materials • Great depth of information	• Not able to generalize (small nonrepresentative sample) • Respondents interact
Web surveys	• Inexpensive • Very quick turnaround • Good design encourages high participation • Probing possible • Ability to demonstrate materials	• Response rates • Cannot be too long • Hard to elicit responses from technology-averse populations
Mail surveys	• Inexpensive • Ability to show materials (limited)	• Poor response rate • Must be short • Very slow turnaround • Very limited probing
Telephone surveys	• Long duration of interviews • High response rates • Quick turnaround • Probing possible	• No demonstration • More expensive than mail surveys
In-person interviews	• Very long duration • Detailed probing possible • Respondents can be shown materials	• Very expensive • Slow turnaround
Experiments	• Very "real" • Definitive conclusions	• Slow turnaround • Can be expensive
Competitive intelligence	• Because usually involves secondary research, generally less expensive and faster than primary research • Avoids tunnel vision, because seeks and triangulates multiple information sources • Designed to encourage action, not just "nice to know"	• Quality of intelligence limited by types and quality of information available • Quality of intelligence limited by researcher's analytical and intuitive skills

be an exhaustive treatment of all possible uses of research by law firms. Almost any marketing situation can benefit from additional information, and it is the marketing situation that should dictate the proper research design. Research should not be undertaken for the sake of using a methodology (as in,

"Litigation isn't doing well this year. Maybe we should do some focus groups.").

Internal Situation Analysis

Many firms assume that their first market research endeavor should be directed toward new industry groups, practices, or geographic areas. However, most firms would be much better served by beginning their research activities with introspection. Decisions regarding "where a firm should go" are best grounded in a thorough understanding of where the firm is and where it has been. The easiest steps to increased profitability come from correcting past errors and improving the way future business is done. Analysis of data from the firm's accounting system is usually a very productive first step.

Analysis of Accounting System Data

Analyzing data from a firm's accounting system clarifies its current position regarding revenues and profits contributed by practice areas, industries served, geographic locales, and leading clients. These data are studied both to provide a snapshot of the current situation and to identify past trends that have led to the current situation. Among other purposes, this endeavor will answer the following questions:

- Is the firm overly reliant on a few key clients?
- How many of the firm's clients are lost each year?
- How many of the firm's top clients remain top clients year after year?
- What is the average tenure of the firm's clients?
- How are the firm's revenues and profits distributed geographically (that is, what percent from downtown, the metropolitan area, in-state, domestic, international)?
- How are the firm's revenues and profits distributed by office?
- How are the firm's revenues and profits distributed by practice area?
- How are the firm's revenues and profits distributed by industry group?
- Which practice areas are growing or declining in terms of revenue and profitability?
- Which geographic areas are growing or declining in terms of their revenue and profitability contributions?
- Which industry groups are growing or declining in terms of revenue and profitability?
- How many different services are being provided to each client?
- How does the number of services received differ by industry group, years served, geographic location, and specific services received (for instance, do clients receiving tax services use more total services than clients receiving estate planning services)?

The analysis of accounting system data generally involves the following steps:

(1) *Design Meetings*: First, a meeting of those involved in the marketing of the firm is held to decide the exact purposes of the project and the types of data necessary to accomplish those objectives. Next, a meeting is held including representatives of the firm's marketing group and data processing group. A "computer savvy" marketing consultant is sometimes included to act as interpreter between the two internal groups. This meeting is held to present functional requirements to the data processing group and to discuss the intended uses of the data. If possible, the marketing group should present mock-ups of the actual computer-generated reports they would like to receive. It is likely that this meeting will result in substantial give-and-take as the data processing group discusses the data that reside in the existing databases and the tools available to extract and manipulate that data.

(2) *System Specifications*: The next step in the process is for the data processing group to prepare and present to the marketing group a set of formal, detailed system specifications. These specifications will describe in detail the data elements being used and the reports to be generated. The marketing group will review the system specifications and either accept the design or submit suggestions to be considered in redesign. The marketing groups in some firms prefer to receive data as spreadsheet files rather than printed reports. This allows them to conduct ad hoc analyses without data processing assistance and to generate their own printed output.

(3) *System Development*: The data processing group then develops the system according to the approved specifications. This process can take anywhere from a few weeks to several months, depending upon the software and hardware in use, the size and expertise of the data processing group, and the other demands on that group.

(4) *Implementation*: When the system is in place, reports should be routinely generated as part of the normal end-of-month accounting cycle, although some firms generate the marketing reports only quarterly.

Once the system has been in place for a few months, it is not unusual for the marketing group to request that modifications or enhancements be made to the system to better meet their needs.

With the exception of the possible use of a consultant to facilitate the process, this research should not involve any outside expense for the firm.

Some firms choose to conduct an analysis of their accounting database only on an ad hoc basis, perhaps once every year or two. This is generally not an efficient approach. The data processing group is required to do more work in the long run, and less information is provided.

The firm enjoys several benefits from this internal data analysis process. It learns the origin of revenue and profits—by industry, practice area, and client location. Because the reports spot growth and decline in specific business areas, the firm can capitalize on growth opportunities and move to remedy problems. The firm can also identify and target clients receiving only one or two types of legal service (as opposed to those being effectively cross-sold).

Focus Groups Among Firm Members

Before embarking upon any external marketing program, a firm must consider the opinions of its own members. By conducting a series of focus groups of its members, a firm can determine how the members believe the firm is currently positioned in the market and how it should be positioned. Such a study may also explore the firm's actual strengths and weaknesses—as opposed to those perceived by the market—and how those should be capitalized upon or corrected.

A separate but very valuable benefit to conducting focus groups of firm members is the support that doing so develops for the subsequent marketing plan. Making the members feel that they are part of the process, and that their opinions are important to its planning, results in increased support of the marketing program.

The sessions usually consist of eight to ten lawyers each. The participants are usually selected so that each group includes only peers (associates might be intimidated by senior partners). Members from the same practice area are placed in separate groups whenever possible, so the ideas presented in each group represent as fresh a mix as possible. Someone from the marketing group or from a research firm should prepare the discussion guide. It is important that the moderator be of sufficient credibility and experience as a moderator to control the flow of the discussion and prevent domination by any participant.

Following the sessions, transcripts of the discussions should be prepared. It is important that the names of the participants be omitted from the transcripts. *What* is said is important. *Who* said it is not. A report should be written based upon the transcripts. The report should focus on the members' perceptions of the firm's current position and where it should be headed. The report should play an important role in the development of the firm's marketing plan. A plan that is contrary to members' wishes, or that does not consider where the members believe the firm should be headed, is likely to fail.

Client Satisfaction Survey

During a client satisfaction survey conducted by a large Southeast firm, a client said, "If our lawyers would just pay a little more attention to us, take us to lunch once in a while—without billing for the time . . . if they would treat us like they care . . . I'd give them all of our business in the entire state of Florida!" Statements of this sort are not at all uncommon in client satisfaction interviews. Of all investments of a firm's marketing budget, none is as cost-effective as a client satisfaction survey. One firm in three has conducted some sort of client satisfaction survey.

A law firm's existing clients are an important source of continuing and new business for the firm. In fact, the most efficient way to bring in business (and one that is not prohibited by the ABA Model Rules of Professional Conduct) is to sell additional work to existing clients—clients who must remain satisfied with the firm if they are to keep buying.

Purpose

Surveying the firm's clients is an effective method of monitoring satisfaction. It is the first step toward improving client relations and increasing revenue from the current client base. A well-designed client satisfaction survey can help a firm do the following:

(1) *Prevent the Loss of Important Clients*: By identifying individual client problems now, the firm can take the steps necessary to correct those problems before they become irreconcilable differences.

(2) *Identify Specific Cross-Selling Opportunities*: A client might have legal service needs that are currently being met by other law firms or that are not being met at all. When a firm identifies such needs, it can actively pursue that work. During a client satisfaction survey for a San Francisco law firm, a respondent said that he was planning to use another law firm for a service he thought the San Francisco law firm could not provide. The San Francisco law firm was notified of this fact while the survey was still in the field. The firm contacted the respondent, told him that the firm did provide that service, and convinced him to use that firm service. The survey paid for itself before it was out of the field.

(3) *Improve Its Service Mix*: A client satisfaction survey identifies the services that are now required by clients. It also reveals clients' anticipated service needs. Armed with this information, the firm may choose to add high-demand services that it does not currently offer.

(4) *Improve the Positioning of Its Services*: Client satisfaction surveys provide a clear understanding of the image of the firm. It may be that the firm is seen as specializing in one practice area when the firm really

wants to project the image of a full-service law firm. With this information, the firm can design and implement marketing strategies that change the firm's image.

(5) *Identify Weaknesses in Competitors*: Once the firm knows what clients do not like about other law firms, it will know which attributes should be promoted as its strengths. For example, if lack of personal attention is a common complaint about other law firms, the firm may want to emphasize the personal service it provides.

(6) *Anticipate Changing Client Needs*: Clients can tell the firm how they expect their legal service requirements to change in the near future. This makes it possible for the firm to make decisions regarding its marketing, its recruitment, and even its service mix on the basis of likely changes, not just guesswork.

(7) *Identify Perceived or Substantive Issues That Detract from Client Relationships*: The firm may have problems that it does not even suspect. One client satisfaction survey uncovered a major client's impending move to another law firm. Why? It seems that the client's personnel were very conservative and were made uncomfortable by the aggressive partner who handled their work. That partner was immediately replaced in that engagement with a more conservative partner who put the client at ease. When last checked, that relationship was still intact.

Methodology

The first step in designing a client satisfaction survey is to decide what is to be gained from the effort. The objective may be to maintain a high level of satisfaction within a few key organizations, or it may be to obtain a complete picture of where the firm stands with all its clients. The firm may wish to learn how it compares with its competitors, or to explore what opportunities exist for new business from existing clients. The goals the firm sets will determine whether the research can be conducted in-house or requires the help of a research firm.

Client satisfaction surveys should be conducted by telephone whenever possible. Mail surveys typically achieve response rates of only 10 to 60 percent, while the author's experience has been that the average response rate for telephone surveys is about 90 percent, if conducted as described below. Also, mail surveys do not collect data with the same qualitative richness as telephone surveys. They are limited in terms of the amount of time a client will spend filling them out. Mail surveys also do not communicate the same degree of caring about the client as do telephone surveys. Although in-person interviews are a superior methodology, the substantial increase in cost and time over telephone surveys may not be justified by the increase in the quality or quantity of data collected.

A client satisfaction survey is useful for making improvements that are both tactical (client by client) and strategic (firmwide). The following issues should be addressed in a client satisfaction survey conducted by telephone:

(1) *Services Received from the Law Firm*: It is important to gain understanding of the respondents' perceptions of which services the firm provides to their organizations. The firm will also want to know how satisfied the respondents are with those services, particularly in the case of large clients with individuals who may be involved with only one aspect of an organization's legal work. Discovering "who knows what" within client companies can give the firm a better idea of how communication flows within those organizations. Even smaller clients may not have a thorough understanding of the work the firm does for them; they may underestimate the worth of the services being provided.

(2) *The Competition*: Once the firm knows how clients view it in terms of services offered, it will want to learn about the competition. When the firm asks its clients about services provided them by other law firms, it should also ask why the firm was not selected to handle that work and what could be done to persuade those clients to use the firm for those services. However, the firm should avoid asking clients to name the other law firms they use. Clients may be reluctant to provide such information or even be offended by being asked, perhaps to the point of discontinuing their interviews. (This type of sensitive questioning is best left to professional, third-party interviewers.) Moreover, even without the names of competitors, answers to these questions will provide a wealth of information about the competition and the firm's position in the market.

(3) *Future Legal Needs*: The firm can stay one step ahead of the competition by anticipating what the future may hold. The firm can ask its clients whether they expect to require additional legal services in the near future. Based upon the answers received, the firm can begin preparing for that need by letting clients know the firm would like to handle the work, and introducing those clients to the members of the firm who are involved in those practice areas.

(4) *Awareness of Additional Legal Services Offered*: Now that the firm knows which legal services its clients are receiving from other law firms and which additional services are perceived as future needs, it should ask the respondents if they are aware that the firm offers those services. The responses will indicate how the firm is perceived in terms of service offerings. For instance, if a large percentage of clients say they are not aware of any of the firm's additional service offerings, the firm may want to begin a marketing campaign to

change its image to that of a full-service law firm. Or, it may be discovered that many of the firm's clients are unaware of a specific service offering (estate planning or products liability, for instance), explaining why the firm is not as busy as it would like to be in that area. A caveat worth noting is that when a client satisfaction interview includes questions designed to assess a client's future legal needs and the client's awareness of the firm's capabilities, the interviewer must avoid any attempt to market or sell the firm's services *during* the client satisfaction interview. Otherwise, the client will likely resent the interview being turned into a "sales pitch."

(5) *Level of Satisfaction*: To correct existing problems and prevent future ones, the firm will want to discuss respondents' levels of satisfaction in many areas. These discussions should start with specific areas that are potentially problematic, such as general handling of telephone calls, how "simple" questions are handled, and fees and billing (including whether to use partners or associates—some respondents prefer the experience or prestige of partners, while other more cost-conscious clients prefer that associates be used whenever possible). The firm should also ask respondents about their levels of satisfaction with the specific lawyers who handle their work. Finally, the law firm should inquire about its clients' overall satisfaction with the firm and ask for suggestions for improvement. This series of questions will reveal what the firm does right; positive feedback can do a lot to improve attitudes and encourage continued high-level performance.

Random or representative sampling is a must when developing a sampling frame for a client survey. For reasons of statistical inference, findings can be assumed to apply to a larger population only if the respondents represent a random or representative sample of that population. Therefore, if the firm wants to survey some of its clients and generalize the findings to all clients, it must start with a randomly selected or representative sample of all clients. However, if the firm has a relatively small client base, the necessity of random sampling can be avoided by using the entire population of clients as the sampling frame.

If the firm does not need to generalize the findings to the entire client base, then it can select potential respondents on the basis of criteria that are relevant to specific research goals. It is important to remember that the results of a survey with a nonrandom sample cannot be generalized to any population. It is still possible, however, to study each interview individually and draw conclusions about the specific respondents who were interviewed.

The number of clients interviewed will depend upon the purpose of the survey. In any client survey, certain clients may be especially desirable to interview because of their current worth to the firm and their potential for future business. In addition, it may be beneficial to include at least one client controlled by each partner in the firm. Or the firm may choose to interview a large number of individuals in one or two key client companies. If generalizations about a large group of clients are desired, the sampling frame should include a minimum of one hundred randomly selected members of that group. This provides 95 percent confidence that the percentage of respondents giving a particular answer is within 10 percentage points of the percentage of the population that would give the response. If the population of interest is small, interviewing all members of the group is recommended.

A simple telephone questionnaire (survey instrument) that will not be subject to statistical analysis or used in comparing participants can be developed by someone in the firm. The questionnaire designer must be a logical thinker with good writing skills. Questions should initially be written in rough form and then rephrased and refined until they flow well and appear to elicit the information desired. This process is illustrated in Table 4.

In the example provided in Table 4, writing the questions was a three-step process. It started with the desire to know if clients were aware of services other than those they use. It ended with a series of questions (services provided by competitors, future requirements, and specific service awareness) that *should* provide that information. "*Should*" is emphasized, because it is not possible to be 100 percent certain about the effectiveness of a question until interviewing begins. For that reason, a questionnaire pretest is always required. (See the earlier discussion about pretesting in the section entitled, "Telephone Surveys.") The pretest is needed to test the instrument *and* the in-

Table 4: Survey Questions

The basic research question:	Do our clients know about other services we offer?
Rephrased:	Do you know that our firm offers services in addition to the ones we provide to your company?
Questionnaire form:	*After asking which services are provided by other firms and which services may be required in the future, ask the following:*
	Are you aware that Jones & Jones offers X* service?
	*A series of these questions should be asked, with the X being replaced by the specific types of services.

terviewers. (The *instrument* pretest is discussed below.) The *interviewers* should be tested to ensure they possess the following skills essential for successful interviewing:

(1) *A Pleasant Voice*: The interviewers should not speak too quickly or too slowly, mumble or whisper, sound raspy or too "sing-song," or sound childish or bossy. Any one of these qualities could make a respondent uncomfortable and detract from the quality of the interview.

(2) *A Sharp Mind*: The interviewers must be knowledgeable and quick-witted. They should be familiar with legalese and terms common in the client's business. If the interview is qualitative, the interviewers must be skilled at probing for information, while at the same time sounding conversational in tone. If the questionnaire is to undergo statistical analysis, it is extremely important that the questions be asked in exactly the same way for each respondent. A fine line marks the balance between verbatim recital of questions and probing when necessary.

(3) *Patience*: Some respondents speak slowly or are difficult to understand. Others continually put the interviewer on hold. Still others ask to have every question repeated, regardless of how clearly it was stated the first time. For interviewers, patience is not only a virtue, it is a necessity.

(4) *Responsibilities*: Keep in mind that interviewers represent the firm and its public image. If they fail to call participants at scheduled times or leave the office after asking someone to call back, new problems will be created rather than old ones discovered.

(5) *Availability*: The interviewers should be available for interviewing all day, and be free from all other responsibilities. In some cases, they will need to conduct interviews before or after work hours, or even on the weekend, if they are to reach very busy executives and individuals in other time zones.

(6) *Experience or Training*: If the firm's staff members possess all the previous attributes but lack experience and training, they are not ready to interview the firm's clients. Untrained interviewers can negate all the gains that a survey is intended to produce.

Individuals who hold lower positions than, and do not have direct contact with, the respondents make the best interviewers. Clients feel more comfortable talking with "unknown" interviewers who are not in positions of authority within the firm.

Because the respondents are clients, it is a good idea to send them letters explaining what the firm is doing and why. Though studies have shown that in most circumstances a "prior letter" has no positive influence and possibly some negative effect on survey response rates, that is not the case for client satisfaction surveys. Clients will be pleased that they have been selected to help assess the firm, and they will be waiting, sometimes eagerly, for the interview call. A sample prior letter is shown below.

Dear Client:

Jones, Jones & Jones is always looking for ways to improve the service we provide to our clients. Toward this end, we will be conducting a Client Satisfaction Survey and would like you to participate. We want to know how satisfactory our service has been and whether you have any complaints or suggestions.

A representative of Jones, Jones & Jones will call you within the next few days to set up a telephone interview. We will make every effort to accommodate your schedule.

We hope you will be able to participate in this study. You are of great importance to Jones, Jones & Jones, and we are very interested in your opinions.

Sincerely,
Your Lawyer

Before the interviewing begins in earnest, the survey instrument should also undergo a pretest. For the pretest, select those clients who are easiest to deal with and who are least likely to have problems with the firm. For a client satisfaction survey, five to ten pretest interviews should be an adequate number to uncover flaws in the questionnaire and the interviewer. Questionnaire flaws may include the following:

- awkward arrangement of the questions
- questions that are difficult for the interviewer to recite
- questions that are difficult for the participant to understand
- questions that are not appropriate for all respondents
- ambiguous questions that do not always elicit the correct information
- incomplete response sets (lists of probable responses to a question)

After the pretest, the questionnaire should be revised, interviewers should be replaced as necessary, and scheduling can begin.

When conducting a client satisfaction survey, it is important to schedule the interviews. Clients will appreciate the firm's interest in accommodating their needs and allowing them to choose the most convenient times for them. A scheduling tracking form should be used to avoid missed appointments or forgotten callbacks.

Unlike the process with most other surveys, the firm may assign one person to schedule the interviews and another person to conduct them, an approach that appears more professional to some law firm clients. However, because some respondents will want to participate immediately rather than schedule later interviews, the scheduler should be capable of conducting "on the spot" interviews or the interviewer should be readily available to take those calls.

The interviews should be conducted in as private a room as possible (a conference room, an office, or an insulated partitioned area), on a telephone with no incoming calls. Background noise creates an unprofessional atmosphere, and interruptions likely will annoy the respondents and lessen the quality—and possibly the duration—of the interviews.

Respondents should be permitted to talk as much as they desire; a lot of useful information can be obtained from unsolicited comments. In addition, the interviewer should not comment on any response—either positively or negatively—because respondents are easily conditioned to respond in the manner that gets the best reaction from the interviewer.

Although audiotaping interviews may seem like a convenient way to capture all the unsolicited information a respondent may volunteer, it is unethical and, in most locales, illegal to do so without the respondent's consent. It has been our experience that respondents do not like having their comments recorded. Even asking a respondent if he or she minds if the interview is taped can cast a pall over the conversation, making it difficult to achieve the rapport necessary to a productive interview. Instead, interviewers simply must be able to write or type quickly enough to record respondents' unsolicited comments accurately.

Using a Research Firm

A client satisfaction survey that will help identify cross-selling opportunities, discover problems, and obtain suggestions for improving a firm's service can be successfully completed in-house by even the smallest law firms. A survey that uses a simple questionnaire and internal support staff to conduct telephone interviews may realize substantial benefits. However, any law firm that plans to conduct a survey in-house should consider engaging a research firm. An experienced survey research firm can assist with overall project design to ensure the survey will provide required results. A researcher can design or review the questionnaire, train the interviewers, help analyze interview data, and develop strategies directed toward individual respondents or client companies. If a law firm wants a large amount of information from a few clients, a large number of client interviews, or an aggregate statistical analysis providing an overall perspective of the firm, then the firm will probably need a survey research firm to handle the entire survey.

Using a research firm's expertise has a variety of benefits, including proper participant selection and questionnaire construction. Participant selection is not always straightforward. If the study is to include an aggregate analysis of data, extreme care must be exercised when compiling the client sampling frame. Decisions must be made regarding the number of client companies, the number of individuals within each of those companies, and the specific companies to include. An experienced survey research consultant can ensure that the sample design is consistent with the firm's goals.

Questionnaire construction is often perceived to be a simple, straightforward task. In reality, writing a good questionnaire is the most complex aspect of survey research. Individual questions are the result of much thought and refinement. Each question must be considered in terms of the statistical techniques to be used in its analysis and in terms of that question's interaction with the other questions in the survey. A professional should be employed to write all but the simplest of survey instruments.

Responses to some questions are so predictable that they should not be allowed to consume valuable survey time. A research firm with client satisfaction survey experience will be aware of these "universal findings" and can provide this information without including the questions in the questionnaire. Following are some examples of these findings:

- Clients deservedly expect to be pampered. They should be taken to lunch or informally visited and telephoned without specific business purposes. They should not be charged for such "goodwill" activities.
- Clients should be introduced to the key individuals working on their accounts. The firm can thereby demonstrate its "bench strength" and provide the clients with known persons to call should their primary contacts be unavailable in times of need.
- Clients should be introduced to other senior members of the firm, so they may become aware of the full range of services provided by the firm and meet the people responsible for supplying other services they may need.
- The firm should not be afraid to "market" its services. Clients like to be courted and do not think less of a firm that aggressively (but professionally) tries to win and keep their business.
- Many clients want to receive brief, on-point newsletters in formats they enjoy, and to attend firmwide seminars on topics that allow them to stay ahead of fast-breaking case law, legislation, and regulations. Such newsletters and seminars should be timely, relevant, and useful, rather than simply interesting.
- General counsel worry incessantly about their legal budgets and are under continuing pressure to reduce them.

- Professional competence is the most important attribute considered in selecting a law firm. (Other attributes are also found to be very important, but these vary in importance by industry and individual client.)
- Clients react very positively to a client satisfaction survey, perceiving it as a sign that the firm cares about them and their opinions.

Most other questions elicit information that differs substantially from client to client. Such questions should be tailored to each law firm and included in the questionnaire.

A research firm will have access to a large number of experienced and available telephone interviewers. This will allow the firm's project to be completed more quickly than in-house staff could manage. In addition, skilled interviewers will use probing techniques to elicit information that in-house staff might miss. Using objective third-party interviewers will also encourage the firm's clients to respond more openly. If the aggregate data is to be analyzed, experienced interviewers will follow the rules that ensure unbiased responses.

Using the Information

When a law firm conducts an in-house client satisfaction survey, an individual interview summary should be written immediately for that interview. This tactical summary should present the collected data in an easy-to-read format. Each summary should be studied independently to guide future handling of the individual respondent or client company. It should be reviewed by the individual or committee that is handling the survey and then passed on to the lawyer responsible for that client. Those clients with problems or immediate needs should be contacted promptly without waiting until the survey is completed. These summaries will help the firm develop specific tactics for continuing or expanding the business received from each respondent or, in some cases, for saving the client relationship.

When the survey is conducted by a research firm, the data should be analyzed in two distinct ways. As with the in-house research, each interview should be studied individually for tactical guidance. If a large enough random sample of the firm's client base is used, the interviews also can be viewed in the aggregate, providing an overall client perspective of the firm that can aid in strategic planning. The analysis of aggregated data from the survey requires an experienced research firm. Statistical analysis is complex, and the interpretation of the resulting tables and charts requires still more expertise. Numerous techniques are used, including formulas that compensate for imperfections in the random selection of respondents.

Using a research firm provides the additional benefit of perspective. A research firm that has conducted thousands of client satisfaction interviews is able to judge responses relative to an accumulated body of responses to such questions. For instance, many respondents may object to the price of the firm's services. An experienced researcher will be able to judge whether the amount of price objection encountered is unusually high or low.

The most important action that a firm should take following the client satisfaction survey is to schedule individual meetings between the lawyers and their participating clients to discuss the survey; a lunch is often a good setting to keep the discussions informal and unstructured. The client should not be billed for these meetings! The degree of detail in the discussions will be dictated by the personalities involved and the magnitude of any opportunities, problems, or dissatisfactions uncovered during the survey.

Marketing plans should be created for each respondent. These plans should begin with the immediate correction of any current problems in the client relationship. They may further include plans to do the following:

- introduce new professionals to the client
- exploit specific cross-selling opportunities
- redefine service positioning and communication strategies
- take work away from competitors

Developing tactical marketing plans for each interviewed client requires manpower and marketing expertise that might not be available in a firm. Therefore, even if the firm conducts the research in-house, it may want to engage a research firm to assist with this step of the survey process.

The aggregate perspective is useful in setting strategic direction. As a result of such statistical analyses, firms often decide to take certain actions, such as the following:

- change the assignment of lawyers to clients
- offer new services
- change the practice areas sought when hiring laterals
- embark upon public-relations campaigns to strengthen perceived expertise in certain service areas
- prepare brochures targeted to specific markets or services
- change firm policies regarding communication strategies, client contact with junior staff, or underwriting of marketing efforts

Assessing a firm's top client base annually seems to be an effective cycle. Such an interval allows the firm enough time to make changes based upon the last survey's results and to allow those changes to take effect. The next survey tests those strategies and lets the clients know that their lawyers have not forgotten them.

When embarking upon a client satisfaction/loyalty research program, it is very important to start small. A firm should conduct no more interviews than it is sure it can follow up. The act of surveying a client causes that client to expect that his or her investment of time will be rewarded with better service, or at least follow-up, from the responsible lawyer. When a firm starts a client survey program with one hundred clients, there inevitably ensues a triage to determine which clients will receive follow-up from the firm's very busy partners. As a result, relationships with several of the firm's most important clients can be harmed, rather than helped, by the survey process.

Another advantage of starting small is that the return on investment of the first few interviews creates confidence among the firm's partners that a properly implemented survey process (and essential follow-up) strengthens client relationships rather than annoying clients. By starting small, confidence is instilled in the partnership before it makes the large investment required by a large client loyalty program.

Both the firm and its clients should find the survey project a "win-win" endeavor. The clients can expect to receive better service, the firm to enjoy more business. The firm also should feel more comfortable about the long-term stability of its client base, finding that the following two maxims hold true: It is generally much easier to keep a client than to develop a new one, and it is easier to sell additional work to an existing client than to a nonclient.

External Studies

A law firm should carefully examine its current situation and client base before embarking upon studies of new markets or practice areas. At some time, however, it becomes necessary to look beyond the current business base and study ways to expand the firm. Such growth can come from seeking new clients in industries already served, new industry foci, or new practice areas. This next section discusses the tools for studying these growth opportunities.

Market Profiles and Trends

Market profiles can provide a firm with powerful information regarding future opportunities for growth, as well as upcoming changes that might lessen the demand for services. From the analysis of accounting system data, the firm should have a good handle on trends regarding the types of services being sold to its clients and the industries served. By comparing this information with projections regarding the market as a whole, it is possible to forecast both opportunities and potential problems for the firm.

As an example, suppose a firm discovers that its real estate practice contributed 28 percent of last year's billings, and that these billings have been increasing at a rate of 15 percent per year over the past three years. Another 18 percent of last year's billings came from employee benefits and ERISA work, but that work has been declining at an average annual rate of 4 percent for the past three years. The firm should conduct a comprehensive study of projections regarding its market over the next few years. Sources for such information include the U.S. Census Bureau (population growth), local newspapers and magazines (projected changes in the local real estate market), chambers of commerce and boards of trade (growth trends for local industry segments), universities (economic projections), and private firms providing regional or local economic projections.

The analysis of these forecasts might lead the firm to conclude that the commercial real estate market will probably decline over the next five years. However, assume the firm learns that as of late, the state development agency and the local chamber of commerce have been unusually successful in attracting large companies to the area, and this success is expected to accelerate during the next three years as real estate prices become more competitive. The firm might conclude that major companies new to the area should be targeted as potential clients and that the volume of real estate work in the immediate area will decrease (though real estate loan work-outs will probably increase).

On the basis of its internal situation analysis and these external projections, the firm may decide to assign marketing teams to approach each of the major companies moving into the area regarding their needs for employee benefits and ERISA work. Seminars would be planned to support this effort, and a brochure regarding the firm's employee benefits and ERISA services would be prepared. On the real estate side, added effort would be made to solidify relationships with the remaining local developers and financial institutions. During that time, special cross-selling efforts would focus upon the firm's loan work-out expertise. To maintain the current work level for the real estate practice, efforts would be made to market this practice beyond the immediate metropolitan area. The firm might decide not to recruit additional associates for the real estate practice, and to hire two lateral partners from a local boutique firm specializing in employee benefits work.

Studies like this, which focus upon trends in local markets, often prove very useful and are often low-cost, even if conducted by research firms.

Corporate Profiles

While research usually is strategic in intent, research tools can also be applied to selling legal services to a specific target company or companies. The more a business development team knows about a target company, the better it will understand the company's need for legal services and the processes the company is likely to undertake in selecting outside counsel. The following information is particularly useful in developing a sales plan for a specifically targeted company (a great deal of other useful information is usually discovered while seeking this information):

- name, title, address, and telephone number of everyone substantially involved in the selection of legal services
- biographical data on those involved in the selection of outside counsel (including, for example, education, hobbies and interests, professional and civic associations, age, presence and ages of children, and information about spouses)
- identification of the subset of the above individuals responsible for final selection of law firms
- description of the processes through which the company evaluates and selects law firms
- information regarding the degree to which different company locations can independently select providers of various types of legal services
- court cases in which the company has recently been involved
- the law firms now or recently engaged by the company
- industry or industries in which the company is involved
- company size and growth over the past five years (in terms of employees, revenues, and number of offices)

Before the formal research process begins, the members of the business development team should record all they know about the target company. Generally, the research process then proceeds through the following four stages:

(1) *Secondary Research about the Prospect, Utilizing Free and Readily Available Sources*: To minimize cost and effort, formal research generally should begin with using on-line and printed materials to conduct secondary research. These sources include the company's annual reports, the company's Web site, industry Web sites, industry publications, business magazine indexes, and court records. Most of this information is readily available for publicly held companies, but is more difficult to uncover for privately held companies.

(2) *Secondary Research Utilizing Subscription and Competitive Intelligence Databases*: Secondary research may continue with searches in various on-line databases such as LexisNexis, OneSource, Hoovers, Westlaw™, Thomson Financial, Dow Jones Information Service, and others. These services can provide information regarding the company's court cases and business activities, such as mergers and acquisitions, growth trends, changes in leadership, innovative practices, and new products or services.

(3) *Primary Research to Tap the Wisdom of Coaches and Guides Close to the Prospect*: By this time, the business development team should know enough about the company to begin knowledgeable inquiries

through the lawyers' own individual networks. Friends and business acquaintances should be asked for information about the company, especially its legal staff. The firm's internal client relationship management systems are very useful in identifying who knows whom and the nature of those relationships.

(4) *Primary Research through Interviews with the Prospective Client*: The final stage in the research process should be to conduct telephone interviews with the company's senior legal personnel: the general counsel and his or her immediate staff. These interviews should be treated with as much professionalism as client satisfaction interviews. The interviews should be scheduled for the convenience of the respondents, follow a formal questionnaire, and be conducted by the business development team members themselves or by professional interviewers with appropriate experience. These tactical surveys of potential clients usually achieve at least 50 percent participation rates.

Information collected by this research process should form the basis of a formal plan for selling legal services to the target company.

Market Surveys

Market surveys are intended to provide the information necessary to design an effective and efficient marketing plan for a specific industry or market segment (whether or not the firm is already active in that area). In addition to this central strategic purpose, market surveys also collect much of the tactical information sought in the development of the corporate profiles described above. When designing a marketing plan to sell legal services to a specific market segment, answers to the following questions are needed:

(1) *The Firm*: What portion of the targeted market segment is aware of the firm? What image (if any) do the companies have of the firm? What services is the firm known to provide? How is the firm perceived by opinion leaders and referral sources?

(2) *Competitors*: How many competing firms are there? What services do they offer? How large are the firms? Who are their clients? How are the competing firms perceived by their clients, potential clients, opinion leaders, and referral sources?

(3) *Work Demand*: How much legal work exists within the target market group? How much of that need is being met? How satisfied are the clients with the services received? In what ways are they dissatisfied?

(4) *The Purchase Process*: Within buying organizations, who influences the purchase decision? Who makes the actual purchase? Upon what criteria are purchase decisions based?

Answering these questions will allow the firm to develop an effective positioning strategy and select the most appropriate marketing tools to promote the firm's services to this group. Although some of the questions require the use of secondary research tools, answers to most can be obtained through a market survey using the telephone survey methodology (see section entitled, "Telephone Surveys"), with a few added steps. As an example, the following steps would be taken to study a region's market for legal services within the healthcare industry:

- A design meeting is held to define the research objectives and the actions that should result from the information gained. This process includes a precise definition of the population to be studied. It will further specify the degree of accuracy required (and thus the sample size) and list the research questions to be addressed.
- The questionnaire is written.
- The sampling frame is developed. A list of potential respondents for healthcare organizations usually is not readily available, so it must be developed. First, a list of organizations in the industry is purchased from a list vendor or developed from a reliable database of industry participants, such as OneSource or LexisNexis. This list would include all members of that industry within the law firm's market area. In addition to its use as the survey sampling frame, this information should be kept for use in future mailings of brochures or newsletters, invitations to firm events, and marketing efforts.
- A call is made to each healthcare organization (each hospital, clinic, or practice group, for instance) to identify the purchasers of legal services. In the case of large organizations like hospitals or health maintenance organizations (HMOs), the call can usually be made directly to the legal department. In the case of smaller organizations such as practice groups, the main numbers should be called. The operator, secretary, receptionist, or whomever answers the telephone is asked who should be contacted regarding the organization's use of outside legal services. This process may require two or three calls to the organization, but it almost always results in identification of at least one person involved in the selection of outside counsel.
- The questionnaire is pretested.
- The survey is fielded.
- Data preparation occurs. This includes coding scheme development, questionnaire coding, data entry, and verification of the accuracy of the entries.
- The initial data analysis occurs.
- A meeting is held to discuss the initial findings and to discuss follow-up analysis tasks.

- Detailed data analysis is undertaken.
- The research report is prepared.
- The findings are presented to the marketing and the sales groups responsible for this market segment.
- Implementation strategies are developed and action responsibilities are assigned.
- Implementation begins.

It is important that some sort of accountability is established to check on progress toward the various action items assigned.

If an outside firm is engaged to conduct a market survey, it should be expected to do the following:

- work with the firm to custom design a telephone survey instrument and to develop the list of potential respondents (sampling frame), ensuring that the right people are asked the right questions
- identify the specific individuals to be interviewed
- pretest and field the questionnaire
- prepare the data for analysis and conduct successively more complex stages of statistical analysis to answer the questions motivating the survey, testing hypotheses suggested by previous stages of analysis whenever possible
- prepare a report that translates the complex statistical printouts into implementation-oriented charts and text easily understood by any lawyer or marketing professional in the firm

Such a study would take a research firm between nine and twelve weeks to conduct, and would cost between $80,000 to $120,000 for the first hundred interviews, depending upon questionnaire length, the complexity of the sample design, and the accessibility of the potential respondents.

This type of market survey allows a firm to:

(1) identify the most likely purchasers of the firm's services, as well as the attributes upon which decision makers in this market segment base their purchase decisions,
(2) create a marketing plan that exploits the weaknesses of competitors while effectively positioning the firm's offerings for this market segment,
(3) design business development/sales plans that are targeted toward specific industries, clients, and prospects aligned with the firm's business development goals, and
(4) design media plans that optimize the effectiveness of the firm's expenditures for printed materials and public relations directed toward this market group.

Practice Area Development Surveys

Surveys to expand the billings of a particular practice area are conducted using the same basic methodology as market surveys. The primary distinction lies in the development of the sampling frame.

When conducting a survey of a given type of legal work, the sample is developed to include companies known or expected to require that particular legal service, regardless of their industries. For instance, a large Midwest firm was considering a substantial expansion of its environmental practice by merging with a successful small firm specializing in environmental work. Before proceeding with the merger, it engaged a research firm to conduct a survey of consumers of environmental legal services. In constructing the sampling frame, the researchers included all organizations in the area that, by nature of their business, were expected to require environmental services. These included hospitals, waste haulers, waste disposal companies, chemical manufacturers, and laboratories. The list was supplemented by a list of all area companies or institutions that had applied for any sort of environmental permit within the past three years. Two hundred of these organizations were then surveyed to determine the extent of their needs for environmental services, whom they used for those services, their satisfaction with their current service providers, and their expectations for additional environmental work in the coming three years.

The survey responses showed that the firm had overestimated the demand for environmental legal services. The demand that did exist was being well met by three other large firms. The purchasers of those services were generally quite satisfied with the services received. The expected need for additional services also proved to be modest. As a result, the firm commissioning the study chose not to proceed with the merger. In this instance, the survey's value was obvious—it was the difference between the relatively small cost of the survey and the considerably greater cost of what would have been a failed merger.

Other Types of Market Research Studies

The studies discussed thus far involve studies of a firm's internal accounting system, its clients, and companies desired as clients. Market research techniques can be applied to other information needs as well, in areas such as the development and use of promotional materials, media use, lawyer recruiting, law firm mergers and acquisitions, and the opening of new offices and practices.

Development and Testing of Marketing Materials

As has already been discussed at length, several types of market research studies are useful in developing a positioning strategy for a firm. Both market surveys and client surveys yield a great deal of information regarding a firm's current position and the position that would be most effective in marketing the firm's services. Once a marketing plan and positioning strategy are in place, the firm is ready to select and develop its marketing materials—materials such as Web sites, advertising, brochures, newsletters, and new business proposals, to name a few.

Focus groups—probably most commonly used in product industries to test advertising concepts—are an effective means to test the marketing materials developed by law firms. In this application of the focus group methodology, participants are selected to be representatives of the population of potential purchasers (or referral sources) of legal services. Presidents of small technology companies might be chosen, for instance. (Focus group participants should not be restricted to those individuals the firm expects can be easily recruited, however. Almost any desired participant—offered the proper incentives—can be successfully recruited.) When the sessions begin, the participants are asked a few introductory warm-up questions about their companies and their use of law firms. They are then shown mock-ups of various marketing materials. A questionnaire that records individual reactions usually follows the displays of the materials. This is then followed by discussion of preferences, reasons for preferences, and the expected effect of the materials. On the basis of these discussions, choices between competing concepts can be made and the selected concepts refined.

It must be kept in mind, of course, that focus groups are not conclusive research and that the opinions expressed are not necessarily representative of the population of interest. Focus group sessions like this would require four to six weeks to complete and cost about $7,500, plus travel and incentives if a research firm is engaged.

Media Use Analyses

Developing the marketing materials is only the first step, for the firm must then decide how the materials will be deployed. A firm may decide to underwrite public television and radio programs, for instance, having selected a message and form for its plan. The firm must then select the most efficient programs for reaching the target audiences.

If the desired audience can be defined in terms of standard demographics (such as age, sex, and income), then the firm can turn to services such as Nielsen and Arbitron for audience statistics, contact the stations for pricing information, and calculate which programs will command the attention of the largest number of targeted individuals per dollar spent. On the other hand, should the firm wish to reach a specific group—say, general counsel in companies with annual revenues of at least $100 million—viewership statistics are not available. Happily, many firms have an easy resolution for this matter. If these individuals represent the market of greatest interest to the firm, the firm likely will be conducting periodic surveys of that group. The firm can easily add to its questionnaires a few questions about viewing public television programs and listening to public radio stations. The answers can provide the basis for calculating the efficiency of underwriting the various programs under consideration.

The cost of this type of study is very low if the audience data can be collected as part of another survey.

Search for Lateral Hires

Research methodologies have been used by some firms to assist in the recruiting of lateral partners. Executive search firms are often retained at substantial expense to assist in hiring individuals who may, or may not, prove to be "right" for the firm. The lawyers may have been available for recruitment because they had poor business development skills or were "problems" at their previous firms. Such lateral recruits often come to the new firm without a strong book of business. Applying survey research techniques can minimize these problems while reducing the cost of identifying the best candidates for a job.

The purpose of such research is to identify lawyers who are considered the best lawyers in their practice areas, as judged by purchasers of those legal services. This is accomplished by interviewing a number of purchasers of the legal services of interest. For instance, a firm was recently interested in hiring two partners to head a new suburban branch office. That office was intended primarily to serve the needs of fast-growing technology companies in that area. To find the best lawyers for those positions, a research firm was engaged to conduct interviews with one hundred of those technology companies. The following steps were taken:

- ♦ A meeting was held to discuss the exact types of lawyers needed and the types of companies that were to be served by the new office.
- ♦ Using secondary resources, the research firm prepared a sampling frame of two hundred companies fitting the firm's criteria.
- ♦ The research firm prepared a brief questionnaire asking about the company's use of outside counsel and about which lawyers in their area had the best reputation for providing the sorts of services they typically needed.
- ♦ The research firm pretested the questionnaire and then began full fielding. When each company was called, a person responsible for the selection of outside counsel was identified and the process of trying to interview that person began. (This list was subsequently used for sales leads by the new branch office.)
- ♦ Analysis of the questionnaires revealed that eight lawyers stood out as having the best reputations in the area.

- The firm chose not to contact the lawyers directly, but instead engaged a search firm (at substantially reduced fees) to discuss the positions with the eight candidates. One was on the verge of retirement and so withdrew himself from consideration. Four others were very satisfied with their current firms and would not consider the positions. The other three met with the firm, and two were hired to head the new office.

This type of study provides a firm with a list of lawyers who are the best candidates for a job—as viewed by the companies desired as clients. The firm is not limited to selecting from a group of individuals looking for a way out of their current situations. (As an added benefit, the lawyers hired usually bring a substantial book of business along.) Although this application of research methods is not yet common, it seems to be of substantial value. Such projects can be expected to cost approximately $20,000, and take between four and eight weeks to complete.

Due Diligence for Law Firm Mergers and Acquisitions

Another application of market research that is commonly employed by corporations, but rarely employed by law firms, is the vetting of merger and acquisition candidates. A survey of the candidate firm's clients is conducted to measure the depth and strength of that firm's client relationships. This is used to evaluate the real worth of the firm as related to the likely post-acquisition stability of client relationships, and to determine future cross-selling opportunities.

These surveys can also be used to measure constructs such as the "brand equity" of the acquisition candidate, optimal naming and positioning for the combined firm, and the most effective structure and staffing of the combined firm's various offices.

Secondary research that utilizes court records and transactional league charts and databases can also reveal a great deal about a firm's client base and the breadth of those relationships. Likewise, macro-metrics about the financial performance of the two hundred largest U.S.-based firms are published annually by the *American Lawyer* magazine. Financial metrics about many firms can be found in syndicated studies published annually by Price-Waterhouse and Citibank. Longitudinal analyses of these financial metrics can be helpful in appreciating a firm's collective assets, as well as how specific firms have managed themselves through good times and bad.

Opening New Offices

Opening a new office in a new city or country is an expensive proposition for a law firm and a decision rife with risk. Look at the register of law firm offices that were opened and closed in the early 1990s and early 2000s and you will see an August sky of shooting stars. Just because some firms have offices in New York and Washington does not mean they are warranted for other firms. Then again, maybe they are. A firm cannot make an informed decision until it conducts appropriate market research.

The first question to answer through market research is whether a new office makes financial sense. Market research is indicated even more strongly when a firm must choose between geographic options or when another new-office failure will not be tolerated. Table 5 summarizes some questions and issues to explore about a new office, as well as the types of research that can help inform such a decision.

Table 5: Opening a New Office

Questions and Issues to Explore	Research	Research Type
How many prospective buyers are there (the potential demand)?	Telephone survey of a representative sample of prospective buyers	Primary
Which competitors are serving the market today?	Analysis of local court records, transactional databases, news stories, law firm and business directories, and law firm Web sites	Secondary
How satisfied is the market with current providers?	Geography, regional economic conditions, trends by industry, and competition from local and national firms	Secondary
Where is the optimal location in the region for a new office?	Client and potential client mapping	Secondary
Are regional economic conditions favorable?	Profiles of local industries and a full listing of potential clients	Secondary
What costs (rental rates) or threats (other firms) raise red flags?	Analysis of recent economic reports and news stories, and interviews with key business reporters and local business mavens	Primary and secondary
What do local business leaders think of the plans?	Opinions of local business leaders	Primary
Which practices are most likely to succeed?	Telephone survey of a representative sample of prospective buyers	Primary
How should the office be staffed?	Telephone survey of a representative sample of prospective buyers	Primary
Which companies are waiting for a call?	Telephone survey of a representative sample of prospective buyers	Primary

How to Select a Research Firm

Unfortunately for law firms, many research vendors approach all problems with the same limited set of tools (methodologies). Either they offer only one sort of research (such as secondary research), or they are limited in their understanding of the many tools available. In such cases, a less-than-optimal fit between need and solution is usually achieved.

It is not uncommon for a law firm desiring information about how to better market its services to be sold a citywide or nationwide subscription study or a statistical analysis of financial data about local companies, neither of which more than tangentially addresses the firm's needs. Engaging a research firm should not be based upon the attractiveness of a particular research product or service. Rather, the law firm should clearly articulate its information needs and determine which research firm can best provide that information.

The following steps are recommended in selecting a research firm:

(1) Issue a detailed request for proposals, requiring fixed cost and time frame, at least five references, qualifications of the personnel to be assigned to each task, *reasons for methodology recommendations*, guaranteed survey response rates, and descriptions of anticipated analytic steps.

(2) Interview the finalists to determine whether they are competent researchers, understand your firm's business situation requiring research, can develop research implications and help you translate them into actionable plans, make you comfortable with them as people, and can easily communicate with you despite your different sets of jargon ("researchese" versus "legalese").

(3) Ask to see (not keep) an example of their reports. (They may insist that the reports be neutered to protect the confidentiality of their clients, which is fine.) Make sure the reports are easy to understand and include many explicit recommendations for action, explaining the meaning of the findings in terms of their marketing implications.

Keep in mind that you want to receive actionable *intelligence* that will inform and improve the difficult decisions your firm must make, not just data or interesting information.

Members of the Legal Marketing Association can log on to the association's Web site at **www.legalmarketing.org** and review and download a six-page advisory entitled, "Research Guidelines to Be Followed by the Legal Marketing Association (LMA) When Conducting Market Research and Advisory Guidelines for Law Firms Wishing to Commission and Conduct Market Research."

Conclusion

Market research is not yet universally employed by the legal industry. However, its proven value in almost every other type of business and its growing acceptance in the legal profession suggest that it will quickly become an indispensable risk management tool in the marketing of legal services.

A wide variety of research methods have been successfully applied to the various information needs involved in law firm marketing. Of these, the research practice of greatest long-term worth and most immediate return on investment is usually the customer satisfaction survey. Such studies have proven effective in demonstrating the worth of market research to lawyers who were previously skeptical of the whole idea of marketing legal services.

Customer satisfaction surveys are worthwhile endeavors for all law firms. Other market research tools should be applied when relevant information needs arise.

We close by noting, as we did at the beginning, that as firms compete fiercely for market position and market share, the legal marketplace is maturing quickly. Law firms are facing major marketing decisions—about products, pricing, place, and promotion. Research that yields reliable intelligence to improve law firm decisions has become an essential risk management tool for those who market and manage law firms. The costs of conducting research that yields reliable intelligence to support these major decisions must be weighed against the costs of taking the wrong actions or no action at all. The vast difference between these two costs defines the value of reliable research.

Afterword

Deborah McMurray

The theme of this book—boldly stated or not—is "change." It's your business imperative if you want a more satisfying career in the practice of law. In the last thirty years, most lawyers in private practice have made more money than they ever dreamed possible. Consequently, there is a naïve (and in some cases, arrogant) belief among many lawyers that doing what they've always done will produce the same fine results.

None of the authors of these chapters, Jim Durham, nor I believe that's possible.

Countless things inhibit a lawyer's success, yet most lawyers know what needs to be done and what needs to change. Lawyers know what to do, but many are simply not doing it. In a timeless book by Jeffrey Pfeffer and Robert I. Sutton, *The Knowing-Doing Gap: How Smart Companies Turn Knowledge into Action* (Harvard Business School Press, 2000), the authors point out that many organizations spend countless hours "planning" to do things, but they seldom take action: "Planning is essentially unrelated to organizational performance . . . [p]lanning can be a ritualistic exercise disconnected from operations and from transforming knowledge into action."

Unfortunately, in many law firms, planning *is* a substitute for action. There are file cabinets and shelves full of lofty ideas, mission statements that mean little to anyone but those who wrote them, and overly general goals and objectives that could never be managed or measured. These plans failed because there was no accountability for action or for changing the firms' current environment or the lawyers' behavior.

Pfeffer and Sutton say, "In a world where sounding smart has too often come to substitute for doing something smart, there is a tendency to let planning, decision making, meetings and talk come to be a substitute for implementation. . . . Managers come to believe that just because a decision has been made and there was discussion and analysis, something will happen. As we have seen, that is often not the case."

There is plenty of awareness about marketing, client service, business development, public relations, etc. in the legal industry. And, there is plenty of motion. But, to get the results that readers of this book deserve, we need more decisive action, accountability, and a belief that an investment of time and money *should* produce a measurable return.

The right kind of change will occur when lawyers set measurable marketing and business development goals, and vow to care *even more* about what keeps your clients up at night. And follow Ernest Hemingway's advice: *Never mistake motion with action.*

Resources

Beckwith, Harry, *Selling the Invisible* (Warner Books, 1997)

Burley-Allen, Madelyn, *Listening: The Forgotten Skill* (John Wiley & Sons, 1995)

Carnegie, Dale & Associates, Inc., *The Leader in You*

Covey, Stephen R., *The 7 Habits of Highly Effective People* (Covey, 2001)

Davis, Stan and Meyer, Christopher, *Blur: The Speed of Change in the Connected Economy* (Perseus Publishing, 1998)

Ewalt, Henry W., *Through the Client's Eyes: New Approaches to Get Clients to Hire You Again and Again,* Second Edition (ABA Law Practice Management Section, 2002)

Hiebeler, Robert , Kelly, Thomas B., and Ketteman, Charles, *Best Practices: Building Your Business With Customer-Focused Solutions* (Simon and Schuster, 1998)

Hildebrandt, Bradford W., and Kaufman, Jack, *The Successful Law Firm: New Approaches to Structure and Management* (Aspen Publishers, 1998)

Hornsby, Willam E. Jr., *Marketing and Legal Ethics: The Boundaries of Promoting Legal Services,* Third Edition (ABA Law Practice Management Section, 2000)

Levinson, Jay Conrad, with Lynch, R.W., *Guerrilla Marketing Attack for Attorneys*

Lundin, Stephen C., Ph.D., Paul, Harry, and Christensen, John, *Fish! A Remarkable Way to Boost Morale and Improve Results* (Hyperion Press, 2000)

Maister, David H., *Managing the Professional Service Firm* (Free Press, 1997)

Peters, Thomas J., *A Passion for Excellence* (Warner Books, 1998)

Peters, Thomas J., *In Search of Excellence* (Warner Books, 1998)

Randall, Kerry, *Effective Yellow Pages Advertising for Lawyers: The Complete Guide to Creating Winning Ads* (ABA Law Practice Management Section, 2002)

Ries, Al, and Trout, Jack, *Marketing Warfare* (McGraw-Hill, 1997)

Siskind, Gregory, Klau, Richard P., and McMurray, Deborah, *The Lawyer's Guide to Marketing on the Internet,* Second Edition (ABA Law Practice Management Section, 2002)

Snyder, Theda C., *Women Rainmakers' Best Marketing Tips,* Second Edition (ABA Law Practice Management Section, 2003)

Weishar, Hollis Hatfield, editor, *Marketing Success Stories,* Second Edition (ABA Law Practice Management Section, 2004)

Whiteley, Richard, and Hessan, Diane, *Customer-Centered Growth: Five Proven Strategies for Building Competitive Advantage* (Perseus Publishing, 1998)

Zander, Rosamund Stone, and Zander, Benjamin, *The Art of Possibility* (Penguin USA, 2002)

Zemke, Ronald, *The Service Edge: 101 Companies That Profit from Customer Care* (Random House, 1991)

Zeughauser, Peter D., *Lawyers Are from Mercury, Clients Are from Pluto* (Client Focus Press 1999).

About the Editors

James A. Durham is president of The Law Firm Development Group, Inc., a firm dedicated to changing the way lawyers and clients work together. Mr. Durham has practiced business law for over fifteen years, during which time he also worked with Mintz, Levin, Cohn, Ferris, Glovsky and Popeo, P.C., one of New England's largest law firms. As Mintz Levin's Director of Client Development, he developed uniquely successful client service and client satisfaction programs, in addition to having senior responsibility for marketing strategies, practice development, and marketing training. Jim was the General Counsel and Vice President of Marketing for Senior Tour Players, Inc. from 1988 to 1990. He also has served as the Senior Vice President of Sponsorship and Affiliate Relations for MLB Advanced Media, which operated thirty-one Web sites for Major League Baseball.

A master in the art of client relationship strategies and business development, Mr. Durham has led firms worldwide in seminars, trainings, and retreats designed to attract new clients, increase referrals, maintain a first-class image and reputation, develop alternative fee structures and partnering relationships, win "beauty contests," develop strategic plans, and create effective branding and positioning strategies. Using his expertise in client relations and business development, he has developed an interactive CD-ROM training program entitled "Just Think . . . about Clients™," a revolutionary training tool helps lawyers—individually and at their own speed—the importance of client service, as well as how to develop better relationships and time management. Mr. Durham has interviewed hundreds of clients of behalf of law firms to assist them in developing management, client service and marketing strategies. He has also done extensive leadership and planning work with Practice Group Leaders and Managers. He currently spends considerable time in a management consulting role, assisting law firm management in the implementation of innovative changes.

Mr. Durham is a graduate of Emory University School of Law and Harvard College. He is a frequent speaker for the Legal Marketing Association, Association of Legal Administrators, and other professional organizations.

Deborah McMurray is a Principal of Deborah McMurray Associates, a strategic marketing consulting firm to the legal industry. She advises law firms on marketing initiatives that focus a firm's strategy and its investments. She develops targeted positioning and branding strategies for firms throughout the U.S., including the creation of collateral, advertising campaigns, Web sites, and other print and electronic materials.

Ms. McMurray is an industry leader in law firm marketing metrics, helping firms measure and track return on investment. She created Couch Money®, a law firm cost recovery program and marketing budgeting system that finds "lost" money and helps firms reallocate their dollars more strategically. She works with marketing departments and firm leadership to help firms find typical amounts of at least $1,000 per lawyer.

She trains lawyers and other professionals in the areas of client relationship management and communications. She created "Leveraging your Business . . ." interactive communications training programs that have been used nationally by Merrill Lynch, as well as law firms, accounting firms, and legal departments.

Ms. McMurray has nineteen years of experience in strategic marketing, positioning, and communications, seventeen years in professional services marketing, and served for eleven years (1987–1998) as the first in-house marketing director at Texas-based Johnson & Swanson/Gibbs and Hughes & Luce, LLP.

She has served on the Legal Marketing Association's national board of directors, and is a frequent speaker at national programs. She has written articles for the *National Law Journal, New York Law Journal, Legal Times, Law Practice Management, Of Counsel, Texas Lawyer, STRATEGIES: The Journal of Legal Marketing*, and various local and state bar publications. She is also a coauthor of *The Lawyer's Guide to Marketing on the Internet*, Second Edition, published by the American Bar Association's Law Practice Management Section.

Please visit **www.deborahmcmurray.com** or contact her at **mcmurray@airmail.net**.

About the Authors

Burkey Belser is president and creative director of Greenfield/Belser, the country's leading brand design and strategy agency for law firms. His firm's work and research on finding and choosing lawyers has been instrumental in the revolution of legal marketing communications.

In 1997, Mr. Belser received a Presidential Design Award from President Bill Clinton for Nutrition Facts, the food label that now appears on billions of food packages worldwide. Only a handful of design firms have been so honored.

Mr. Belser has been featured or quoted in dozens of publications, including *The Wall Street Journal, The New York Times, The Washington Post, Fast Company*, and the leading publications in the field of graphic design. He was elected a fellow in the College of Law Practice Management in 1998.

Most recently, Mr. Belser is featured in *Who's Really Who*, a new compendium by the dean of information design, Richard Saul Wurman, that includes "succinct bios of the 1,000 most interesting and creative individuals living in the U.S."

Suzanne Donnels spent three years developing marketing technology systems as the director of marketing technology and strategy, then left Orrick, Herrington & Sutcliffe, LLP, for the sole purpose of working with law firms to leverage their investment in marketing technologies. These technologies include CRMs (Client Relationship Management), proposal centers, data organization, and procedures that improve the business development process. She has more than fifteen years of law firm marketing experience focusing on business development. Before joining Orrick, she spent six years in marketing at Nossaman, Guthner, Knox & Elliott, LLP, with five of those years as the director of client services. Ms. Donnels offers insights into the challenges experienced in the deployment of marketing systems combined with a thorough understanding of the business development and competition processes, having successfully coached attorney teams in numerous high-stakes competitions. She is located in San Francisco, California, and can be reached at **sdonnels@donnels.com** or at 415.971.0151.

Terri Pepper Gavulic leads the marketing consulting practice for Hildebrandt International. She provides strategic and tactical counsel to law firms. More than eleven years of her twenty-five-year career were spent as an in-house law firm marketing director in Atlanta, Georgia. She has pioneered many marketing initiatives in the law firm environment, which shaped her personal philosophy about how to successfully market the professional services firm. That philosophy is to understand each client so deeply that the delivery of professional services is completely aligned with the client's business goals.

Ms. Gavulic's commitment to these beliefs has enabled her to be a change agent and coach at every level, from boards of directors and management committees, to practice groups and marketing staff, as well as individual lawyers and their staff. Additionally, it has gained her industry recognition and she is a sought-after speaker at conferences and other forums. Client feedback and relationship management, strategic marketing planning and positioning, and marketing staffing and support analyses are particular areas of expertise for Ms. Gavulic.

Ann Lee Gibson, Ph.D., is a business development and competitive intelligence consultant to law firms. She helps law firms win new business in situations where real opportunities exist to do so; she has helped her law firm clients win new business worth nearly $400 million in legal fees. Before becoming a consultant, she was the marketing director at Nossaman Guthner Knox & Elliott and at Gibson Dunn & Crutcher. Ms. Gibson can be reached at 417.256.3575 and at **agibson@annleegibson.com**.

Mark T. Greene, Ph.D., has probably conducted more market research for law firms during the past two decades than anyone else in the world. Before founding The Brand Research Company in 2002, he had worked with law firms for more than seventeen years—first with MIICORP, then with his own company, Market Intelligence, and finally as managing director of research for FGI, Inc.

Mr. Greene regularly conducts studies in the United States and overseas for clients such as Citicorp, MCI, General Electric (where he has worked for twenty-one GE companies), and Sun Microsystems, as well as many other Fortune 500 companies.

A Six Sigma Black Belt, he has pioneered the application of cutting-edge corporate research and management techniques to professional services marketing in such areas as client satisfaction surveys, brand development and tracking, advertising development, office and practice feasibility analysis, and recruiting research.

A prolific author and speaker, Mr. Greene frequently addresses professional organizations around the world. He has served as an adjunct professor and lecturer at the University of North Carolina and several other universities and has published many articles and book chapters concerning research for the legal industry and the corporate world.

William E. Hornsby is staff counsel in the American Bar Association's Division for Legal Services. Prior to joining the Legal Services Division in 1990, he was counsel to the Standing Committee on Professionalism in the ABA Center for Professional Responsibility.

Mr. Hornsby has written several articles on legal ethics, law firm marketing, and technology for publications such as the *National Law Journal*, the *Georgetown Journal of Legal Ethics* and the ABA Law Practice Management Section's *Law Practice* magazine. He authored the ABA book *Lawyer Advertising at the Crossroads* and the third edition of the ABA Law Practice Management Section book *Marketing and Legal Ethics: The Boundaries of Promoting Legal Services*.

Mr. Hornsby is currently a member of the Illinois Attorney Registration and Disciplinary Commission Hearing Panel and an adjunct faculty member at the John Marshall Law School, where he teaches the first law school course on the professional responsibility of a technology-based law practice.

Rick Klau is a graduate of the University of Richmond School of Law, where he founded and edited the first student-edited law journal in the world to publish exclusively online. Mr. Klau has co-authored (with Erik Heels) a technology column in American Bar Association periodicals for ten years, and has co-authored two books for the ABA. Mr. Klau maintains a Weblog focused on law and technology at **http://www.rklau.com/tins/**, and regularly presents at technology conferences on the impact of technology on the practice of law. Mr. Klau lives outside of Chicago with his wife and two children. He can be reached at **rick@rklau.com**.

Robert N. Kohn and **Lawrence M. Kohn** are brothers and principals of Kohn Communications located in West Los Angeles and Monterey, California. They specialize in helping lawyers bring in new clients by focusing on interpersonal interaction. Established in the early 1980s, their firm was one of the early pioneers of a technique called "executive coaching." The technique is to use a series of one-on-one, confidential consulting sessions via telephone. Robert Kohn is the past-chair of the California State Bar Law Practice Management and Technology Section. Both speak regularly across the country to law firms and bar associations.

ABOUT THE AUTHORS

Linda S. LaBrie is a consultant to law firms and other professional services companies. She conducts primary qualitative research and advises firms on ways to leverage client feedback and market intelligence to improve client satisfaction and loyalty, win new business, and achieve a strategic and competitive advantage in the marketplace. Her research methods include face-to-face interviews, key client panels at firm retreats, focus groups and roundtables, and lost business reviews. Throughout the 1990s, Ms. LaBrie served as the chief marketer for two major northeast law firms and is credited with spearheading client satisfaction and loyalty programs designed to achieve excellence in client service and to create a "delighted" and loyal client base. She presents frequently at national and regional conferences and seminars and served as a faculty member for five years at the Law Firm Marketing Director Institute. Ms. LaBrie has written articles on various legal marketing topics, including a recent white paper titled *The Critical Follow-up Strategy*.

Susan Raridon Lambreth is a director with Hildebrandt International, the largest international management consulting firm for the legal profession. She earned her JD from the University of Pennsylvania Law School and her M.B.A. from Villanova University. She has more than nineteen years of experience as a consultant to the legal profession. Ms. Lambreth consults on leadership, practice management, and strategic issues affecting the future of law firms and the legal profession. She works with managing partners, practice group leaders, and executive committees. Ms. Lambreth has helped many of the largest firms in the U.S. implement strong practice group management (including over 30 percent of the AmLaw 100) and train their Practice Group Leaders. She has trained over 1,800 lawyers holding firm or practice management roles how to lead and manage more effectively.

Ms. Lambreth is nationally recognized as one of the top leadership and practice management consultants for law firms. She chairs the Hildebrandt Institute Practice Group Leader Workshop, a practice group leader management-training program. She has made presentations to the American Bar Association, the national and regional chapters of the Association of Legal Administrators and Legal Marketing Association, the Arizona Women Lawyers Association, the Incorporated Law Society of Ireland, Pennsylvania Bar Association, Philadelphia Bar Association, and many other law-related organizations.

Elizabeth Lampert is executive vice president of Levick Strategic Communications. She works with clients to develop strategic focus, and manages implementation of their communications plans nationally and in Europe. She can be reached at 925-932-4420.

About the Authors

Richard S. Levick is president of Levick Strategic Communications, and is one of the most sought-after speakers on strategic media and marketing for the legal industry. He was named by PR News as the 2002 Public Relations Professional of the Year for U.S. Agencies.

Levick Strategic Communications is a worldwide leader in legal media, securing media for the world's leading law firms and their clients. It has represented nearly half of the hundred largest law firms in America and more than one-third of the largest law firms in the world, and pioneered many of the media relations tactics—from third-party commentary to feature roundtables that are popular today. The firm's litigation media expertise has been applied in the highest-profile cases, including Napster, Enron, the Catholic Church, and Rosie O'Donnell. It has represented most of the transatlantic merged firms, and has spearheaded campaigns on behalf of the dominant law firms in virtually every major U.S. market and many European markets.

Mr. Levick has contributed to five other books, including *Inside/Outside: How Business Buy Legal Services* and *Stop the Presses: The Litigation PR Desk Reference*. He can be reached at **rlevick@levick.com**.

Roberta Montafia is a consultant to the legal industry with over fifteen years experience. She spent several years working in the legal industry in Europe and Bermuda, and was Global Director of Marketing for one of the world's largest law firms. Ms. Montafia specializes in providing client development initiatives and marketing planning services to a variety of clients, covering a range of services such as brand development, practice and industry group development and attorney training. She is on the advisory board of the Legal Sales and Services Organization and is the former President of the Legal Marketing Association. She has written articles on various legal marketing topics including a recent white paper titled *The Critical Follow-up Strategy*. Ms. Montafia can be reached at **rmontafia@ameritech.net**.

Felice Wagner is a successful lawyer and business development expert with over fifteen years of experience building businesses and leading successful teams. She founded Sugarcrest in 1998 in response to a growing need from law firms and legal service providers for sales and marketing solutions that work. In the past six years, she has built an industry-leading consulting practice with a satisfied client roster that includes major law firms and corporations throughout the United States and Canada.

Ms. Wagner is a regular speaker at national conferences and firm retreats. Her articles on client development and relationship management have appeared in several print and Web publications, such as *Marketing for Lawyers*, *Legal Times*, *Strategies: The Journal of Legal Marketing*, Law.com,

LawCommerce.com, FindLaw, The Law Marketing Portal, Martindale-Hubbell's LegalBiz Online, and lexisONE. She is currently President of the Legal Marketing Association's Mid-Atlantic Chapter.

Ms. Wagner is a cum laude graduate of Georgetown University Law Center and a magna cum laude graduate of the University of South Florida.

Hollis Hatfield Weishar is president of Hollis Weishar Marketing, East Greenwich, Rhode Island, a practice devoted to working with professionals, primarily lawyers, accountants, and architects. Ms. Weishar is a frequent speaker and is the author of *Marketing Success Stories: Personal Interviews with 66 Rainmakers,* published by the ABA Law Practice Management Section. She was co-editor of *The Complete Guide to Marketing Your Law Practice,* also published by the ABA Law Practice Management Section. She has worked as a marketing consultant to professional service firms throughout the United States and Canada since 1986. She assists her clients with the creation, development, and implementation of marketing, client relations, and business development programs.

Ms. Weishar has a bachelor's degree in marketing from Central Missouri State University. She has been actively involved for a number of years with the Legal Marketing Association, the Society for Marketing Professional Services, and the Association for Accounting Marketing. She resides in East Greenwich, Rhode Island, with her husband and two children.

Peter Zeughauser is widely regarded as one of the legal industry's premier strategists. A broadly skilled consultant and speaker, Peter specializes in law firm mergers and combinations, firm-wide strategic business planning, and devising strategies for increasing revenues and profitability and strengthening firm values and culture. He also works with firms to develop and align practice group and office growth strategies with firm-wide strategy, and to craft client strategies that promote long-term relationships.

Mr. Zeughauser is the author of *Lawyers Are from Mercury, Clients Are from Pluto* (ClientFocus Press, 1999). Since 1996 he has shared his insights on the legal profession as a contributing editor of *The American Lawyer* magazine, for which he writes a regular column on management, business development, and leadership issues. Frequently quoted and featured in publications as diverse as *The Wall Street Journal, Fortune, Business Week, The Washington Post, American Lawyer,* the *ABA Journal, California Lawyer, Corporate Counsel Magazine,* the *New York Law Journal,* the *Recorder,* and the *Daily Journal,*

A fellow of the College of Law Practice Management, Mr. Zeughauser graduated from the University of Wisconsin at Madison and St. Louis University School of Law, where he was elected to Alpha Sigma Nu.

Index

ABA/BNA Lawyers' Manual on Professional Conduct, 211
ABA Commission on Billable Hours Report, 158
ABA Model Rules of Professional Conduct, 202, 211
   Rule 1.5, 206
   Rule 5.4, 206
   Rule 7.1, 202, 204, 209, 210
   Rule 7.2, 205, 206
   Rule 7.3, 207–208, 209
   Rule 7.4, 209
   Rule 7.5, 209
2001 ACCA Partnering with Outside Counsel Survey, 159–160
Accountability, 6
Accounting system, analysis of, 250–252
Active listening, 126–127
Advertisements, 201
   copies of, 205
   cost of, 206
   labeling, 208
Advisories, 113–114
Agency, public relations, 73–74
Aggregators, 187
Alabama Bar
   communication of legal services rules, 205
   disclaimer rules, 206
Alerts, 114

American Corporate Counsel Association, 159
American Lawyer, 273
Andrew Skurth LLP, 174
Announcements, 93–94, 114
Asset-Backed Securities, 148

Bag & Baggage, 184, 186, 187
Bashman, Howard, 184
Bieser Greer & Landis, 174–175, 178
Billable hour, 157–158
Billing. *See* Fees
Biographies
   on Web site, 178
   writing, 112–113
Blawg Ring, 187
Blawgs. *See* Weblogs
Blended hourly rates, 163
Blogger, 182–183, 185
Bloglet, 187
BlogRolling, 187
Blogs. *See* Weblogs
BlogSpot, 182
Blow-outs, 164
Bonuses, 151–152
Branding, 77–78
Brochure, firm, 87–90, 111–112
   client focus for, 89
   design goal for, 88
   design strategy for, 88–89
   messages for, 88

Budget
  marketing, 23
  phased, 152
Bulletins, 114
Burton, Congressperson Dan, 117
Business cards, 125, 138

Caddie Relief Act of 1997, 117
Campbell, Donald T., 244
Capped fees, 162–163, 165
Carrington Coleman Sloman & Blumentahl LLP, 174
Client interviews
  interviewer, 55–57
  90/10 rule for, 58–59
  preparation for, 57–58
  questions for, 59–60
Client relationship management (CRM), 5
Clients. *See also* Client interviews; Client satisfaction surveys; Relationship with client
  annual legal review, 121
  crisis management, 79–81
  existing, 23–24
  feedback from, 13, 20, 49–63
  as marketing focus, 17
  prospective, 24, 121–132
  reactions to marketing, 8
  reasons for terminating representation, 223–224
  sales dialogues with, 120–121
  testimonials, 203–204
  value perception by, 50–52
Client satisfaction surveys, 26, 120–121, 253–262
  letters prior to, 258–259
  methodology for, 254–260
  purpose of, 253–254
  questions for, 257
  research firm for, 260–262
  summary of, 262
  use of information, 262–264
  for Web sites, 173–174
The Cluetrain Manifesto, 188
Commercial speech, 202
Communication
  in crisis, 79–81
  false and misleading, 202–205
  within firm, 5, 11–12
  open lines of, 125
  with reporters, 81–82
  sales, 119–132
Compensation systems, 4–5, 10
Competition, 7–8, 17
Competitive intelligence (CI), 247–248
  strengths of, 249
  types of research in, 224
  use of, 148–149
  weaknesses of, 249
Conclusive market research, 220–221
Connectables, 125
Connecticut Bar, solicitation rules, 207
Contingency fees, 161–162, 164
Controlled group discussion, 225
Conversations as marketing. *See* Sales conversations
Corporate Board Member, 213
Corporate profiles, 265–267
Courtlink™, 148
Crisis management, 79–81
Culture of firm, 4
Cybersquatting, 174

Daily Whirl, 187
The Deal, 148
Detod, 187
Direct mail, 208
Disclaimers, 205–206
Discounted fees, 163, 166–168
Division of fees, 206
Domain names, 174–175, 210
Dow Jones Information Service, 266
Due diligence, 273
Durham, Jim, 51

E-mail, use of, 98, 132
Endorsements, client, 203–204
Ernie the Attorney, 181, 184, 186, 187
Ethics, 8, 201–212. *See also* ABA Model Rules of Professional Conduct
  content of marketing material, 202–205
  copies of communications, 205
  disciplinary actions, 211
  disclaimers, 205–206
  domain names, 210
  false and misleading communication, 202–205
  firm name, 209

housekeeping rules, 205–207
money flow and, 206–207
multijurisdictional compliance,
   210–211
resources, 211–212
solicitation, 207–209
specialization, 209
state rules, 202, 205–207
trade names, 209
Experiments, 244–247
strengths of, 249
types of research in, 224
weaknesses of, 249
Exploratory market research, 220, 221

Family, sales dialogues with, 121–122
Feedback program, client, 13, 20, 49–63
client selection in, 54
elements of, 54–62
follow-up in, 60–61
interviews, 55–60
methodology for, 54–55
profitability from, 52–54, 62–63
Fees
alternative, 159–160
arrangements, 157–165
blended hourly rates, 163
capped, 162–163, 165
contingency, 161–162, 164
discounted, 163, 166–168
discussion with prospective clients,
   129–130
division of, 206
fixed, 152, 161
flat, 161
goals of, 157
hourly, 157–158
quality and, 165–166
relationship-building, 164–165
in request for proposal, 151
retainers, 162
retrospective based on value, 162
risk/reward allocation with, 160
strategies for, 26
volume discounts, 163
Finding and Working with Lawyers on the Web, 173, 175, 177
Firm culture, 4
Firms. *See* Law firms
Fixed fees, 152, 161

Flannery, Bill, 143
Flat fees, 161
Florida Bar
communication of legal services
   rules, 205
disclaimer rules, 206
solicitation rules, 208
Focus groups, 225–230
cost of, 229
elements of, 225
firm members in, 252
steps in, 226–228
strengths of, 249
types of research in, 224
use of, 225–226, 229–230, 271
weaknesses of, 249
Fondo, Michael C., 116–117
Friends
sales dialogues with, 121–122
solicitation of, 208

Gardere Wynne Sewell LLP, 174
Goals, marketing, 22–23, 32, 83–84
Godwin Gruber LLP, 173
Goldstein & Howe, 184
Google™, 176, 181–182
Goulston Storrs, 178
Greene, Dr. Mark, 225, 229
Greenfield/Belser, 229–230

Haloscan, 186
Heels, Erik, 180
Hirshon, Robert, 158
Holland & Hart's Health Care Blog, 180,
   184
Hoovers™, 148, 266
Hourly fee, 157–158
How Appealing, 184–185
Howell, Denise, 180, 184, 186, 187
Hughes & Luce LLP, 176
Hybrid studies, 247

Image of firm, 32
announcements, 93–94, 114
brochure, 87–90, 111–112
change management, 94–95
developing, 83–99
memory enhancement, 90–95
name, 90
newsletters, 95–96, 113–114

visual identity, 90–93
visual pathways, 90–91
Web sites, 96–99
Individual marketing plans, 22, 26–27
Information, requests for (RFI), 142
In-house counsel, 24
Internet, 96–97. *See also* Online marketing
Interviews, 243–244. *See also* Client interviews; Focus groups; Telephone surveys
   strengths of, 249
   types of research in, 224
   weaknesses of, 249
Iowa Bar, solicitation rules, 207

Kentucky Bar, communication of legal services rules, 205
Keshet, Dr. Harry, 197

Lateral hires, searches for, 272–273
Law firms
   accountability in, 6
   communication within, 5, 11–12
   compensation system in, 4–5
   complacency in, 4
   culture of, 4
   internal situation analysis by, 250–252
   leadership in, 6, 13, 30
   name, 90, 209
   practice management by, 5–6, 12
   public relations function in, 72, 74–77
   teamwork in, 25
   visual identity, 90–93
Lawson, Jerry, 181
Lawyers
   locating, 84–85
   selection of, 85–86, 160
   solicitation of, 208
The Lawyer's Guide to Marketing on the Internet, Second Edition, 185
The Lawyer's Guide to the Internet, Second Edition, 181
Leadership, 6, 13, 30
Legal Marketing Association, 73, 275
Letters, 110
Letters to editor, 110

LexisNexis™, 148, 266, 268
Library research, 224–225
   strengths of, 249
   types of research in, 224
   weaknesses of, 249
Littlefield, Bill, 117
Logos, 90–91

Mail, direct, 208
Mailing lists, 114
Mail surveys, 55, 230–234, 254
   cost of, 234
   strengths of, 249
   types of research in, 224
   weaknesses of, 249
Maister, David, 51
Manning Fulton & Skinner PA, 174
Marketing. *See also* Oral marketing; Strategic marketing planning; Written marketing
   barriers to, 3–8
   comfortability with, 7
   education for, 10–11
   ethics of, 8, 201–212
   external obstacles to, 7–8
   goal of, 22–23, 32, 83–84
   individual obstacles to, 6–7
   institutional obstacles to, 4–6
   leadership in, 6, 13, 30
   online, 171–178
   overcoming obstacles to, 10–14
   reasons for obstacles to, 9–10
   time requirements for, 6–7
   understanding of techniques, 7
Marketing and Legal Ethics, Third Edition, 211
Marketing director, 6, 61–62
Market profiles, 264–265
Market research. *See* Research, market
Market segments, 23–24
Market surveys, 267–269
Martindale-Hubbell, 84, 175
Massachusetts Bar, solicitation rules, 207
Mass Lawyers Weekly, 117
Mayer Brown Rowe & Maw, 177
Media, new, 98–99
Media directories, 108
Media relations. *See* Public relations

Media use analyses, 271–272
Message points, 80
Metrics, 152
Mission statement, 21, 31–32
Missouri Bar, disclaimer rules, 208
Movable Type, 183, 186

Name of firm, 90, 209
National Association of Touring Caddies, 117
.net, 174
Networking. *See* Sales conversations
New Mexico Bar
    barratry rules, 207
    communication of legal services rules, 205
Newsletters, 95–96, 113–114
News readers, 187
Niches, practice, 22, 24–25
Notes, 110

Offices, opening new, 273–274
Olson, Walter, 184
OneSource™, 148, 266, 268
Online marketing, 171–178
    client surveys for, 55, 173–174
    client wishes in, 177
    domain names, 174–175, 210
    industry strength and, 177
    practice descriptions in, 177
    résumés in, 178
    search engines and, 176
    strategy in, 171–173
    tools for, 175–176
    traditional marketing tools and, 175
Op-ed pieces, 110
Oral marketing, 119–140. *See also* Sales conversations; Speeches
.org, 174
Overlawyered, 184

Perceived quality service, 50
Peters, Tom, 51
Phased budgeting, 152
Planning. *See* Strategic marketing planning
Positioning, 21, 77–78, 96
Positioning statements, 90
Powell, Dennis, 141

Practice area development surveys, 270
Practice areas
    management of, 5–6, 12
    specialization, 209
    strategic marketing plan for, 22, 24–25
Press. *See* Reporters
Press releases, 68, 114–116
Pricing. *See* Fees
Primary market research, 218, 219
Proposals, requests for. *See* Requests for proposals (RFPs)
Prospective clients, 24
    family as, 121–122
    friends as, 121–122
    qualified, sales dialogues with, 126–132
    qualifying, 124–125
    strangers as, 123–126
Public relations, 67–82
    agency for, 73–74
    cases, publicity for, 68
    commentary by firm spokesperson, 70
    crisis management, 79–81
    deals, publicity for, 68
    models for internal, 74–77
    press releases, 68, 114–116
    publishing, 70–71, 107–109
    reporters, relationships with, 68–69, 81–82
    research studies, 71
    round table discussions, 71
    speeches, 72, 133–140
    structure, internal firm, 72
    two-tiered approach to, 77–78
Public speaking. *See* Speeches
Publishing. *See also* Written marketing
    marketing with, 70–71
    selection of publication, 107–108
    selling article, 108–109

Qualitative market research, 49, 50, 219
Quantitative market research, 49, 220
Questions
    client interviews, 59–60
    client surveys, 257

close-ended, 229
open-ended, 59, 229
telephone surveys, 237–238
Quote, requests for (RFQ), 142

Radio 8, 183–184, 185
Referral fees, 206
Referral sources, 24
Relationship with client
   annual legal review and, 121
   building, 28, 53
   changes in, 146–147
   fee arrangements for building, 164–165
   leveraging, 121
   sales as expanding, 120–121
   terminating, 223–224
Re-openers, 161, 163, 164
Reporters
   communication with, 81–82
   meetings with, 68–69
   relationship with, 115
Reprints of publications, 71, 109
Reputation building activities, 29
Requests for information (RFI), 142
Requests for proposals (RFPs), 141–156
   appearance of proposal, 153
   automating process, 152
   competitive intelligence for, 148–149
   content of proposal, 153–155
   decision to respond to, 143–146
   evaluating proposal process, 155
   list for, 142–147
   obtaining, 142–147
   opportunity evaluation, 143–146
   process for response to, 150–155
   relationships and, 146–147
   research for, 148–149
   responding to, 147–150
   strategies for responding to, 149–150
   team for responding to, 150–151
   value of, 142
Requests for quote (RFQ), 142
Research, market, 20, 213–276
   application of methodologies, 248–274
   client surveys, 26, 120–121, 253–264
   competitive intelligence, 247–248
   conclusive, 220–221
   confidence intervals, 233
   corporate profiles, 265–267
   definition of, 215
   due diligence with, 273
   experiments, 244–247
   exploratory, 220, 221
   external studies, 264–270
   focus groups, 225–230
   function of, 215–216
   hybrid studies, 247
   internal situation analysis with, 250–252
   interviews, in-person, 243–244
   lateral hires with, 272–273
   library research, 224–225
   mail surveys, 230–234, 254
   marketing materials with, development of, 270–271
   market profiles, 264–265
   market surveys, 267–269
   media use analyses with, 271–272
   methodologies for, 224–248
   for new offices, 273–274
   practice area development, 270
   primary, 218, 219
   qualitative, 49, 50, 219
   quantitative, 49, 220
   research firm selection, 275
   secondary, 218–219
   strategic, 221–222
   tactical, 222–223
   telephone surveys, 234–243, 254
   types of, 217–224
   Web research, 224–225
   Web surveys, 234
Research firm
   selection of, *275*
   use of, 260–262
"Research Guidelines to Be Followed by the Legal Marketing Association (LMA) When Conducting Market Research and Advisory Guidelines for Law Firms Wishing to Commission and Conduct Market Research," 275
Research studies, 71
Responsiveness, 50, 85–86

Résumés
   on Web site, 178
   writing, 112–113
Retainers, 162
Retreat, marketing, 18–20
Retrospective based upon value billing, 162
Risk corridors, 164
Risk sharing, 151–152
Round table discussions, 71
RSS (Really Simple Syndication), 187
Rukeyser, William S., 213

Sales conversations, 119–132
   active listening in, 126–127
   with clients, 120–121
   fee discussions in, 129–130
   with friends, 121–122
   with qualified prospects, 126–132
   self-promotion in, 127–129
   with strangers, 123–126
   voice mail, 131–132
SAS, 241
SCOTUS Blog, 184
Search engines, 176
Secondary market research, 218–219
SiteMeter, 188
Slogans, 90
Society of Competitive Intelligence Professionals (SCIP), 247
Solicitation, 207–209
South Dakota Bar, false or misleading statement rules, 204
Spam, 98
Specialization, 209
Speeches
   arranging engagements for, 139–140
   audience, meeting prior to, 133
   audience participation in, 136–137
   audio/visual equipment for, 136
   benefits of, 133
   content of, 135
   enhancements in, 136
   fear of public speaking, 138–139
   follow-through of, 137–138
   handouts with, 136
   introduction by host, 133–134
   marketing with, 72, 133–140
   memorization of, 135–136
   notes for, 135–136
   opening of, 134–135
   practicing, 138
   preparation of, 134–135
   sound bites in, 135
   timing in, 137
SPSS, 241
Standard Industry Classification (S.I.C.) Codes, 241
Stanley, Julian C., 244
Strangers, sales dialogues with, 123–126
Strategic marketing planning, 15–47
   application of knowledge, 20–22
   client feedback, 20
   components of, 22–29
   designing strategies, 31
   for large firms, 46–47
   leadership in, 30
   levels of, 22, 31–32
   market research, 20
   mission statement, 21, 31–32
   people strategies, 25
   place strategies, 26
   positioning, 21
   price strategies, 26
   process for, 16–22, 30–32
   promotion strategies, 26
   reasons for, 16–18
   sample plan, 33–45
   service strategies, 25–26
   situation analysis, 18
   strategies, 25–26
   vision session, 18–20
   weekly checklist, 27–29
Strategic market research, 221–222
Surveys. *See also* Interviews; Telephone surveys
   client satisfaction, 26, 120–121, 253–262
   confidence intervals, 233
   mail, 55, 224, 230–234, 249
   market, 267–269
   practice area development, 270
   response rates, 230–231
   Web, 55, 224, 234, 249
Svenson, Ernest, 181, 184, 186, 187

S.W.O.T. (Strengths, Weaknesses, Opportunities, and Threats) analysis, 18–20

Tactical market research, 222–223
Telephone surveys, 234–243. *See also* Client satisfaction surveys
    coding schemes, 240
    cost of, 234–235
    data collection, 239–240
    data entry, 240
    goals of, 235
    implementation, 243
    presentation of findings, 243
    pretesting, 238
    questionnaire coding, 240
    questionnaire design, 236–238
    rankings, 239
    rating scales, 238
    report preparation, 242
    research design of, 236
    sample in, 236
    statistical analysis, 241–242
    statistical programming, 240–241
    steps in, 235
    strengths of, 249
    types of research in, 224
    use of, 254
    weaknesses of, 249
Tennessee Bar, communication of legal services rules, 205
Testimonials, client, 203–204
Texas Bar
    communication of legal services rules, 205
    disclaimer rules, 206
    domain name rules, 174
Thompson & Knight LLP, 174, 266
Thomson Financial, 148
Toastmasters International, 138
Tonkon Torp LLP, 178
Trade names, 209
Trade publications, 70–71, 107
Training, 191–199
    case study, 197–198
    costs of, 197
    expectations in, 197
    extent of, 194–197
    flexibility in, 196–197
    management role in, 196
    nature of, 194–197
    need for, 193–194
    process for, 194–195
    trainer for, 195–196
    types of programs, 199
20 Questions You Should Ask Your Clients and Prospective Clients, 143
TypePad, 186

Userland Radio 8, 183–184, 185

Value, definition of, 50
Vision session, 18–20
Visual identity, 90–93
Visual image. *See* Image of firm
Voice mail, 131–132
Volokh, Eugene, 185
The Volokh Conspiracy, 185
Volume discounts, 163

Wall Street Journal, 116
Weblogs, 179–188
    comments to, 186
    content of, 184–185
    endorsements for, 180
    enhancing, 186–187
    links to other sites on, 181
    location of, 185–186
    marketing with, 180–188
    programs for, 182–184
    publicizing, 186
    subscriptions to, 186–187
    Web sites compared, 179
Web research, 224–225
    strengths of, 249
    types of research in, 224
    weaknesses of, 249
Web sites, 171. *See also* Online marketing
    domain names, 174–175, 210
    expanding, 176–177
    media for, 98–99
    reprints on, 71, 109
    use of, 96–99
    weblogs compared, 179

Web surveys, 234
    strengths of, 249
    types of research in, 224
    weaknesses of, 249
WestLaw™, 148, 266
    Corporate Counsel Marketplace, 97
Womble Carlyle, 229
Work segmentation, 164
World Wide Web, 97–98
Written marketing, 103–118
    advisories, 113–114
    announcements, 93–94, 114
    articles, publishing, 70–71, 107–109
    audience for, 106, 115–116
    biographies, 112–113, 178
    content of, 105–106
    firm brochure, 87–90, 111–112
    idea folder, 106
    letters, 110
    letters to editor, 110
    need for, 103–104
    newsletters, 95–96, 113–114
    notes, 110
    op-ed pieces, 110
    plan for, 105
    press releases, 68, 114–116
    reprints of publications, 71, 109
    résumés, 112–113, 178
    style of, 106–107

YACCS, 186

Selected Books From...
THE ABA LAW PRACTICE MANAGEMENT SECTION

The ABA Guide to Lawyer Trust Accounts. Details ways that lawyers should manage trust accounts to comply with ethical & statutory requirements.

Changing Jobs, 3rd Edition. A handbook designed to help lawyers make changes in their professional careers. Includes career planning advice from dozens of experts.

Collecting Your Fee: Getting Paid From Intake to Invoice. Author Ed Poll outlines the basics and the systems you need to set in place to ultimately increase your bottom line and keep your clients happy while doing it. Learn how to increase your collections, decrease your accounts receivable, and keep your clients happy. CD-ROM with sample forms, letters, and agreements is included.

Compensation Plans for Law Firms, 3rd Ed. This third edition discusses the basics for a fair and simple compensation system for partners, of counsel, associates, paralegals, and staff.

Complete Guide to Marketing Your Law Practice. Filled with dozens of fresh and innovative ideas, this book features the strategies form the country's top legal marketers.

Complete Internet Handbook for Lawyers. A thorough orientation to the Internet, including e-mail, search engines, conducting research and marketing on the Internet, publicizing a Web site, Net ethics, security, viruses, and more. Features a updated, companion Web site with forms you can download and customize.

Do-It-Yourself Public Relations. A hands-on guide (and diskette!) for lawyers with public relations ideas, sample letters, and forms.

Easy Self-Audits for the Busy Law Office. Dozens of evaluation tools help you determine what's working (and what's not) in your law office or legal department. You'll discover several opportunities for improving productivity and efficiency along the way!

Effective Yellow Pages Advertising for Lawyers: The Complete Guide to Creating Winning Ads. This new book by Kerry Randall, "the world's foremost expert on Yellow Pages advertising," shows you how to create more powerful Yellow Pages advertising—the best *lawyers* do not get the most calls; the best *ads* get the most calls.

Essential Formbook: Comprehensive Management Tools for Lawyers, Vols. I & II. Useful to legal practitioners of all specialties and sizes, the first two volumes of The Essential Formbook include more than 100 forms, checklists, and sample documents. And, with all the forms on disk, it's easy to modify them to match your needs.

Flying Solo: A Survival Guide for the Solo Lawyer, Third Edition. This book gives solos, as well as small firms, all the information needed to build a successful practice. Contains 55 chapters covering office location, billing and cash flow, computers and equipment, and much more.

Handling Personnel Issues in the Law Office. Packed with tips on "safely" and legally recruiting, hiring, training, managing, and terminating employees.

HotDocs in One Hour for Lawyers, Second Edition. Offers simple instructions, ranging from generating a document from a template to inserting conditional text and creating dialogs.

How to Build and Manage an Employment Law Practice. Provides clear guidance and valuable tips for solo or small employment law practices, including preparation, marketing, accepting cases, and managing workload and finances. Includes several time-saving "fill in the blank" forms.

How to Build and Manage a Personal Injury Practice. Features all of the tactics, technology, and tools needed for a profitable practice, including how to: write a sound business plan, develop a financial forecast, choose office space, market your practice, and more.

TO ORDER CALL TOLL-FREE:
1-800-285-2221

VISIT OUR WEB SITE:
www.lawpractice.org/catalog

How to Start and Build a Law Practice, Fourth Edition. Jay Foonberg's classic guide has been completely updated and expanded! Features 128 chapters, including 30 new ones, that reveal secrets to successful planning, marketing, billing, client relations, and much more. Chock-full of forms, sample letters, and checklists, including a sample business plan, "The Foonberg Law Office Management Checklist," and more.

Law Office Policy and Procedures Manual, 4th Ed. A model for law office policies and procedures (includes diskette). Covers law office organization, management, personnel policies, financial management, technology, and communications systems.

Law Office Procedures Manual for Solos and Small Firms, Second Edition. Use this manual as is or customize it using the book's diskette. Includes general office policies on confidentiality, employee compensation, sick leave, sexual harassment, billing, and more.

The Lawyer's Guide to Extranets: Breaking Down Walls, Building Client Connections. Well-run extranets can result in significant expansion in clientele and profitability for a law firm. This book takes you step-by-step through the issues of implementing an extranet.

The Lawyer's Guide to Marketing on the Internet, Second Edition. This book provides you with countless Internet marketing possibilities and shows you how to effectively and efficiently market your law practice on the Internet.

Legal Career Guide: From Law Student to Lawyer, Fourth Edition is a step-by-step guide for planning a law career, preparing and executing a job search, and moving into the market. This book is perfect for students currently choosing a career path, or simply deciding if law school is right for them.

Making Partner: A Guide for Law Firm Associates, Second Edition. If you are serious about making partner, this book will help you formulate your step-by-step plan and be your guide for years to come for your decisions and actions within your firm.

Managing Partner 101: A Guide to Successful Law Firm Leadership, Second Edition is designed to help managing partners, lawyers, and other legal professionals understand the role and responsibilities of a law firm's managing partner.

Persuasive Computer Presentations: The Essential Guide for Lawyers explains the advantages of computer presentation resources, how to use them, what they can do, and the legal issues involved in their use. It covers how to use computer presentations in the courtroom and during meetings, pretrial, and seminars.

Running a Law Practice on a Shoestring. Offers a crash course in successful entrepreneurship. Features money-saving tips on office space, computer equipment, travel, furniture, staffing, and more.

Successful Client Newsletters. Written for lawyers, editors, writers, and marketers, this book can help you to start a newsletter from scratch, redesign an existing one, or improve your current practices in design, production, and marketing.

Telecommuting for Lawyers. Discover methods for implementing a successful telecommuting program that can lead to increased productivity, improved work product, higher revenues, lower overhead costs, and better communications. Addressing both law firms and telecommuters, this guide covers start-up, budgeting, setting policies, selecting participants, training, and technology.

Through the Client's Eyes, Second Edition. Includes an overview of client relations and sample letters, surveys, and self-assessment questions to gauge your client relations acumen.

Wills, Trusts, and Technology. Reveals why you should automate your estates practice; identifies what should be automated; explains how to select the right software; and helps you get up and running with the software you select.

Winning Alternatives to the Billable Hour: Strategies that Work, Second Edition. This book explains how it is possible to change from hourly based billing to a system that recognizes your legal expertise, as well as your efficiency, and delivery winning billing solutions—for you and your client.

Women Rainmakers' Best Marketing Tips, Second Edition. This book contains well over a hundred tips you can put to use right away that will have a positive effect on your marketing strategy. Anyone involved in marketing a firm can benefit from the down-to-earth advice in this book.

Order Form

Qty	Title	LPM Price	Reg Price	Total
_____	ABA Guide to Lawyer Trust Accounts (5110374)	69.95	79.95	$_____
_____	ABA Guide to Prof. Managers in the Law Office (5110373)	69.95	79.95	$_____
_____	Anatomy of a Law Firm Merger, Second Edition (5110434)	74.95	89.95	$_____
_____	Changing Jobs, 3rd Ed.(511-0425)	39.95	49.95	
_____	Compensation Plans for Lawyers, 3rd Ed. (5110452)	84.95	99.95	$_____
_____	Complete Guide to Marketing Your Law Practice (5110428)	74.95	89.95	$_____
_____	Complete Internet Handbook for Lawyers (5110413)	39.95	49.95	$_____
_____	Computerized Case Management Systems (5110409)	39.95	49.95	$_____
_____	Connecting with Your Client (5110378)	54.95	64.95	$_____
_____	Do-It-Yourself Public Relations (5110352)	69.95	79.95	$_____
_____	Easy Self Audits for the Busy Law Firm (511-0420P)	99.95	84.95	$_____
_____	Essential Formbook, Vols. I and II	*Please call for information*		
_____	Flying Solo, Third Edition (511-0463)	79.95	89.95	$_____
_____	Handling Personnel Issues in the Law Office (5110381)	59.95	69.95	$_____
_____	HotDocs in One Hour for Lawyers, Second Edition (5110464)	29.95	34.95	$_____
_____	How to Build & Manage an Employment Law Practice (5110389)	44.95	54.95	$_____
_____	How to Build & Manage a Personal Injury Practice (5110386)	44.95	54.95	$_____
_____	How to Start & Build a Law Practice, Fourth Edition (5110415)	57.95	69.95	$_____
_____	Law Firm Partnership Guide: Getting Started (5110363)	64.95	74.95	$_____
_____	Law Firm Partnership Guide: Strengthening Your Firm (5110391)	64.95	74.95	$_____
_____	Law Office Policy & Procedures Manual, 4th Ed. (5110441)	109.95	129.95	$_____
_____	Law Office Staff Manual for Solos & Small Firms (5110445)	59.95	69.95	$_____
_____	Lawyer's Guide to Marketing on the Internet, 2nd Ed. (5110484)	69.95	79.95	$_____
_____	Living with the Law (5110379)	59.95	69.95	$_____
_____	Making Partner, Second Edition (511-0482)	39.95	49.95	$_____
_____	Managing Partner 101, Second Edition (5110451)	44.95	49.95	$_____
_____	Persuasive Computer Presentations (511-0462)	69.95	79.95	$_____
_____	Practicing Law Without Clients (5110376)	49.95	59.95	$_____
_____	Running a Law Practice on a Shoestring (5110387)	39.95	49.95	$_____
_____	Successful Client Newsletters (5110396)	39.95	44.95	$_____
_____	Telecommuting for Lawyers (5110401)	39.95	49.95	$_____
_____	Through the Client's Eyes, Second Ed. (5110480)	69.95	79.95	$_____
_____	Wills, Trusts, and Technology (5430377)	74.95	84.95	$_____
_____	Winning Alternatives to the Billable Hour, Second Ed (5110483)	129.95	149.95	$_____

*Handling
$10.00-$24.99 .... $3.95
$25.00-$49.99 .... $4.95
$50.00+ $5.95   MD residents add 5%

**Tax
DC residents add 5.75%
IL residents add 8.75%

Subtotal
*Handling $_____
**Tax $_____
TOTAL $_____

PAYMENT

☐ Check enclosed (to the ABA) ~ ☐ Bill Me
☐ Visa   ☐ MasterCard   ☐ American Express

_____
Account Number   Exp. Date Signature

Name _____ Firm _____
Address _____
City _____ State _____ Zip _____
Phone Number _____ E-mail address _____

Mail: ABA Publication Orders, P.O. Box 10892, Chicago, Illinois 60610-0892
♦ **Phone: (800) 285-2221** ♦ **FAX: (312) 988-5568**
E-Mail: service@abanet.org ♦ **Internet: http://www.abanet.org/lpm/catalog**

Source Code: 22AEND499

CUSTOMER COMMENT FORM   ABA

Title of Book: _____

We've tried to make this publication as useful, accurate, and readable as possible. Please take 5 minutes to tell us if we succeeded. Your comments and suggestions will help us improve our publications. Thank you!

1. How did you acquire this publication:

- ☐ by mail order
- ☐ by phone order
- ☐ other: (describe) _____
- ☐ at a meeting/convention
- ☐ at a bookstore
- ☐ as a gift
- ☐ don't know

Please rate this publication as follows:

	Excellent	Good	Fair	Poor	Not Applicable
Readability: Was the book easy to read and understand?	☐	☐	☐	☐	☐
Examples/Cases: Were they helpful, practical? Were there enough?	☐	☐	☐	☐	☐
Content: Did the book meet your expectations? Did it cover the subject adequately?	☐	☐	☐	☐	☐
Organization and clarity: Was the sequence of text logical? Was it easy to find what you wanted to know?	☐	☐	☐	☐	☐
Illustrations/forms/checklists: Were they clear and useful? Were there enough?	☐	☐	☐	☐	☐
Physical attractiveness: What did you think of the appearance of the publication (typesetting, printing, etc.)?	☐	☐	☐	☐	☐

Would you recommend this book to another attorney/administrator? ☐ Yes ☐ No

How could this publication be improved? What else would you like to see in it?
_____
_____
_____

Do you have other comments or suggestions? _____
_____
_____

Name _____
Firm/Company _____
Address _____
City/State/Zip _____
Phone _____
Firm Size: _____ Area of specialization: _____

We appreciate your time and help.

BUSINESS REPLY MAIL
FIRST CLASS   PERMIT NO. 16471   CHICAGO, ILLINOIS

POSTAGE WILL BE PAID BY ADDRESSEE

AMERICAN BAR ASSOCIATION
PPM, 8th FLOOR
750 N. LAKE SHORE DRIVE
CHICAGO, ILLINOIS 60611-9851

NO POSTAGE
NECESSARY
IF MAILED
IN THE
UNITED STATES

ABA LawPracticeManagementSection
MARKETING • MANAGEMENT • TECHNOLOGY • FINANCE

JOIN the ABA Law Practice Management Section (LPM) and receive significant discounts on future LPM book purchases! You'll also get direct access to marketing, management, technology, and finance tools that help lawyers and other professionals meet the demands of today's challenging legal environment.

Exclusive Membership Benefits Include:

- **Law Practice Magazine**
  Eight annual issues of our award-winning *Law Practice* magazine, full of insightful articles and practical tips on Marketing/Client Development, Practice Management, Legal Technology, and Finance.
- **ABA TECHSHOW®**
  Receive a $100 discount on ABA TECHSHOW, the world's largest legal technology conference!
- **LPM Book Discount**
  LPM has over eighty titles in print! Books topics cover the four core areas of law practice management – marketing, management, technology, and finance – as well as legal career issues.
- **Law Practice Today**
  LPM's unique web-based magazine in which the features change weekly! Law Practice Today covers all the hot topics in law practice management *today* – current issues, current challenges, current solutions.
- **Discounted CLE & Other Educational Opportunities**
  The Law Practice Management Section sponsors more than 100 educational sessions annually. LPM also offers other live programs, teleconferences and web cast seminars.
- **LawPractice.news**
  This monthly eUpdate brings information on Section news and activities, educational opportunities, and details on book releases and special offers.

Complete the membership application below.

Applicable Dues:
o$40 for ABA members   o$5 for ABA Law Student Division members

(ABA Membership is a prerequisite to membership in the Section. To join the ABA, call the Service Center at 1-800-285-2221.)

Method of Payment:
oBill me   Charge to my: oVisa   oMasterCard   oAmerican Express
Card number _____ Exp. Date _____
Signature _____ Date _____

Applicant's Information (please print):
Name _____ ABA I.D. number _____
Firm/Organization _____
Address _____ City/State/Zip _____
Telephone _____ FAX _____ Email _____

Fax your application to 312-988-5528 or join by phone: 1-800-285-2221, TDD 312-988-5168
Join online at www.lawpractice.org.

I understand that my membership dues include $16 for a basic subscription to *Law Practice Management* magazine. This subscription charge is not deductible from the dues and additional subscriptions are not available at this rate. Membership dues in the American Bar Association and its Sections are not deductible as charitable contributions for income tax purposes but may be deductible as a business expense.

About the CD

The accompanying CD contains excerpted material from the book, as well as new information that supplements key concepts presented in the book. This material is divided into twenty-one sections, including:

- Marketing Plans
- Publicity for Deals and Cases
- Keys to Successful Presentations
- Requests for Proposals
- Internet Marketing
- Practice Group Leader Manual
- Client Satisfaction Program Plan

The two different file formats allow you to easily read (PDF format) and customize (Microsoft Word format) the material to your needs.

For additional information about the files on the CD, please open and read the "**readme.doc**" file on the CD.

NOTE: The set of files on the CD may only be used on a single computer or moved to and used on another computer. Under no circumstances may the set of files be used on more than one computer at one time. If you are interested in obtaining a license to use the set of files on a local network, please contact: Director, Copyrights and Contracts, American Bar Association, 750 N. Lake Shore Drive, Chicago, IL 60611, (312) 988-6101. **Please read the license and warranty statements on the following page before using this CD.**

CD-ROM to accompany
The Lawyer's Guide to Marketing Your Practice,
Second Edition

WARNING: Opening this package indicates your understanding and acceptance of the following Terms and Conditions.

READ THE FOLLOWING TERMS AND CONDITIONS BEFORE OPENING THIS SEALED PACKAGE. IF YOU DO NOT AGREE WITH THEM, PROMPTLY RETURN THE UNOPENED PACKAGE TO EITHER THE PARTY FROM WHOM IT WAS ACQUIRED OR TO THE AMERICAN BAR ASSOCIATION AND YOUR MONEY WILL BE RETURNED.

The document files in this package are a proprietary product of the American Bar Association and are protected by Copyright Law. The American Bar Association retains title to and ownership of these files.

License
You may use this set of files on a single computer or move it to and use it on another computer, but under no circumstances may you use the set of files on more than one computer at the same time. You may copy the files either in support of your use of the files on a single computer or for backup purposes. If you are interested in obtaining a license to use the set of files on a local network, please contact: Manager, Publication Policies & Contracting, American Bar Association, 750 N. Lake Shore Drive, Chicago, IL 60611, (312) 988-6101.

You may permanently transfer the set of files to another party if the other party agrees to accept the terms and conditions of this License Agreement. If you transfer the set of files, you must at the same time transfer all copies of the files to the same party or destroy those not transferred. Such transfer terminates your license. You may not rent, lease, assign or otherwise transfer the files except as stated in this paragraph.

You may modify these files for your own use within the provisions of this License Agreement. You may not redistribute any modified files.

Warranty
If a CD-ROM in this package is defective, the American Bar Association will replace it at no charge if the defective diskette is returned to the American Bar Association within 60 days from the date of acquisition.

American Bar Association warrants that these files will perform in substantial compliance with the documentation supplied in this package. However, the American Bar Association does not warrant these forms as to the correctness of the legal material contained therein. If you report a significant defect in performance in writing to the American Bar Association, and the American Bar Association is not able to correct it within 60 days, you may return the diskettes, including all copies and documentation, to the American Bar Association and the American Bar Association will refund your money.

Any files that you modify will no longer be covered under this warranty even if they were modified in accordance with the License Agreement and product documentation.

IN NO EVENT WILL THE AMERICAN BAR ASSOCIATION, ITS OFFICERS, MEMBERS, OR EMPLOYEES BE LIABLE TO YOU FOR ANY DAMAGES, INCLUDING LOST PROFITS, LOST SAVINGS OR OTHER INCIDENTAL OR CONSEQUENTIAL DAMAGES ARISING OUT OF YOUR USE OR INABILITY TO USE THESE FILES EVEN IF THE AMERICAN BAR ASSOCIATION OR AN AUTHORIZED AMERICAN BAR ASSOCIATION REPRESENTATIVE HAS BEEN ADVISED OF THE POSSIBILITY OF SUCH DAMAGES, OR FOR ANY CLAIM BY ANY OTHER PARTY. SOME STATES DO NOT ALLOW THE LIMITATION OR EXCLUSION OF LIABILITY FOR INCIDENTAL OR CONSEQUENTIAL DAMAGES, IN WHICH CASE THIS LIMITATION MAY NOT APPLY TO YOU.